Getting In

Getting In

*Mediators' Entry
into the Settlement of
African Conflicts*

Mohammed O. Maundi
I. William Zartman
Gilbert M. Khadiagala
Kwaku Nuamah

UNITED STATES INSTITUTE OF PEACE PRESS
Washington, D.C.

United States Institute of Peace
1200 17th Street NW
Washington, DC 20036

First published 2006

Printed in the United States of America

The paper used in this publication meets the minimum requirements of American National Standard for Information Sciences—Permanence of Paper for Printed Library Materials, ANSI Z39.48-1984.

Library of Congress Cataloging-in-Publication Data

Getting in : mediators' entry into the settlement of African conflicts
/ Mohammed O. Maundi … [et al.].
    p. cm.
  Includes bibliographical references and index.
  ISBN-13: 978-1-929223-62-6 (softcover : alk. paper)
  ISBN-10: 1-929223-62-5 (softcover : alk. paper)
  1. Mediation, International—Case studies. 2. Africa—Politics and
government—1960- 3. Political stability—Africa—History—20th century.
I. Maundi, Mohammed Omar.
  JZ6045.G48 2006
  341.5'2—dc22
                  2005035153

To Mike Schatzberg, Steve Stedman, Gilbert Khadiagala, and Theresa Simmons, my colleagues in the African Studies Program at SAIS for more than a quarter-century, who made the program so good and so enjoyable to work on.

I.W.Z.

Contents

Foreword

Even the most casual observer of international politics knows something about the tasks of a mediator, whose sudden arrival into the diplomacy of a conflict is heralded briefly and sporadically in the media: get the warring parties to the negotiating table and find some sort of compromise that stops the fighting—hopefully once and for all.

But the *process* of selecting the mediator, and of the mediator's *getting in* that crucial negotiating venue, are, at best, obscure. Before we see the media clips of the mediator shaking hands with typically taciturn and reluctant interlocutors, there is a very complex and contingent series of decisions among the actors directly involved in or surrounding the conflict. Who is the one person—or several, successive persons—each side believes can maximize its interests (or minimize what it expects in the way of penalties or disadvantages) during the period of the conflict's lifespan known as a "mutually hurting stalemate"? When the warring sides realize that there are no more gains to be had from further warfare, the resort to mediation is typically done in the spirit of "let's cut our losses." Yet why should the leaders of warring factions opt to have an outsider mediate their conflict, especially when the stakes are typically very high?

The "problem" with the study of mediation, as the authors of this work describe at the outset, is that the mediators' *selection* and *entry* into the mediation process is just as complex and crucial to the settlement of the conflict as mediators' subsequent tasks of agenda setting, negotiation, bargaining, diplomatic maneuvering, and cajoling in the hopes of achieving a mutually acceptable settlement. Yet much of the mediation process we are able to witness through media accounts, if at all, comes much later in the process—during breaks in the negotiating sessions, when the conflict's principal representatives stand in front of the familiar phalanx of microphones and cameras, and grimly (or, at best, impassively) assess the progress of the mediation initiative.

A mediator arrives at the front door of a very tense chamber, but how does he or she *get into* that particular venue—that is, how does the mediator get traction in the settlement of the conflict? A large part of the answer to that question is how and why mediators are selected—and who selects them—as the authors of this study explain. The rest of that answer is how the mediator proceeds with his or her particular mandate, the other dimension of the authors' analytical framework in this book. We know mediators are professionals, skilled in negotiating, bargaining, diplomacy, and a host of lesser-known attributes that are geared toward settling deadly disputes. But mediation is an art, not a science; the personal skills of the mediator are just as important as the routine matters of process, and usually the choice of a mediator tells us more about the warring parties than it does about the nature of the conflict and the international community's concern about the conflict's potential to spread beyond its immediate confines.

If the study of mediation can approach anything resembling a level of systematic inquiry, it can be found in this important work. The authors endeavor to identify, if not an iron-clad taxonomy of the early stages of mediation, then at least some discernable patterns of how and when mediators get involved in conflicts. The analysis of the mediation process in some of the most horrific conflicts in the contemporary international milieu is a daunting challenge: organized armies are relatively easy to disengage, but paramilitary groups, informal militias, and entire mobilized populations that seek each other's extermination in various African countries make these mediators' missions extraordinarily complex. The authors of this work are all experts in African politics and conflict, but the value of this book for those who study conflict resolution in other regions is the concluding attempt to apply the lessons of mediation in these African examples to other conflict venues as well.

This study originated as a colloquium at the Johns Hopkins University's Nitze School of Advanced International Studies (SAIS) led by Mohammed Maundi, a graduate student there at the time whose doctoral dissertation served as the basis for the colloquium's weekly discussions. Guiding Maundi in turning the analyses and subsequent academic and practitioner exchanges into the penetrating case studies presented herein was I. William Zartman, who is perhaps the best link between the academic and the practitioner in the realm of mediation and negotiation. Professor Zartman was not only head of the Conflict Management and African Studies Programs at SAIS but also served as a mediator in one of the case studies in this work—stemming from his service as a distinguished member of the Carter Center's International Negotiation Network—so he brings both practical experience and a special analytical acumen to this study of African conflict mediation. He is also no stranger to the U.S. Institute of Peace, having authored or edited many relevant studies published by the Institute's Press, including the revised edition of *Peacemaking in International Conflict,* also appearing this year.

Gilbert Khadiagala, the acting director of SAIS's African Studies Program, contributed substantially to this volume as well, not only authoring one of the case studies but also joining Zartman in the editing process. Kwaku Nuamah also brought his special expertise to this volume's case studies as the project director of the Council on Foreign Relations' G8-Africa Project.

Getting In adds to the list of many other significant published works and special initiatives of the U.S. Institute of Peace on African conflicts and mediation. In that regard, we have to thank four senior members of the Institute for their contributions to this growing effort: Judy Barsalou, vice president of the Institute's newly combined Grant and Fellows Programs, whose grantmaking has funded a variety of penetrating analyses of the study of mediation and of conflicts on the African continent and elsewhere, including the present work; David Smock, vice president of the Institute's new Center for Mediation and Conflict Resolution and director of the Religion and Peacemaking Program, who has just published a new addition to the Institute's Peaceworks series, *Religious Contributions to Peacemaking,* which includes a focus on religion-based conflict resolution initiatives in Africa; Institute board member Chet Crocker, who brought his special expertise to the mediation project as former U.S. assistant secretary of state for African affairs and author of *High Noon in Southern Africa: Making Peace in a Rough Neighborhood* (Norton, 1993); and Pamela Aall, vice president of the Institute's Education Program, who has joined with Crocker and Fen Osler Hampson to produce a variety of bestselling works on international conflict published by the Institute's Press, including *Taming Intractable Conflicts: Mediation in the Hardest Cases.*

At a time when the international community is searching for new, innovative approaches to managing the internecine and destructive conflicts that continue to plague Africa, *Getting In* and other relevant studies published by the U.S. Institute of Peace should find their way onto the required-reading lists of the policymakers and practitioners who have devoted their careers to finding an effective, preventive approach to putting an early end to this deadly violence.

RICHARD H. SOLOMON
PRESIDENT
UNITED STATES INSTITUTE OF PEACE

ACKNOWLEDGMENTS

We wish to express gratitude to the United States Institute of Peace, not simply for the financial support for this work from the Institute's Grant Program, but for underwriting a pleasurable and imaginative collegial venture. The core of the venture and of this work is the doctoral dissertation of Mohammed Maundi, which was the basis of a biweekly seminar on "Entry into Mediation," to which Gilbert M. Khadiagala, Kwaku Nuamah, Saadia Touval, and I. William Zartman, in addition to Maundi, contributed papers for discussion by students and colleagues of the African Studies and Conflict Management Programs at Johns Hopkins University's School of Advanced International Studies in Washington, D.C. In this book, the original work in the introduction and in the case studies of Rwanda, Burundi, and Sudan was done by Maundi, revised and edited, along with the conclusion, by Zartman. The case study of Congo-Brazzaville (the Republic of the Congo) was written by Zartman, the study on Liberia by Nuamah, and the study on Ethiopia-Eritrea by Khadiagala. Touval's contribution to the project was published as chapter 3 in his *Mediation in the Yugoslav Wars: The Critical Years 1990–95* (New York: Palgrave, 2002).

We want to thank Francis M. Deng and Ahmedou Ould Abdallah for reviewing parts of the manuscript. We also want to express our gratitude to Theresa Taylor Simmons for entering multiple rounds of corrections into the manuscript and keeping the project on track. We are also grateful to Peter Pavilionis of the U.S. Institute of Peace Press—a wonderful editor to work with—for his constant assistance.

Getting In

Africa Map

Mediterranean Sea

Tangier • Oran • Algiers • Constantine • Tunis
Rabat • Casablanca
MOROCCO
Marrakech
Ghardaia •
TUNISIA
Tripoli •
Banghazi •

Canary Islands (SPAIN)
Alexandria •
Cairo •

★Layoun
Tindouf •
ALGERIA
LIBYA
EGYPT

WESTERN SAHARA
Al Jawf •
Aswan ★

Tamanrasset •

MAURITANIA
MALI
NIGER
Faya-Largeau •
CHAD
Port Sudan •
Red Sea

Nouakchott •
Nema •
Tombouctou •
Agadez •
ERITREA
Asmera •

SENEGAL
★Dakar
Niamey ★
Zinder •
Khartoum •
Al Fashir •
DJIBOUTI
Djibouti ★

Banjul
GAMBIA
Bamako •
BURKINA FASO
Kano •
N'Djamena •
Maiduguri •
Berbera •

GUINEA-BISSAU
★Bissau
Ouagadougou •
SUDAN
★ Addis Ababa
SOMALIA

GUINEA
★Conakry
Freetown★
COTE D'IVOIRE
Yamoussoukro
TOGO
BENIN
NIGERIA
Abuja •

SIERRA LEONE
GHANA
Lome
Porto Novo
Lagos
ETHIOPIA

Monrovia★
LIBERIA Abidjan ★
Accra
CENTRAL AFRICAN REPUBLIC
Juba •
Lake Turkana

CAMEROON
Douala •
Bangui ★
Yaounde •
UGANDA
Lake Albert
Mogadishu ★

EQUATORIAL GUINEA
Malabo •
Kampala •
KENYA
Lake Victoria

Sao Tome •
Bata •
REP. OF THE CONGO
Libreville •
Kisangani •
Kigali
Nairobi •

SAO TOME and PRINCIPE
GABON
DEM. REP. OF THE CONGO
RWANDA
Bujumbura
BURUNDI
Mombasa •

Brazzaville •
TANZANIA

Pointe-Noire •
Kinshasa •
Kananga •
Kalemie •
Dar es Salaam •

Cabinda (ANGOLA)
Lake Tanganyika

South Atlantic Ocean
Luanda •
Indian Ocean

Kasama •

Lubumbashi •
MALAWI

ANGOLA
Kitwe •
Lake Nyasa
Mahajanga •

ZAMBIA
Lilongwe •
Antananarivo •

Namibe •
Lusaka ★
MAURITIUS
Port Lewis

Harare •
MOZAMBIQUE
★Saint Denis

ZIMBABWE
Beira •
Reunion (FRANCE)

NAMIBIA
Bulawayo •
MADAGASCAR

BOTSWANA
Toliara •

Walvis Bay
Windhoek •
Gaborone •
Maputo •

Pretoria •
Mbabane
Johannesburg •
SWAZILAND

Maseru
Durban •
LESOTHO

SOUTH AFRICA
CapeTown • Port Elizabeth •

1

THE
PROBLEM

This study investigates the conditions for a successful initiation of *entry* into the mediation of violent conflicts in six African cases. It seeks, on the one hand, to explain the motives behind the prospective mediators' involvement in the mediation process, and on the other, to explain the motives behind the parties' consideration of mediation as a policy option and their acceptance of particular mediators. The major question addressed by the study is: How do prospective mediators gain access to internal conflicts? In other words, how does a prospective mediator initiate a mediation process successfully in an internal conflict? The study deals specifically with other questions directly related to the major research concern: What motivates the parties in a conflict to consider the option of mediation? What motivates an aspiring mediator to accept or initiate a mediating role? Why do parties accept or seek the assistance of a particular mediator?

The study considers mediation as an integral part of negotiation that, in turn, is regarded as a succession of processes divided into three major phases. The first is the preparatory phase. Its main objective is to create a conducive environment through which conflicting parties can be brought to the negotiating table. In negotiation theory this phase is referred to as *diagnosis, premediation,* or *prenegotiation.*[1] It can also be referred to as *entry, gaining access,* or simply *getting in* to mediation. The second is the mediation phase, in which parties to a conflict are involved in the actual substantive negotiations with the help of a mediator. And the third is the postsettlement phase, in which efforts are taken to implement the mediated agreement.

This study focuses exclusively on the premediation phase—that is, on how mediation entry is initiated. Although the importance and contribution of the entry phase to the substantive phase of mediation and its outcome are appreciated, the study is concerned with neither the final outcome of the mediation process nor that of the conflict as a whole. It is concerned only with the decisions to initiate, invite, and accept mediation as a policy alternative on the one hand, and the acceptance of a particular mediator on the other. Its focus on entry is based on a number of factors. The first is the fact that the other two phases of the mediation process take place only after the success of the first phase. Simply put, there is no mediation before the success of the entry of a mediator in a conflict. But the process of entry has much to do with the process of mediation and the reasons for its course. It is hard to understand and explain what goes on in mediation without understanding how it got started.

The second is the fact that very little work has been done so far on the entry phase.[2] Most work on mediation focuses on the second phase of the process.[3] Alluding to this shortcoming, John Stephens argues that "a great deal of conflict research has centered on the process of mediation and what factors or tactics speed or hinder settlement of disputes. However, the question of how this process begins has been relatively ignored."[4] Addressing this limitation, Ronald Fisher points out that "there appears to be a gap in both the thinking of conflict theorists and the practice of diplomatic practitioners with regard to the question of how to facilitate movement toward negotiation which is meaningful and ultimately successful. More specifically, there is a lack of knowledge and expertise regarding the process of prenegotiation by which hostile parties move from stalemate to negotiation."[5]

Another factor is that even among the few studies that have so far tried to deal with the entry phase, there are a number of limitations. First, the studies lack comprehensiveness. They either deal with few elements of entry or address the problem of entry indirectly.[6] Second, emphasis has been on interstate rather than on internal conflicts.[7] Furthermore, nothing much has been done to explore the African experience in this area. This study, therefore, aims to fill the vacuum. It attempts, in general terms, to contribute to the understanding of the entry process, particularly to internal conflict. And it attempts, in specific terms, to investigate the characteristics of the African experience in entry initiatives.

Significance of the Study

This study is animated mainly by the call for a broader theory of negotiation that integrates the processes that precede formal negotiation.[8] It is guided by three major theses. The first is that an understanding of gaining access to internal conflicts contributes to a better understanding of mediated negotiation. Second, an investigation on entry facilitates the examination of the mediation process from the perspectives of both the intermediaries and the parties. And third, an objective comprehension of entry requires not only an understanding of the motives for such an initiative but also an identification of its underlying problems. An understanding of the obstacles to entry is extremely useful to the mediation process because, according to Stephen John Stedman, "mediators need to know the conditions that facilitate negotiation, the barriers that negotiations face, and how these barriers can be overcome more effectively."[9] On the basis of the complexities of internal conflict, one of the major objectives of the study is to investigate the possibilities of initiating mediation entry that can lead to a negotiated settlement.

The significance of the study lies in its theoretical and practical values. Understanding the complexities of mediation entry creates a conducive environment that provides the parties with an opportunity to make an informed assessment of each other. Thus, as Janice Stein puts it, "they learn not only about others but also about themselves."[10] The learning process allows the parties to readjust their perceptions toward each other, toward the mediator, and toward the conflict. With an objective of helping the parties to cooperate in seeking a joint solution to the conflict, initiating entry is useful in redefining relationships, re-evaluating alternative means to a final solution, and considering potential intermediary roles.[11] At the practical level, an understanding of entry characteristics provides general guidelines to practitioners for an improved negotiation process.

The relevance of the study lies in the realization that the world is currently experiencing a dangerous wave of violent internal conflicts, particularly in Africa, that threaten national, regional, and international peace and security. A study that deals with the issues of understanding these conflicts and prescribing the means of resolving them is quite relevant and timely.

There are three levels at which the study contributes to knowledge. First, its findings are an additional conceptual contribution to the emerging literature that is trying to understand internal conflicts and the models of their resolution. Second, its findings can also help in determining useful policy recommendations. And third, its findings can also play a catalytic role of provoking further debate and research.

The study is undertaken on the conviction that the understanding of the nature of an internal conflict and its resolution within one region can have some relevance to other regions as well. This conviction takes cognizance of the fact that a conflict in one region can have far-reaching consequences to other regions. This is true for both its contagion as well as its demonstration effects.[12] It is therefore hoped that the relevance of its findings is universal. The findings would provide invaluable learning experiences in dealing with internal conflicts in various parts of the world.

THEORETICAL FRAMEWORK

Conceptualizing Internal Conflict

Conflict refers to parties' attempts to pursue incompatible ends.[13] Thus conflicts are intrinsically nonviolent; they may turn violent, but violence is not their inherent aspect, only a potential form or means that conflicts may adopt.[14] Internal conflicts, like interstate conflicts, can be political, economic, social, cultural/perceptual, and structural, and they can move from normal politics to violence.

Internal conflicts can be *centralist* or *regionalist*.[15] Centralist conflicts are disputes over the central authority. Insurgencies fight in order either to replace the government or to be included in it, and governments fight back to resist being replaced or sharing power with the insurgents. Regionalist conflicts aim at self-determination through secession or regional autonomy.

Two models, "ethnic" and "territorial," are presented by Anthony D. Smith to provide a conceptualization of organizing a national identity that is helpful in understanding the nature of centralist ethnic conflict.[16] According to the ethnic model, a nation-state is identified with one self-defined ethnic group, to which the state belongs and which belongs to the state.

> To turn a motley horde of people into an institutionalized nation, to give them a sense of belonging and identity, to unify and integrate them, to give them a sense of authenticity and autonomy and fit them for self-rule, all require a symbolic framework in and through which they can be mobilized and stabilized.[17]

There are negative implications of this model: internally, it can lead efforts to make the nation-state ethnically pure; externally, it can foster militant irredentism. Political entrepreneurs from the dominant ethnic groups can capitalize on ethnic appeals, enforce homogeneity, repress differences, and promote intolerance and discrimination.[18] In contrast to the ethnic model, national identity in a territorial model is based on individual allegiance to the state, independent of ethnicity. The emphasis in this integrative approach is on the "legal equality of citizen-residents."[19]

Mediating Internal Conflict

Both centralist and regionalist conflicts involve high stakes. Left on their own, the parties strive mainly for zero-sum outcomes, usually attainable only at a very high cost. Both parties in a centralist conflict want to rule the state exclusively; both parties in a regionalist conflict want to rule a part of the state exclusively. It is within this zero-sum context that intermediaries try to intervene in internal conflicts. The objective of the intervention is not to assist either party to gain outright victory over its adversaries, but to break the impasse and bring the parties to a level where they would be able to settle for a win-win outcome. Mediators help them to move from the generally desirable but untenable zero-sum victories to the relatively malleable compromise solutions. Mediation then makes sense when parties to a conflict abandon the option of a zero-sum outcome and embrace a desire for a compromise outcome. This shift entails the lowering of the high stakes each party had previously perceived in the conflict. Once all the parties are genuinely committed to mediation, they should be aware that the agenda for a zero-sum outcome is dead and that a compromise settlement becomes the most rational outcome of the mediation process. In practice, however, mediation can and has taken place even when some parties are not fully committed to compromise. This is one of the major conundrums that this study will explore.

Mediation is one of the specific forms of the intermediary roles in the broader processes of negotiation. While negotiation refers to the peaceful means of resolving conflict through dialogue, mediation, in its intermediary capacity, plays a role of facilitating the dialogue between the conflicting parties, particularly in a situation where they are unable, by themselves, to conduct the negotiations. The notion of inability among the conflicting parties to conduct negotiation by themselves introduces an external component to the conflict. Generally referred to as a "third party" in the literature, the intermediary intervenes, by either invitation or other means, in the middle of what Jeffrey Rubin calls "the interface of cooperative and competitive interests," when the disputants are sufficiently cooperative that they are willing to invite or accept the intrusion of one or more external (third) parties who may be able to break the conflictual stalemate.[20]

Mediators are distinguished between those on "Track One," consisting of official mediators representing states and intergovernmental organizations, and those on "Track Two," constituting either nongovernmental organizations (NGOs) or private persons. Across the two tracks, intermediaries can be discussed either as individuals or as institutions. All mediation—indeed all diplomacy—is done by individuals, and individual interaction is crucial to the practice and study of mediation. Individuals vary widely in their personal attributes, of course, but they also vary according to their institutional capacity. Institutions—states and organizations—do not actually do the mediating; individuals do, but the institutions for which they speak make a crucial difference in their operation and effectiveness. This study concerns mediation as an institutional rather than an individual exercise.

Initiating Entry

Entry is a process of achieving *acceptability* for intermediary involvement in negotiations. It is the process through which a prospective mediator gains access to a conflict. It begins when one party or a potential intermediary considers mediation as a policy option and continues to a point when mediation is formally endorsed by both parties and a specific mediator is agreed upon.[21] Entry can be either mediator-initiated (entry by proposition) or parties-initiated (entry by invitation). Entry is a voluntary process; there is no legal sanction facing the parties in accepting a mediation initiative.[22] In theory, a potential mediator will not gain access to a conflict without the consent of the parties, nor will invited intermediaries be automatically involved in mediation without their prior consent to play such a role. Therefore, consent is the backbone of entry to mediation.

The Problematic Issues

The Imperviousness to External Intervention

Why are we concerned about entry? Entry into internal conflicts becomes a problematic and interesting area of study because of a number of significant theoretical and practical factors. The first is internal conflicts' imperviousness to external interventions. General observations about international relations and conflict management hold that internal conflicts are resistant to outside efforts to bring about a peaceful resolution and usually do not end in a compromise agreement.[23] More frequent is victory for the secessionist insurgency, as in the victory of the Eritrean People's Liberation Front in 1991; or for the anti-centralist insurgency, as in the Ethiopian People's Revolutionary Democratic Front's victory in 1991, the Rwandan Patriotic Front's (RPF) victory in 1994, and the Alliance des Forces Démocratiques pour la Libération du Congo-Zaire's (AFDL) victory in the Congo in 1997; or else for the government, which succeeds in preserving the unity of the country, as in Nigeria in the 1970 Biafran conflict.[24] There are very few cases of governments' victory over insurgencies in centralist conflicts.

The assumption that internal conflicts are impervious to external mediation efforts is based mostly on the parties' perceptions about the nature of the conflict and the high stakes they attach to the perceptions. The higher the stakes the parties attach to the conflict, the more likely they will be willing to make more sacrifices for the realization of their goals, creating an environment not conducive to a compromise solution. Hence, a win-lose scenario becomes the most obvious expected outcome.

Normative and Legal Issues

A second issue emerges from the assumption that intervention in internal conflict violates a country's sovereignty.[25] Thus an intermediary role in an internal conflict will be resisted by the government because, in one way, it undermines its authority and in another, it legitimizes the insurgency. Saadia Touval addresses this point succinctly:

> For state authorities confronted by internal opponents challenging their legitimacy, external attempts at mediation pose difficult dilemmas. When the government itself is a party to the conflict, acceptance of outside mediation carries a bargaining disadvantage. It implies that it recognizes its opponents as being equal in status, entitled to present their point of view to an

outside body, regardless of the government's claim to exclusive jurisdiction over the citizens living in its sovereign territory. Placing the internal opponents of a government on an equal footing with the regime implies that the opponents' claims are no less legitimate than those of the government. Since this inevitably weakens the position of the government and strengthens that of its opponents, governments are usually reluctant to accept external mediation in domestic conflicts.[26]

Because the insurgency also challenges the central authority, the denial of legitimacy then becomes mutual: "When adversaries do not recognize each other as legitimate, a negotiated ending to any conflict between them is most difficult."[27]

Entry could also be resisted by the insurgency if it feels that mediation could undermine its cause or favor the government. An insurgency on the verge of defeating the government obviously will have no interest in engaging the government at the negotiating table and will continue the armed option to its logical conclusion. This was demonstrated by Laurent Kabila's AFDL during its struggle to replace Mobutu in the former Zaire in 1997. When Kabila's forces were closing in on Kinshasa, there was a flurry of diplomatic efforts led by the United Nations envoy Mohammed Sahnoun, South African president Nelson Mandela, and U.S. ambassador Bill Richardson, to obtain Mobutu's dignified exit, to prevent Kabila from taking Kinshasa by force, and to negotiate a lasting solution to the crisis by involving all the parties. The diplomatic efforts failed to achieve all the three objectives simply because the AFDL was in no mood to negotiate at a time when a military victory was in its sights.[28]

Who Takes the Initiative?

A third factor concerns the manner in which entry is initiated. Initiation by the mediator creates the challenge of convincing the parties, first, to accept mediation as a policy option and, second, to accept the initiator as playing the mediating role. In initiation by invitation, the challenge is to convince not only the prospective mediator but also the other party, who can see the invitation as a sign of the initiator's weakness, as a tacit acceptance of the initiator's inability to win militarily, or as an attempt to bias the mediation process by engaging a friend.[29] Either case contains an incentive for the other party to reject mediation and continue with the violent option, convinced that it might gain an outright military victory.

The Scope of Engagement

Another problem about entry involves its scope, or the magnitude of engaging the parties. An internal conflict usually involves many parties, but at the highest level of its escalation, aspiring mediators seem to engage only the government and the armed groups in their efforts to gain entry into the mediation process. The crucial question here is whether it is enough for the prospective mediators to get the consent of entry only from the principal parties. If the other parties' consent and involvement in the mediation is desirable, under what framework should they be involved?

Louis Kriesberg talks about the selection of parties to be engaged as among the strategic choices a prospective mediator must make.[30] Selection connotes partial engagement; other parties will be left out. Including all the parties may be practically impossible, and "all" is an elastic concept. Yet entry is not a single event. Usually, the entry of just one mediator does not result in a mediated settlement. If the mediator is making some progress, others may try to join in the success or, at least, work it in their preferred direction. If the mediator seems to be encountering obstacles, others may try to pick up the challenge. In either case, mediators are not likely to act alone, and the challenging question subsequent mediators must ask themselves before attempting entry is: What can I offer to help the mediation process that the exiting mediator did not have?

Timing of Initiating Entry

Timing is another problem of initiating entry—specifically, at what level in the conflict's escalation should entry be attempted? Analysts seem to agree that timing matters when it comes to both the entry phase and the substantive phase of mediation, but they differ in isolating the propitious moment. Some argue that it is better to attempt entry at a low level of escalation. Frank Edmead, who shares this view, believes that entry should be attempted at an early stage, well before parties cross the threshold of violence and begin to inflict heavy losses on each other.[31] Others are of the opinion that entry should be attempted when a "mutually hurting stalemate" has set in and the parties have already tested their strength.[32] Stephens, who also shares this view, is of the opinion that entry initiatives are of greater relevance if attempted in situations of significant suspicion or antagonism between the parties. He contends that at lower levels of escalation there is little need logically for external parties to assist disputants who trust one another, as they should be able to negotiate directly.[33] A study of entry contributes to a better understanding of this controversy.

The Issue of Asymmetry

The sixth problem for the entry of mediation of internal conflicts emanates from the structure of the conflict. Internal conflicts are characteristically asymmetrical. The government "enjoys international recognition as the legitimate authority and has at its disposal the resources of the state, including its security forces," whereas the insurgency "lacks such legitimacy and possesses far fewer material resources than its opponent."[34]

The issue is whether mediation is possible in such a situation of power and resource imbalance. Kriesberg holds that if the balance of the means of coercion is relatively equal between disputants, it is more likely that mediation will be accepted. If there is a wide disparity, the stronger party will not be prompted to accept mediation and make concessions. Its superior power should enable it to dictate a more favorable outcome to the conflict.[35]

In line with this argument, Kjell Skjelsbaek and Gunnar Fermann posit that usually the weaker party first accepts the services of an intermediary. The stronger party, according to them, may hope to win, or at least to prevail, and consequently regards offers of mediation as detrimental to its interests.[36] In a study that related the parties' power balance to the effectiveness of mediation, Jacob Bercovitch and Allison Houston found a clear pattern showing high mediation impact when power disparity is high.[37]

The Issue of Neutrality and Interests

Neutrality or impartiality and the broader matter of mediator interests are the seventh issue in the study of initiating mediation. It is by now generally recognized that a mediator has interests and engages only because of them, and therefore some degree of partiality is always likely. Indeed, bias may be useful, as the biased mediator is expected to deliver the party toward which it is partial.[38] What is required of a mediator, however, is both avoidance of the reverse (the construction of an outcome favorable to the favored party) and, more positively, reliability on the part of the mediator as a conveyor of ideas and messages. Mediators do not play that role for altruistic reasons alone. They do so in order to promote or protect any interests they may have, even though they are not parties to the conflicts in which they get involved. Keith Webb, for one, states categorically that the act of mediation

is not a neutral one. According to him, it is a moral and political act undertaken by the mediator to achieve desired ends. He further notes that
although a mediator may claim to be neutral with respect to the values and
claims of the combatants, the activity of mediating is still a declaration of
values held by the mediator.[39]

In agreement with Webb, C. R. Mitchell asserts that all intermediaries
possess motives and reasons for undertaking that role quite apart from any
desire to bring about a satisfactory peace settlement.[40] Peter Carnevale and
Sharon Arad agree that mediators have interests and motives that provoke
them to get involved in conflicts. Their detailed research experiments demonstrate that effective mediation may well be undertaken by biased or partial
mediators, and that decisions concerning the acceptability of mediators do
not simply reflect the mediators' bias.[41]

Costs to Intervenors

Finally, beyond whatever motives drive prospective intervenors to engage in
intermediary roles, it is important to realize that there are costs involved in
the exercise. On the one hand, there are costs incurred from laying down
the infrastructure for the mediation process itself and its maintenance to the
point where the process is concluded or breaks down. And, on the other
hand, there is a personal bill to prospective intervenors because they invest
capital in order to gain benefits from the process. Whereas the costs of the
first type are mostly in the form of finance and material, those of the second
type include time, perseverance, endurance, and frustration. In view of the
fact that mediation can drag on for months, prospective mediators, in a
typical cost-benefit consideration, look at the financial, material, and psychological price tags before making a commitment to get involved. These
considerations have a restraining effect on some potential mediators who
would want to play the intermediary role.

Mitchell addresses the subject of costs in the context of the impact of
intervenors' decision to mediate on their relationship with the parties and
on their domestic constituencies. He contends that using mediation to
increase dependence (and hence influence) on one or both of the parties
may backfire, and mediators may be left with less influence, an escalated
level of violence, and less opportunity to establish what they regard as a
satisfactory relationship with the parties.[42] As far as the domestic support is
concerned, Mitchell argues that costs can also come in the form of dimin-

ished support and approval from internal constituencies. "Adopting the role of intermediary when there are strong domestic factions feeling that the full weight of governmental or organizational effort should be thrown behind a favored party can be a dangerous action for the leadership making a choice."[43] Mitchell's specific conclusion is that it is necessary to recognize that although somewhat asymmetric, there is always a balance of potential benefits and costs in undertaking the role of mediation.

THE ANALYTICAL APPROACH

This study is guided by a realist interpretive framework of international relations whose notions of interests, power, and rationality are relevant to the analysis of entry.[44] The realist perspective helps us to construct a theoretical model that can relate the motives for initiating and accepting mediation and a particular mediator to the self-interests of the parties and the mediators. The construction of the model is inspired by Stephens's work, the one model that tests the reasons that some mediation initiatives are accepted while others are rejected.[45]

Stephens's model consists of dependent factors that determine parties' decisions on a mediation initiative and independent factors that help explain such decisions. Three related assumptions flow directly from the dependent factors. The first is that a mediation initiative's success or failure is based on the decisions by the parties' leaderships. Success or failure refers to, respectively, acceptance or rejection of the initiative. The second assumption, which is a corollary of the first, is that parties to a conflict are distinct entities, with recognized individuals as leaders, and that the leadership is not homogenous, which creates the potential for intraparty factions. And the third assumption concerns the level of antagonism between the parties, which ranges from very low to very high. The hypothesis here is that the higher the level of antagonism between the parties, the more likely that mediation will be considered.

Two judgments stem from the three assumptions. The decision of the parties' leadership to accept or reject mediation depends on, first, whether the preconditions for negotiation exist, and, second, whether a particular mediator is acceptable. Four preconditions for negotiation are provided. The first is a low or decreasing probability of attaining conflict goals unilaterally through violence. The second is a decreasing value of conflict goals relative to the direct costs of pursuing those goals and relative to other goals. The third is some common or compatible interests between the parties. The last precondition is flexibility by each leadership to consider negotiation. Stephens also provides two judgments on the acceptability of a particular mediator: a party's *trust* in the prospective mediator and a party's perception that the potential mediator is *independent* of the adversary's opponents.

Stephens's model then focuses on the independent variables that are relevant to the decision of whether or not to accept mediation. The identity and resources of the prospective mediator and the nature of the issues in conflict are identified as the central variables. Identity is constituted by three interlinked components: status, prestige, and constituency. Status is defined as the nature of the link between the persons who would mediate and their constituency. Prestige is the parties' perceptions of the mediator's attributes; these include authority, skill, or fame. Constituency refers to the mediator's authority base, which ranges from political to economic to ethnic.

The resource variable is separated into technical, moral, diplomatic, and material forms. Technical resources are defined as communication links, a meeting place, and secretarial support. Moral resources emanate from the potential mediator's perceived authority and worthiness. Diplomatic resources involve the potential for action in political forms that could support principles, initiate censure, or promote other assistance for, or persuasion toward, one or more of the parties. Material resources are goods and financing that a mediator can offer to compensate for concessions made in the negotiations.

On the variable of the nature of the issues in conflict, Stephens underlines the complexity of defining them and identifying their sources, their relative importance, and their links as the conflict unfolds. Underscoring the different perceptions and values parties attach to the issues, Stephens warns that the difference in the definition of the issues among the parties should be expected. Hence, he provides a caveat in applying the model especially to the analysis of the nature of the issues involved in a conflict. The caveat is that while one label is convenient for discussing the issues, each party's definition and explanation of "the issue" must be included.

A general assumption has been that entry is supposed to be initiated by potential mediators and not by the parties. The assumption is based on the perception that parties would be constrained to take such an initiative, first, by their zero-sum perceptions of the conflict, which rules out mediation as a policy option, and, second, by the considerations of sovereignty, legiti-

macy, and the structure of the conflict. A government's initiative to invite
mediation would translate into accepting interference in its internal affairs,
legitimizing the insurgency, and admitting its weakness in facing up to the
rebels. An insurgency would hesitate to take such an initiative in order, first,
to prevent the mediation process from rescuing an unacceptable regime
that it is determined to replace and, second, to avoid giving an impression
of weakness. An insurgency would additionally hesitate to take the initiative on the assumption that its stigmatic label of being a "rebel" would not
attract a positive response in an international environment that holds high
the concept of sovereignty.

This study focuses on the assumption that entry can be initiated by both
the mediators and the parties. The assumption is based, first, on the rational
and cost-benefit premise of parties' actions and, second, on the changed
international political environment and its impact on sovereignty, legitimacy
of insurgencies, and the structure of the conflicts. A party's self-interest can
be a driving force for taking the initiative in mediation and inviting a mediator. On the other hand, human rights issues, injustice, and accountability
are currently challenging the traditional interpretation of the concept of
sovereignty as related to intervention. Those challenges provide the justification for insurgencies to invite intervention and for prospective mediators to
respond positively to such an invitation. Issues of minority rights and self-
determination also play a positive role in encouraging insurgencies to take
the initiative. A conflict's structural change also can force the government to
take the initiative to invite entry of a mediator particularly when the power
balance is not in its favor.

Whether the initiative for mediation comes from the parties or from
outside, the mediator is always an outsider to the conflict. This means that
while a third party may have interests in the conflict to the extent of accepting a mediating role, that does not make it a party to the contested issues
and outcomes of the conflict.

Thus Stephens's analytical model needs to broaden its scope to cover
entry by invitation from one or more parties, as well as by proposition from
the potential mediator. Stephens's model confines itself exclusively to the
mediation attempts initiated by the intermediaries.[46] Another problem with
the model is that all the preconditions for accepting mediation it presents
have the sole objective of a compromise settlement; yet mediation initiatives
have more objectives than just a compromise settlement.

Stephens's model also needs to be expanded to analyze mediation initiatives from the intermediaries' perspective. Although the model addresses the parties' motives for accepting mediation, it does not address the motives of intermediaries to initiate mediation. A model is needed that is comprehensive enough to help participants understand the entry phase of mediation from the perspectives of the intermediaries and the parties in the conflicts. From the potential mediators' perspective, the model's central objective is to facilitate an understanding of why they present themselves to play the intermediary role. And from the parties' perspective, the objective is to provide an understanding of why they accept mediation and why some mediation initiatives are readily accepted, some face initial resistance, and others are rejected outright.

The model assumes the rationality of actors in making policy decisions on the basis of self-interests and cost-benefit considerations. According to Touval, actors weigh costs and benefits of alternative policies and prefer those they believe to be least costly and most effective.[47] This model is applicable both to the parties and to the aspiring mediators in initiating entry into the mediation of internal conflicts. This means that beyond altruistic motives prospective mediators are driven by self-interests in their attempts to enter into a conflict. Also, the disputants' self-interests are central in their decisions to accept mediation and a particular mediator. Hence, the model is applied in the following analysis of the various types of mediation initiators. Its adoption has been inspired by the fact that there has been a conspicuous neglect of tying mediation initiatives to self-interests of the parties and the mediators. According to Mitchell, there has been an overemphasis on the belief that "any intermediary is wholly or, at worst, largely motivated by a desire to bring about a settlement restoring peace and stability to the adversaries' relationship and terminating the conflict in some satisfactory manner."[48] As a result, it is often forgotten that intermediaries possess goals and objectives that they attempt to further through mediation. The central focus of the analysis is to examine the motives behind the intermediaries' initiatives and those of the parties for accepting both mediation and the mediators.

In his instructive analysis of mediation in international conflicts, Thomas Princen argues that in its application to the mediating role the realist framework's traditional focus on state actors should also be extended to include nonstate actors.[49] This extension recognizes the important role that regional and international organizations and also private individuals and NGOs play in the area of conflict management.

According to Princen, states' active involvement in facilitating mediation moves them beyond the traditional focus on and roles of alliance power politics, characteristic of the Cold War era, to a new level whereby power is used not in its coercive sense to force conflicting parties to submission in a balance of power context, but in its persuasive sense to influence them to move to compromise solutions.

The model has two interlinked sets of propositions. One set is the outcome of the problematic issues outlined previously in this chapter. The other arises from the conditions that satisfy the relationship between (a) the motives for initiating and accepting mediation and a particular mediator and (b) the self-interests of the parties and the mediators.

What then motivates potential mediators to either propose mediation or accept an invitation to mediate? The response comes directly from the study's analytical model: they are motivated by self-interests. The self-interests are as diverse as the aspiring intervenors and are particular to specific mediators. What follows is a presentation of the prospective intervenors and what motivates them to play the intermediary role.

States

From a realist perspective, states' intervention in an internal conflict of another state is analyzed within the context of the conflict's impact on national interests of the other states. Regardless of its size and strength, a state may be motivated to initiate or accept an intermediary role in an internal conflict if that conflict affects its national interests. The degree of a conflict's impact on a state's national interest is a function of the state's moral principles, its physical proximity to the conflict, and the closeness of its bilateral relations. A state's humanitarian, democratic, and justice principles may motivate it to intervene in an internal conflict where these principles are seriously violated by the state in conflict. A state sharing borders with the state in conflict will be motivated to initiate mediation as a result of the conflict's contagion and demonstration effects.[50]

A conflict in a neighboring state produces refugees, who become a socioeconomic burden to the host state. It likewise encourages discontented groups in neighboring countries with similar latent disputes to take up arms against their governments. A conflict in one country destabilizes regional peace and security and undermines regional trade and communication. But a state may also be motivated to play a mediating role as "a strategy to avoid having to choose sides in a dispute from which it cannot remain wholly aloof."[51] The avoidance of choosing sides has the advantage of either establishing or maintaining good relations with both parties, as persuasively argued by Touval.[52]

The above reasons by themselves are not always sufficient to inspire a neighbor to play a mediating role. In discussing the concept of "triangulation," which explains the relationship between conflicting parties in an internal conflict and neighboring states, I. William Zartman emphasizes that the relationship may bc either friendly or hostile, but scarcely indifferent.[53] The neighbor has an option of supporting either party according to how it perceives the nature of the conflict in relation to its own national interests. This option creates a triangular relationship whereby the conflict becomes internationalized and the neighbor becomes an interested party. By being an interested party, a neighbor may restrain itself from initiating mediation and discourage others from playing such a role if the negotiation between the parties will affect its interests in the conflict. Characterizing mediation as "a means to a particular end rather than an end in itself," Webb argues that "there may be cases where those ends are more likely to be achieved through not mediating" and by allowing a conflict to run its course.[54]

Apart from the option of supporting either party, "there are also narrow but specific conditions under which the host neighbor will also find it in its interest to mediate the internationalized conflict."[55] One of these specific conditions is when the neighbor's support to either party becomes unbearably costly. It is when the triangular relationship reaches this stage that the neighbor not only becomes interested in playing a mediating role but also becomes the best placed party to play that role. This is so because "the host-neighbor has leverage over the insurgency, by virtue of its sanctuary, and also leverage over the government by virtue of its ability to produce a solution. It also now has a motive to mediate, reduce its own costs, and increase its influence."[56]

A state thousands of miles away may be as strongly affected by an internal conflict as a neighboring state if it has stronger strategic bilateral relations with either the state in conflict or its neighbors. It is most likely that such a state might be motivated to either initiate or accept a mediating role. Such a state might as well be motivated to intervene as a way of preventing the intervention of other powerful external actors that could lead to the internationalization of the conflict.[57]

Such a state might likewise intervene because of domestic public opinion on the conflict. The public opinion pressures might be a result of general humanitarian concerns or of interests of a particular important constituency.[58] According to Mitchell, governments frequently take up the role of honest broker in order to "buy off" domestic pressure to support one side or another—a pressure that can become a major factor in domestic politics in countries where domestic cleavages mirror the external conflict. Often these pressures relate to external influences and pose serious problems for a government that might best be resolved by adopting an intermediary role.[59] He discusses the relationship between domestic public opinion and states' decision to play the intermediary role under the concept of *constituency arena.* He defines the benefits accrued from this relationship as those emerging out of the state's domestic "internal audience," which simply means the state's domestic support.

Intergovernmental Organizations

Intergovernmental organizations' intermediary role is motivated by their members' interests and by the interest of the organizations' executive secretariats. The two are not always in harmony with each other, or indeed with themselves in the case of the members' interests. International organizations decide or agree to mediate when their members see it as in their interests to do so rather than taking sides or staying unengaged; it must be remembered that an international organization is primarily a place, not a thing, with "individual, sovereign state members acting to authorize its action."[60] That decision will be based on the sum of the members' self-interests combined with their judgment between two conflicting interests for the self-preservation of the organization—the question is whether reconciling the parties to the conflict is worth the risk of offending members of the organization, the parties themselves, and their friends. Whether the organization (thus understood) is mediating between two or more of its members, its members must weigh their interests against the effect of intervention on the life and interest of the organization. Because an international organization is established to broker some specific purposes and principles, the members must see the potential mediation and its likely outcome as consistent with those goals.

Related to internal institutional interests is the issue of the organization's standing among other international institutions with similar objectives. It is prestigious to the members of an organization with peace objectives to become involved in a conflict and succeed in mediating a lasting solution. It is an indication that the organization is achieving its objectives.

But an internal organization can also defer to its secretary-general or his representatives who have their own interests and who represent the organization's corporate interests as well. An organization's success is the success of its staff: "For an international civil servant rewards may be the sense of gratification from a job well done or an attempt made in difficult circumstances. More mundanely, there may be an increase in personal standing or career prospects within an organization,"[61] but also a chance to enhance the prestige and purpose of the organization. Mitchell discusses the intergovernmental organization's symbolic rewards accrued from the organization's constituency arena. An internal conflict in a member state can have a negative effect on the organization's institutional objectives as well as on its physical existence. The intermediary role is then to demonstrate the organization's efforts in restoring the political stability of the member state in conflict as well as in preserving its own unity.

NGOs

Like the intergovernmental organizations on the first track, the second-track NGOs' entry into internal conflicts is driven by their institutional interests. Moral values are part of the humanitarian and religious NGOs' interests, yet, in pursuing their mission, such organizations cannot ignore the question of their relative standing within their own framework of reference—the system comprising other humanitarian and religious organizations performing similar work. In such situations, political motives may accompany moral and humanitarian ones.[62]

The moral-value interests provide a strong incentive to NGOs to find lasting solutions to internal conflicts. This commitment explains the successful involvement of the World Council of Churches and the All Africa Conference of Churches in the first Sudanese civil war that culminated in the 1972 Addis Ababa Agreement and that of the Community of Sant'Egidio in Mozambique that helped in the mediation that ended the civil war.[63]

It is on the advantages that NGOs bring to an environment of an internal conflict, compared with other prospective intermediaries, that they hinge their hope of being accepted by the parties to play the intermediary role. In an environment where the entry of intergovernmental organizations and states may be resisted strongly by the parties on the basis of sovereignty and interference in internal affairs, an NGO can gain access merely for being nonpolitical and nongovernmental and, hence, not a threat to the state's sovereignty. According to Hizkias Assefa, the intermediary involvement of such a third party would not necessarily confer international political status on the insurgents and would not threaten the sovereignty of the incumbent government.[64] This would make a government more willing to accept the mediating role of an NGO than that of a state or an intergovernmental organization.

Assefa also points out NGOs' infrastructural advantages in comparison to formal intervenors. NGOs, especially the international ones, have a very wide infrastructural network that can provide an invaluable access and information base that is rarely available to states and intergovernmental organizations. The infrastructure can be usefully harnessed for peacemaking. Apart from the infrastructural advantages, the humanitarian nature of many NGOs provides an additional advantage. In conflicts that entail large-scale humanitarian suffering, according to Assefa, humanitarian agencies have a great advantage over many other organizations in obtaining access to the conflict.[65]

Some circumstances call for the quiet, informal services of "unofficial diplomats," individuals without official status, operating on the second track. While they have no political, economic, or military clout, they have the freedom to be flexible, to disregard protocol, to suggest unconventional remedies or procedures, to widen or to restrict the agenda or change the order of items, to propose partial solutions or package deals, or to press the case for constructive initiatives or magnanimous gestures.[66]

Individuals who get involved in mediation are not just ordinary people. They are prominent personalities who carry with them a lot of weight and influence. They can be prominent retired politicians, seasoned international diplomats and former heads of state, religious leaders, or renowned academics. Some of them initiate mediation because of moral and humanitarian interests. Others do so for personal prestige and reputation, and others do so from sheer joy of professionalism. Whatever motivations push them toward an intermediary role, they all accept the role on the basis of their professional background. Hendrik van der Merwe argues that the most important advantage of private intermediaries is their detachment from an "official status," although this has become a liability rather than an asset in intermediary roles.[67]

As individuals who generally play the intermediary roles are prominent personalities in their societies, it is doubtful whether their freedom can be as unlimited as van der Merwe suggests. Touval warns that sometimes these prominent personalities find it difficult to be unaffected by political considerations and may feel bound to take into account the views of their governments. He cites the example of President Carter, who was initially restrained from mediating the civil war in Ethiopia at a time when his government viewed such an initiative as unfavorable. Carter had to take the initiative in 1989, when the U.S. government's attitude had changed, but when the moment was no longer ripe (if it ever had been).[68] Foreign governments tend, erroneously, to view the status of a private individual such as Carter as completely official. Yet most private individuals will consult with their government before undertaking mediation, whether they follow its counsel or not.

Individual Consultants

Apart from conventional intermediaries, another innovative category of mediation initiators at the premediation phase is that of the problem-solving consultants.[69] This is a group of prominent scholars and practitioners of conflict resolution who play a facilitative and diagnostic role in assisting the parties in analyzing their conflict and searching for mutually acceptable solutions. Keashly and Fisher define the problem-solving consultation as "the intervention of a skilled and knowledgeable third party (usually a team) who attempts to facilitate creative problem solving through communication and analysis using social-scientific understanding of conflict etiology and process."[70] Problem-solving consultation is generally conducted through workshops.

Problem-solving consultation is relevant to the entry phase of the mediation process because it not only helps in analyzing the nature of the relationship among the parties, their perceptions and attitudes, and the underlying causes of the conflict, but it can also have a useful influence on the parties to accept mediation and its final outcome.

While problem-solving consultation places more emphasis on the subjective factors, highlighting social-psychological elements such as perceptions, attitudes, communication, and various characteristics of the relationship, mediation emphasizes the objective side and attempts to work around the subjective elements even though it is cognizant of them and their effects.[71]

The consultants' entry into a conflict is generally governed by the same rules that guide the entry of other potential mediators. This is true for the motives and acceptability for such a role. Like the other aspiring individual mediators, consultants also are motivated by personal interests. Their biggest motivation is the belief that they have something to contribute toward peace, which is their expertise. Collectively, problem-solving consultants constitute a unique and significant reservoir of intermediary experts that can be exploited by potential mediators as resource persons or can play a contributing role to the mediation. But they are unlikely to be able to carry the burden of mediation alone.

MULTIPLE MEDIATORS

Mediators are attracted to conflict because that is their business, although, at the same time, potential mediators are highly selective, even wary, about taking up the challenge. The result is that several mediators are often operating on the same case. Coordinated, this situation can have its advantages; uncoordinated, it weakens and often defeats the process. Multiple mediators can increase the resources and influence available in the mediation process. "Different members of the coalition may be more acceptable than others to certain parties and their patrons in the conflict."[72] United, multiple mediators can combine ideas, expand communications, and compound pressure on the parties to the conflict. Even rivals, jealous of protecting their individual interests, can engage in joint mediation when it is in their interest.

Furthermore, the collective approach can compensate for the individual deficiencies in terms of the intervenors' attributes, skills, and resources. The cooperation of individuals with different but complementary skills and expertise creates the requisite skills and knowledge base that no one mediator can possess. The team approach provides an opportunity for an expanded range of ideas, options, and strategies to be considered in order to cope with problems that may arise during the mediation.[73]

PARTIES' ACCEPTANCE OF MEDIATION

When entry is analyzed from the disputants' perspective, acceptability has two levels. One is the decision to turn to mediation, and the other is the decision to accept or invite a particular mediator. What influences the parties in reaching those two decisions? In line with the study's model, both decisions are explained by the parties' interests. Motivated by self-interest, the parties accept mediation because either they wish to make a fundamental change of policy orientation or they wish to enhance the prevailing policy track.

The desire to change a party's policy orientation is an outcome of its realization that it cannot achieve its initial preferred outcome of the conflict through the military track. That realization is in turn a result of the party's change of perception about the conflict's final outcome—from a zero-sum to a win-win mindset, or from a competitive to a cooperative mindset. This dramatic change of policy is explained by such cost considerations as "mutually hurting stalemate."[74] It comes at a time when a party realizes that it is too costly to pursue a unilateral solution and recognizes the importance of a joint-solution alternative. Zartman characterizes this change as a "shift to a conciliatory mentality where parties believe that the solution is to be found with, not against, the adversary and are prepared to give a little to get something, to settle for an attainable second-best rather than hold out for an unattainable victory."[75]

This acceptance can be conceptualized as a "perceptional acceptability" because it is an outcome of perceptional change on how the conflict will finally be resolved. The fact that parties may not arrive at the hurting stalemate at the same time poses the challenge of how the other party would be brought to this level. The relevant question is how a mutually hurting stalemate could be induced to facilitate mediation entry. It is the aspect of inducing ripeness to the other party that makes an intermediary's role the more important. It might appear that once the conflict reaches the level of mutually hurting stalemate and parties recognize the importance of a joint solution, an intermediary role would become redundant because parties can now afford to engage in direct negotiation. However, while this is theoretically possible it is generally impractical because the mutual feeling of "pain" does not remove the parties' mutual hostility toward and suspicion of each other. Hence, the intermediary role is still relevant because "mediation will provide a more favorable settlement than could be achieved by facing the adversary alone in bilateral negotiation. The parties may also accept mediation in the hope that the intermediary will help them reduce some of the risks entailed in concession making, protecting their image and reputation as they move toward a compromise. They may also believe that a mediator's involvement implies a guarantee for a negotiated agreement, thus reducing the risk of violation by the adversary."[76]

In contrast to perceptional acceptability, potential intermediaries gain access to internal conflicts also through what could be called "expedient acceptability." This acceptability is not motivated by a desire for a compromise solution but to enhance their given policy. Such "devious objectives" include time to regroup and reorganize, internationalization of the conflict, the search for an ally, empowerment, legitimization of parties' negotiation positions and current status, face saving, and avoiding costly concessions by intending to prolong the process of mediation itself.[77] Rather than steering a party toward a compromise solution, expedient acceptability is geared toward the enhancement of the competitive course.

PARTIES' ACCEPTANCE OF AND INVITATION TO PARTICULAR MEDIATORS

On the basis of rational cost-benefit calculations, parties accept or invite particular mediators according to the roles they are expected to play in line with their interests. The choice among the various types of potential intermediaries depends on how the prospective mediators' qualities and resources match with the roles they are supposed to perform. Qualities refer to the calabashes contained in the mediator's basket that can be useful in fulfilling the parties' objectives. The choice of a particular mediator is based on what he or she brings to the negotiation and its relevance to the interests of the parties.

States may be preferred if the parties' objective of accepting entry is to get a compromise solution because of the resources they command and their ability to guarantee the compromise agreement. If entry acceptance has the objectives of empowerment, legitimization, or internationalization, then an international organization could be the appropriate choice. An international organization would also be preferred, according to Touval, if parties want to "deflect the pressure that a single state mediator might bring to force an undesired settlement."[78]

Kriesberg addresses the riddle of what he calls the "officiality" of the mediator in relation to what an intermediary brings to the negotiation. He notes that persons with a position in a state or an organization may bring greater authority to their efforts, yet may be constrained by protocol or the organization's policies and principles. On the other hand, a mediator without such a position may have greater freedom to meet with people and suggest concessions but, without an organization's backing, lack sufficient influence with the disputants.[79] The sufficient influence Kriesberg is alluding to is a requirement not only of impressing upon the parties the need to strike a deal but also of convincing them that the mediator will guarantee that the agreement holds and will be implemented. Such an assurance can be provided by powerful states and intergovernmental organizations such as the United Nations, the North Atlantic Treaty Organization, and the European Union.

There are two other forms of accepting a particular mediator. One is what Stephens calls "unavoidable mediator"[80] and the other is what could be conceptualized as the "patrons-preferred mediator." Stephens defines unavoidable mediation as a situation "when an adversary outweighs accepting the initiative, even if the judgments on negotiation preconditions and mediator acceptability are negative."[81] Touval provides a list of the mediation initiatives that a party may find difficult to reject. One of these is the initiative from a friendly state that a party is attached to by numerous close ties. Another is a variety of initiatives that are based on international legal and humanitarian justifications. These initiatives include an intervention of a regional or international body that has a preauthorized agreement for such an intervention to which a state party is a member. Yet another is the intervention by the same organizations on the pretext of peace and humanitarian concerns.[82]

Patrons-preferred mediation is a phenomenon arising from the tendency for protracted internal conflicts to involve other governments and organizations as patrons of the domestic parties.[83] This patron-client relationship turns the original conflict into a vehicle through which the patrons' interests are played. The original conflict then turns into a proxy war.[84] Acceptability of entry in such a conflict is a function not only of the parties' interests but also, more important, of their patrons. This simply means that the parties do not have a free hand in choosing a particular mediator. They will be forced to accept the intermediary role of either one of the patrons or another mediator sanctioned by the patrons. Patrons become potential mediators when they find their commitment to their clients is becoming increasingly costly. They use their leverage to force their clients not only to accept them as mediators but also to accept outcomes that serve their own interests as well.[85]

Self-Interest, Asymmetry, and Partiality

The self-interest explanation of the acceptance of mediation and a particular mediator challenges the assumptions that, on the one hand, mediation is more likely to be accepted by the weaker party than the stronger one,[86] and, on the other hand, impartiality is central to the parties' decision of accepting a mediator. Acceptance of mediation is a question of the parties' individual interests more than just a matter of power relationship. Regardless of a conflict's power balance, parties will accept entry of mediators as long as the entry serves their particular interests. The parties' interests need not be the same in order to accept mediation entry; each must expect a better outcome from the mediation.[87]

Despite a conflict's asymmetry, both parties can perceptively and expediently accept entry of mediation. For the stronger party, perceptual acceptance is based, first, on cost considerations (though it is the strongest party, continuing with the military track can still be too costly) and, second, on the advantage of negotiating from the stronger position. Expedient acceptance can be motivated by a quest for international approval for talking instead of fighting. For the weaker party, expedient acceptability avails it not only of recognition but also of legitimization and empowerment. In the meantime, perceptual acceptability guarantees the party's participation in whatever government structure the final outcome of the mediation would be.

On the other hand, the parties' cost-benefit calculations make impartiality not a necessary condition of acceptance. As long as acceptance is related to a mediator's ability to deliver the acceptable outcome, even a biased mediator could be acceptable. The closer a mediator is to one party, the greater the chances of delivering that party to a compromise solution.[88]

The Hypotheses

The following hypotheses are drawn from the two sets of the study's propositions and are tested through the case studies:

1. The higher the stakes the parties attach to the issues in conflict, the more likely that mediation attempts will be rejected.

2. When the costs of pursuing the objectives of the issues in conflict increase, then it is likely that mediation will be accepted.

3. A third party is likely to try to intervene or accept an invitation to mediate when the conflict threatens its interests or when playing such a role contributes positively to its interests.

4. The more determined third parties are to intervene, the more likely that they will gain access.

5. The more the parties believe that a potential mediator will help them attain their objectives, the more are the chances that the entry initiative will be accepted.

The Case Studies

The investigation is based on six case studies: Rwanda from October 1990 to June 1992; Burundi from October 1993 to June 15, 1998; Congo (Brazzaville) from December 1991 to August 1993, from June to October 1997, and from June to December 1999; Sudan from May 1983 to May 1993; Liberia from December 1989 to August 1996; and Ethiopia from May 1998 to July 1999.

The Rwandan conflict was triggered by the Rwandan Patriotic Front invasion in October 1990. The Great Lakes Region's efforts to initiate mediation succeeded in June 1992, when the Arusha Peace Process was launched under the Tanzania's government mediation on behalf of the region.

The Burundi crisis of October 1993 was sparked by the assassination of the first democratically elected and Hutu president during a coup engineered by the extremist elements within the Tutsi-dominated army. In early 1994, the GLR, with the support of the Organization of African Unity (OAU), mandated former Tanzanian president Julius Nyerere to mediate the Burundi conflict. Nyerere's mandate had the blessing of the United Nations and the international community at large, and he was thus bestowed the title of an international mediator for Burundi. Until the July 25, 1996, military coup, Nyerere had not yet been successful in bringing the conflicting parties together, despite his prestigious title. However, as a result of the sanctions imposed on Burundi by the leaders of the region, Nyerere was successful in bringing the conflicting parties to the negotiating table on June 15, 1998.

The repeated crises in Congo-Brazzaville (the Republic of Congo) accompanied the sudden democratization of the Afro-Marxist single-party state by means of a Sovereign National Conference (CNS in the French abbreviation) in 1990. When the country's first contested elections of 1991 gave rise to protests and then to the mobilization of party militias, a large number of local and international mediators began to offer their services. In the end, a Special Representative of the Secretary-General of the OAU and the president of a neighboring state, Gabon, restored peace and order in August 1993. But when the next round of elections approached, in 1997, violence again broke out, led by the militias that had not been disarmed as the 1993 agreement had stipulated. Again, numerous mediators stepped forward but the same pair took the lead. Just as they crafted an agreement, reinforcements from neighboring Angola carried the rebels to victory against the elected regime. Yet fighting continued, bringing back mediators from a variety of international sources who finally arranged the surrender and amnesty of a number of militias at the end of 1999. However, after elections under a reimposed single-party system in 2002, violence broke out again.

Civil war began in Liberia on Christmas Eve 1989, when a small band of dissidents entered the country and roused the deep-felt opposition to the regime of Samuel Doe. Local and international NGOs, great powers, and African neighbor states operating as the regional organization all entered the competition as mediators. Over the course of the next six years, thirteen agreements were negotiated until one could be devised in mid-1996 that brought the fighting to an end long enough to hold elections the following year. The Economic Community of West African States (ECOWAS) and its dominant member, Nigeria, were the most active of the mediators.

Sudan's civil war was triggered in May 1983 following the abrogation of the 1972 Addis Ababa Agreement that ended the first war of nearly two decades. The agreement was instrumental in ending the first civil war in 1972 by granting regional autonomy to the south. Numerous entry initiatives have been attempted in trying to mediate a lasting political settlement, but the mediators have usually exited without obtaining a compromise agreement. The Inter-Governmental Authority on Development (IGAD) succeeded in gaining access to the conflict in May 1993. Although the organization has seriously tried to engage the conflicting parties, it has not so far succeeded in moving them toward a compromise settlement. Regardless of its dismal performance, IGAD has not exited from the conflict. It still remains the only internationally recognized mediator.

War broke out between Ethiopia and Eritrea in 1998, five years after their separation into two independent states. African states operating alone and under the aegis of the OAU and great powers outside Africa hastened to mediate, as did an array of private groups. The conflict, basically over a contested border but more deeply over the political psychology of separation, continued for a year, alternating with mediation that gained one side's agreement but not the other's, with the agreement changing from side to side. Finally, in mid-1999, a coalition of African and U.S. efforts produced an end to the war and the beginning of an attempt to define the border.

The cases all come from Africa, where internal conflict is a major occurrence. They involve the most important instances of civil war and mediation, so that notions about entry can be tested in a wide variety of circumstances. The focus on more than one case facilitates a comparative analysis that can allow the development of insights and generalizations that would be applicable to a broader spectrum of mediation entry initiatives. The case studies are classic examples of longtime, deep-rooted, and relatively intractable internal conflicts. They also are clear cases of internal conflicts whose intensity and commitment demanded a third-party intervention.

Four cases—Rwanda, Burundi, Liberia, and Congo-Brazzaville—are centralist conflicts, where a national rebellion contested the incumbent government. All of these rebellions had an ethnic coloring, although it was the politics of exclusion rather than any innate opposition that led to the conflict. Sudan is a mixed case, combining centralist and regionalist features in an unstable relationship, with religion added to ethnic identity as an underlying element of conflict.

One interstate case, the Eritrean-Ethiopian border war of 1998–2000, is included as a "control" to test intrastate findings in an interstate conflict. But it is also the consummation of a regionalist conflict that turned centralist—into the Ethiopian thirty-year civil war—and, as such, needs to be considered among the most important instances of African conflict. The lessons for mediation in these six case studies are, like the cases themselves, African. Although our observations of the entry phase of mediation in conflicts around the world suggest a valid generalizability, it is only by testing the instant study's conclusions against cases elsewhere that we will know whether their lessons are uniquely African or are more broadly relevant.

The organizational structure of the study consists of three major parts. Chapter 1 constitutes the first part that defines the objectives and the scope of the study. Apart from raising the problematic issues, it also provides a theoretical framework for the study's analysis. Chapters 2 to 7 constitute the second part of the study, presenting the six case studies through which the propositions and the hypotheses emanating from chapter 1 are tested. Chapter 8, the last part, draws out the study's specific theoretical and practical findings and conclusions. This is a historical case research that tries to explain a complex puzzle—the entry phase of mediation.

2

RWANDA,
1990–1992

Rwanda has experienced a disturbing and prolonged cycle of violent conflict since 1959, three years before it gained its independence. The conflict, which has been characteristically political and socio-economic in nature, has played out mainly on the basis of ethnicity and regionalism. Although the first phase of the conflict was set off during the process of the country's decolonization that began in the late 1950s, its seeds were sown during the colonial period itself.[1] It was first German and then Belgian colonialism that created and nurtured the country's ethnic rivalry between the majority Hutu and the minority Tutsi. The rivalry was constructed on the basis of a myth of Tutsi superiority over the Hutu in order to serve both the colonial policy of divide-and-rule and the colonial division of labor. The Tutsi were designated as the administrative supervisors and the Hutu as the labor force of the extractive colonial economy. It was on the basis of this specialized division of labor that the country's socio-political and socio-economic relations were established prior to independence.

The objectives of the 1959 revolution, which brought the Hutu to power, were to end colonialism and to change the socio-political and socio-economic relations that it had created. Unfortunately, though it succeeded in changing the colonial socio-political relations, it failed to crush the ethnic stereotypes that continue to haunt the country. Hence, if there was any-thing revolutionary about the 1959 revolution, it was the elitist role-reversal whereby Hutu elites succeeded in taking the reins of power from the Tutsis. Since independence, both Hutu and Tutsis elites continued to manipulate ethnic hatred for socio-political advantage. The second phase of the conflict came during the early 1970s, when Juvénal Habyarimana initiated a coup that replaced the nationalist president Grégoire Kayibanda. Although this phase of the conflict had interethnic connotations and implications, it was more of an intra-Hutu regional conflict—a protest of the northern Hutu, represented by Habyarimana, against the exclusionist tendencies of the Kayibanda regime, which was mainly dominated by the Hutu of the south and central part of the country.[2] The third phase of the conflict was the Tutsi return to power, sparked by the October 1990 invasion of the Rwandan Patriotic Front (RPF). The most common characteristic of all the phases of the Rwandan conflict has been the killing of tens or even hundreds of thousands of innocent civilians and the forcing of hundreds of thousands of others into exile as refugees.

This chapter focuses on the mediation efforts in the third phase of the conflict. Its time frame ranges from October 1990, following the RPF's invasion, to June 1992, when the Great Lakes Region's efforts to initiate mediation succeeded in launching the Arusha Peace Process under the Tanzania government's facilitation.

The following questions will form the basis of the chapter's analysis: What was the nature of the Rwandan conflict in this phase? Who were the major protagonists? What were the specific issues of the conflict? Who tried to intervene and what were their motives? What were the prospective inter-mediaries' perceptions of the nature of the conflict? Were these perceptions in line with those of the parties to the conflict? Why did the protagonists accept mediation and the particular prospective mediators? The chapter concludes with specific theoretical and practical lessons from the mediation experiences in Rwanda.

THE RWANDAN CIVIL WAR OF THE 1990S

The October 1990 civil war was a classic case of a centralist internal conflict based on the struggle for the control of central authority. A number of external and internal factors contributed to the timing of the RPF invasion from Uganda.

First the Rwandan government's policy of denying hundreds of thousands of refugees, scattered all over the world, the right to return to the country of their nationality amounted to a process of denationalizing them or condemning them to permanent refugee status—and thus an invitation to a forceful return. The policy was based on the argument that the country did not have enough land to resettle the returnees, and that its high population density made it all the more exigent that the refugees remain in the host countries. Against this backdrop, the refugees—the majority of whom, by the history of previous events, happened to be Tutsi—decided to organize to return by force.

Second, the role of the Rwandan refugees—who later constituted the backbone of the RPF—in helping bring Yoweri Museveni to power in Uganda in 1986, their numerical presence, and the high positions some of them attained in the Ugandan National Resistance Army (NRA) raised hostile nationalistic sentiments among Ugandans themselves, especially those who were opposed to Museveni.[3] These xenophobic sentiments and the subsequent sidelining of the Rwandan top officials within the NRA created among the refugees a feeling of being unwanted and a fear of future harassment and hastened preparations for their return. Thus the invasion was neither accidental nor spontaneous. It was carefully planned.

Within Rwanda, the RPF was helped by growing internal opposition against Habyarimana's regime. These were the 1990s, and, like everywhere else in Africa, Rwandans were being blown by the winds of political change. Thirty years of dictatorial leadership, human rights abuses, dismal economic performance, nepotism, corruption, and the north-south political rift provided an impetus for civil society to mobilize for political transformation. Inspired by the democratic changes taking place in other African countries and donor nations' conditionalities that tied foreign aid to political reform, courageous politicians, intellectuals, and journalists called for the introduction of a multiparty system. This call posed, for the first time, a serious threat to Habyarimana's single-party rule. In July 1990, he succumbed to these pressures and promised to form a national commission to study the issue. In September, a group of thirty-three agitators declared that there was no need for a commission to study the relevance of democratic changes. Rwanda was more than ready for multiparty politics.[4]

Another internal factor was Habyarimana's apparent change of heart on his refugee policy. In February 1988, he had formed a joint commission with Uganda to deal with the refugee problem, but nothing serious was done. Following the world congress of the Rwandan refugees held in Washington, D.C., in August 1988, which passed a resolution on the "right of return," even by force if necessary, Habyarimana started to pay more serious attention. During its third session, held in July 1990, the joint commission came up with a document that spelled out the modalities that would have guided the Rwandan officials to determine the list of the refugees to be repatriated from Uganda, effective in November.[5] However, the return came earlier and much differently than the joint commission envisioned.

The RPF invasion in October was a calculated pre-emptive move to prevent Habyarimana from making positive inroads in the political sphere and in the refugees' problem. The RPF militants were in danger of losing support from the refugees if the refugees would now be able to return peacefully, and of losing their political platform if Habyarimana were to install a multi-party system. Accordingly, as Gerard Prunier observed, the RPF militants "accelerated their preparations to beat the November deadline."[6]

Of lesser importance, but still significant, was the absence of both Museveni and Habyarimana in their capitals during the eleventh hour of the invasion. Both were in New York attending a United Nations Children's Fund conference on children's problems in the Third World. Hence, "Museveni would be able to distance himself from any RPF activities until it was too late to stop them, while in Habyarimana's absence, the regime in Rwanda would also find it more difficult to respond effectively."[7]

Despite initial setbacks the RPF proved within a short time to be a credible challenger to the Rwandan government. The Front suffered a shocking major loss on just the second day of the invasion, when its chief commander, Major-General Fred Rwigyema, was killed in ambiguous circumstances. After recovering from its initial shock, the government forces, the Forces Armées Rwandaise (FAR), backed by the French, launched a serious counteroffensive. Within two weeks, they succeeded not only in pushing back the invaders but also in killing two other RPF high-ranking commanders with a score of fighters as well as senior officers.[8] These initial losses threw the RPF in disarray and they were forced to retreat. But after lying low for two months, the RPF was able to regroup and relaunch what its new chief commander, Major-General Paul Kagame, called "the beginning of a protracted popular war."[9] This second offensive rooted the insurgency in the ground and established its credibility. It would take the RPF four years of military and diplomatic campaign to get rid of Habyarimana's regime and elevate itself to power.

THE PARTIES TO THE CONFLICT AND THEIR PATRONS

By early 1992, the conflict was already a triad in itself even before the involvement of an intermediary. Although the RPF invasion reduced the conflict to a two-party scenario, between itself and the government, the internal opposition was actually a third party. Each of the three parties had specific objectives, so it is important to explore how each party was constituted, what it stood for, and who its cheerleaders were.

The RPF

The RPF was constituted mainly by the Rwandan refugees, with Tutsis in the majority. Whereas its initial core leadership and the backbone of its fighters were refugees from Uganda, many others from the diaspora joined the organization as the war continued. The RPF's eight-point political program, adopted some years before the invasion,[10] called for national unity, democracy, an end to corruption and nepotism, a self-sustaining economy, improved social services, a national army, a progressive foreign policy, and an end to the system that generates refugees. Out of this comprehensive program, two objectives stand out: the return of refugees and the transformation of the Rwandan political system and all that it stood for.

The RPF faced a number of dilemmas in its effort to achieve the two objectives. The first dilemma was the tactical question. Defining one's objectives is one thing, deciding how to achieve them is another. Given the political circumstances prevailing then in Rwanda, military insurgency seemed to be the rational choice to guarantee the return of the refugees. But this approach created another dilemma. How could an exclusionist political system be transformed by an institution exclusively dominated by one ethnic group without being accused of the very ills that it was determined to eradicate? It dawned on the RPF that this would not have been possible without adopting an integrative approach; it was expedient to give the organization a national character in both its leadership and membership. This character was provided by the objective of overhauling the political system, as spelled out in the eight-point program, and appears to be the credible explanation for the inclusion and involvement of a few Hutu among the RPF combatants and in its leadership.

The RPF was fully aware that the involvement of the Hutu within its ranks could not be a cosmetic or a short-term expediency. It would never have been able to realize the objective of turning Rwanda into a democratic society under the RPF's leadership without a mass participation of the Hutu in it. Short of making the organization a truly integrative national movement, there was no way that the RPF could win and be legitimized by a free and fair multiparty election. The indication of that awareness could be deduced from its political agenda, which spelled out not only a democratic objective but also national unity and a national military. The RPF simply could not achieve national unity, let alone a unified national military, without adopting an integrative approach.

Two distinct categories of Hutu were attracted to the RPF. The first consisted of the Hutu who were political exiles and refugees like the Tutsis in Uganda. The RPF's objective of the "right of return" resonated with the plight of these Hutu as well. The political exiles included prominent Hutu personalities such as Colonel Alexis Kanyarengwe and Pasteur Bizimungu, who became top-ranking Hutu cadres in the RPF. The initial few Hutu fighters in the RPF were descendants of Hutu agricultural migrants who had moved to Uganda in the 1920s and 1930s to escape the harshness of Belgian colonialism and take advantage of the economic opportunities Uganda then offered. During Milton Obote's anti-refugee repression in Uganda in the early 1980s, the Hutu were targeted the same way as the Tutsi refugees. Some Hutus joined Museveni's NRA for the same reasons the Tutsi refugees did, and later on joined their Tutsi comrades-in-arms in the RPF.[11]

The second category of the Hutu who joined the RPF included those who were specifically attracted by its broader national political agenda to bring down Habyarimana's authoritarian regime. Admittedly, the political agenda took time to gain credibility among the population, but as the war dragged on and the RPF was scoring some impressive victories, some young Hutu men left their villages and enlisted in the RPF army. Some government soldiers also defected to the RPF side.

Some interpret the Hutu involvement in the RPF merely as opportunistic: it provided an avenue for combatants to earn a living, a stepping stone for quenching the megalomania of those who joined the ranks of its leadership, and a cover-up of the organization's Tutsi ethnic character in order to deceive the world.[12]

Though opportunism cannot be completely ruled out in individual cases, it should not, at the same time, be taken as the only credible explanation for Hutu participation in the RPF. Some Hutu combatants joined the RPF to earn a living, although the RPF was not paying its fighters. The proponents of this view may argue that the combatants did it as a long-term investment, expecting to be paid once conscripted in the regular army following the RPF victory. Though plausible, this would have been a really costly investment. How could they be sure that the RPF would succeed, or that they themselves would survive the war in the first place?

For the Hutu who joined the RPF leadership for opportunistic motives, doing so would have been equally costly and risky. Would it not have been cheaper for them to wait on the sidelines until the RPF took care of the Habyarimana regime and then pursue their political ambitions through the bandwagon of a democratic system by joining opposition parties? The most credible explanation for the presence of the Hutu in the RPF is that they were really committed to its nationalistic approach in dealing with Rwanda's political problems. Given the historical ethnic hatred between the two, it was an extraordinary measure of courage for the few Hutu and the Tutsi to trust each other and work together for a shared objective. Much credit should be given to the few Hutu who were courageous enough to risk their necks and join the RPF. Their action could serve as a much-needed bridge to link the people of Rwanda for a meaningful political transformation, irrespective of their deep-rooted ethnic animosity.

Uganda was the major supporter of the RPF. Its support was so obvious that it ran the risk of robbing the organization of its international sympathy and raising fears of the revival of the Hima Empire in the region. Many countries saw only "Museveni's hand in the RPF conspiracy" and downgraded the real plight of the Tutsi refugees, which was one of the issues that had forced the RPF to launch the war.[13] Yet it should not be difficult to understand the rationale of Uganda's support for the RPF. Museveni owed much to the RPF for the role its members played in the NRA. In addition, the RPF was almost a copy of Uganda's National Resistance Movement, the political wing of the NRA, in both policy and tactics. Both claimed to be broad-based nationalist movements, and both launched military insurgencies in order to replace the central authority. Also Museveni felt obliged to assist a seemingly "progressive" movement, such as the RPF in order to expand the new brand of African "progressive" leadership on the continent.

The Government

By the time the civil war broke out the government consisted of a political wing represented by the ruling party, the Mouvement Révolutionnaire National pour le Développement (MRND), and a military wing represented by the FAR. The government was dominated by the Hutu, particularly those from the north, where Habyarimana originated. The deliberate and institutionalized marginalization of the Tutsi was based on an exclusionist ideological myth that equated democracy with demography. The logic was that the Hutu majority automatically made the Hutu-controlled government both legitimate and democratic.

Throughout the Habyarimana years there was not a single Tutsi *bourgmestre* (equivalent to district head) or *préfect* (provincial head), only two Tutsi members of parliament out of seventy, only one Tutsi minister out of a cabinet of between twenty-five and thirty members, and only one Tutsi officer in the army, whose members were even prohibited by regulations from marrying Tutsi women.[14] The government's objective was to resist both the ethnic and regional threats to its power monopoly posed by the Tutsi under the guise of the RPF and by the southern and central regions' Hutu under the guise of the opposition parties, respectively. Against the RPF, the government was fighting for its survival—that is, not to be replaced by it. Against the internal opposition, it was fighting for its monopoly of power, refusing to open its doors to participation in government.

In the government's struggle for survival, France was the most reliable ally—it became the major supplier of arms to the Rwandan government, trained its various branches of the armed forces, including the notorious *interahamwe* militia, and advanced a vigorous diplomatic campaign in support of the government. One of the obvious steps in the transformation of Habyarimana's foreign policy in accordance with his internal initiative toward absolute power was the marginalization of Rwanda's former metropole, Belgium, as a primary foreign ally in favor of France.[15] It was beneficial to Rwanda to join the larger and more prestigious Francophonia club rather than remain in the smaller and less glamorous Belgian camp.

One of the indicators of this change of policy was Rwanda's attendance at the Francophonia summits that began during the Giscard d'Estaing administration and became more prominent during the Mitterrand administration. It is only France, among the former colonial powers that once ruled Africa, that "has kept the will and the political breathing space, both at home and on the African continent, to use military power whenever it feels the need to add muscle to its policies in defense of its 'special relationship' with Africa."[16] Gérard Prunier contends that there are personal material rewards from this policy: Africa is used as a money-laundering machine:

> Overpriced government contracts are given to good trusted friends and dull public money becomes vibrantly alive in private hands. . . . There is a high degree of symbiosis between French and francophone African political elites. It is a mixture of many things: old memories, shared material interests, delusions of grandeur, gossip, sexual peccadilloes—in short, a common culture for which there is no equivalent among ex-colonial powers with the possible and partial exception of Portugal.[17]

France's paranoia of the Anglo-Saxon influence and the danger it posed to French interests is another explanation of its deep involvement in the Rwandan crisis. Referred to as the "Fashoda Syndrome" (reminiscent of the 1898 clash of British and French colonial ambitions at a small village in southern Sudan), the French Anglo-Saxon paranoia is very much a part of French foreign policy thinking, particularly in Africa, where France's post-colonial interests are concentrated and important.

The Internal Opposition

Rwanda's internal opposition gained prominence the very moment that the RPF invaded the country. There was a kind of reciprocity between the two groups: While the internal political situation was one of the influencing factors in the RPF's timing of the invasion, the invasion in turn acted as a catalyst for internal political agitation. It took just a month after the invasion for Habyarimana to agree to political change. In a speech on November 11, 1990, he promised that a multiparty system would soon be allowed and that there would be a constitutional referendum in June 1991.[18] On the basis of this promise, a new constitution was proclaimed on June 10, 1991, which allowed the existence of a multiparty system. By the beginning of 1992, the internal opposition comprised five major political parties.

The Mouvement Démocratique Républicain (MDR), formed in March 1991, adopted a name of an old party, the Mouvement Démocratique Rwandais, Kayibanda's transformed Parmehutu, which was abolished in 1973 following Habyarimana's coup. It had to change its name to shed its negative image associated with the anti-Tutsi massacres during the 1959 revolution. Like Kayibanda's old MDR, the new one also drew its membership from Hutu in the north, especially Ruhengeri, where Habyarimana came from, and the south and the central part, particularly Gitarama, Kayibanda's birthplace. The Gitarama membership outnumbered that of Ruhengeri by two to one, and then potentially inherited the Hutu regional rivalry that was characteristic of the Kayibanda period as well as Habyarimana's time. Ideologically, the MDR adopted a populist approach.

The Parti Social Démocrate (PSD) was a center-left party that drew its membership from the civil service and other professions. Based in the southern province of Butare, the PSD was a moderate party that tolerated a bit of ethnic mix, unlike the MDR.

The Parti Libéral (PL) was a center-right party with no specific geographical or ethnic base. It was therefore the only party that could boast of being a real national party by being able to attract both the Hutu and the Tutsi to its ranks. These liberal leanings, however, resonated more with the urbanites than with the rural people; hence, its following was confined to prominent and well-to-do Hutu and Tutsi.

The Parti Démocrate Chrétien (PDC) was smaller than the other three parties. Given the strong and warm relations between the Catholic Church and the Habyarimana regime, it was not an easy job for the PDC to make inroads into the political arena on the basis of a religious ideology.

The Coalition for the Defense of the Republic was also very small but one of the most significant parties in the future politics of the country. It was one of the most extremist Hutu parties, and its anti-Tutsi ideology took it to the fringes of racism. It benefited from the fact that the internal opposition depended more on the conducive international and regional political environment that favored political transformation in Africa than on specific external support as such.

ENTRY INITIATIVES AND THE ROAD TO ARUSHA

The Early Responses and the Internationalization of the Conflict

Responses to the RPF invasion were immediate and varied, according to the way the actors perceived the conflict. The government of Rwanda, while aware of the internal sources of the conflict, quickly tried to internationalize it by turning it into an interstate conflict between Rwanda and Uganda. After all, the invaders came directly from Uganda, and the initial 2,500

RPF invaders were all soldiers of the Ugandan army who entered Rwanda still in Ugandan army uniform and ranks, armed and equipped with Ugandan army weapons and materiel. Habyarimana hoped that his characterization of the conflict as an interstate one would make the outside world sympathetic to Rwanda for being "invaded" by Uganda.

Buying the "invasion-from-outside" perception, France, Belgium, and Zaire responded quickly by sending troops. Although France and Belgium justified their action on the excuse of protecting their nationals, France's subsequent behavior indicated beyond doubt that it sent in troops to assist the Rwandan government; Belgium withdrew its troops by the end of the month after a brief stay and called for the formation of an African peacekeeping force.[19] As for Zaire, Mobutu had long been a patron of Habyarimana and so Zairian troops quickly joined the FAR in fighting against the RPF, although they were withdrawn later for indiscipline.

The Belgians, nonetheless, had a two-track response. They sent troops to Rwanda and, at the same time, initiated a diplomatic offensive by dispatching a powerful delegation to Rwanda, Kenya, Uganda, Tanzania, and Ethiopia to hold talks with the heads of state of those countries and the secretary-general of the Organization of African Unity. The offensive was aimed at encouraging the regional leaders and the OAU to prevail on Uganda to stop the invasion rather than to force Habyarimana into accepting mediated talks with the RPF. The diplomatic initiative appears to have been taken on the basis of the *perception* of the *interstate* conflict.

Whereas France and Belgium responded immediately as a result of their historical ties with Rwanda, the other major powers did not respond at all, or their response came a bit late, and the most probable explanation for their late responses is that the conflict itself was a victim of timing as far as some of the major powers were concerned. The conflict started on the eve of the most spectacular world changes, as the international community moved from the Cold War to the uncertain post–Cold War era. The conspicuous absence of the former Soviet Union's response to the Rwandan conflict can be explained by these world changes. The Soviet Union was, at this time, undergoing its own internal upheaval.

The U.S. delay in responding was attributable to a number of reasons— chief among them, the standard U.S. policy of not paying attention to African conflicts that did not have a direct impact on its national interests. This prioritization of foreign policy concerns was compounded by its newfound status as the only superpower after the collapse of the Soviet Union; the United States was undergoing a soul-searching exercise on how to respond to numerous world crises that were emerging. Second, the attention of the United States, together with some of the European major powers, particularly Britain, Italy, and Germany, was focused elsewhere at the time—within its "sphere of influence" in the Philippines, Panama, and Haiti, or together with the European powers in the Persian Gulf, Yugoslavia, Angola, and Somalia. And third, attention during the initial stage of the Rwandan conflict was pre-empted by the early response of the French and the Belgians; so long as these two took care of their "neighborhood," the United States felt no need to meddle. The United States' and Britain's delay in responding was also encouraged by two specific considerations: to minimize the French paranoia of the "Anglo-Saxon conspiracy" and to avoid being labeled as "accomplices" to the so-called "Museveni interests" in the Rwandan war.[20]

The Regional Response: October 1990–August 1991

The regional response was initiated by Tanzania and Zaire and continued later on with the active involvement of the OAU. It was agreed at this stage that Mobutu should be the region's and the OAU's mediator of the conflict. Mobutu's early response was one of the reasons that led to his endorsement by the region and the OAU for the mediating role; his patronage of Habyarimana was another reason. The logic here was that he was the leader in the region most likely to prevail over Habyarimana, delivering the agreement of the party that the mediator favored.[21] Although the other regional leaders were aware of Mobutu's domestic problems, they recognized the fact that he was still around and they could not just wish him away.

The early regional response was motivated by security concerns. Considering that Rwanda had perceived the conflict as between itself and Uganda, the regional leaders feared the possibility of an interstate war. Their early intervention was also intended to prevent further internationalization of the conflict as demonstrated by the French and Belgian response. Furthermore, the region intervened as an ad hoc collective security mechanism to prevent the conflict's spillover effects.

The effectiveness of mediation depends on the proper understanding of the nature and character of the conflict. The summitry approach adopted by the early regional response was determined by these regional misperceptions of the Rwandan conflict. There were those—Zaire and, to a certain extent, Kenya—who bought Habyarimana's argument that the conflict was between Rwanda and Uganda. Others perceived the conflict in the traditional "government-versus-rebels" terms.[22] Still others saw the refugee problem as the major cause of the conflict. Because the nature and character of the conflict were not properly comprehended, the summitry approach was bound to face difficulties.

On the basis of the "interstate conflict" and "government-versus-rebels" misperceptions of the conflict, the flurry of regional summits that took place at various venues between October 17, 1990, and September 7, 1991, concentrated on engaging the heads of state of Uganda and Rwanda. The RPF initially was not directly involved in the talks because, from the interstate-conflict perspective, it was not a party to the conflict, and, from the government-versus-rebels perspective, it was regarded as illegitimate. Accordingly, the heads of state negotiated with their peers Habyarimana and Museveni, hoping to end the conflict without directly involving the RPF on the basis of the assumption that Museveni would deliver the RPF agreement. On the basis of the perception that the conflict was a one-factor crisis, the summits focused more on the issue of refugees. Presumably, the logic was that if it was the refugee problem that forced the RPF to invade Rwanda, its resolution would have ended the conflict automatically.

The unexpected launching of the war on October 1, 1990, led to Belgian shuttle diplomacy in the region to encourage the regional leaders to intervene diplomatically. The region responded by convening the Mwanza summit on October 17; the Gbadolite summit on October 26; and the Goma summit on November 20. The Mwanza summit was attended by the presidents of Tanzania, Rwanda, and Uganda. High on its agenda was the issue of the refugees, identified by the heads of state as one of the major factors underlying the conflict. Consequently, it was decided that a regional conference on the problem of the refugees should be organized in order to find a lasting solution to the problem.[23] The Gbadolite summit was attended by the presidents of Zaire, Rwanda, and Burundi. It reaffirmed, among other things, the decision of the Mwanza summit to hold a regional conference on the refugee problem. The Goma summit, attended by the presidents of Zaire, Rwanda, and Burundi, and the third deputy prime minister of Uganda, dwelled at length on the refugee problem as well.

The RPF's successful attack at Ruhengeri, the home province of President Habyarimana, on January 23, 1991, prompted the Zanzibar summit on February 17, the Dar-es-Salaam summit on February 19, and the N'sele summit on March 29. The Zanzibar mini-summit was a precursor to the regional conference on the problem of Rwandan refugees held in Dar-es-Salaam. Attended by the presidents of Tanzania and Rwanda, it had more of a consultative than a substantive nature. The convener of the regional conference on the Rwandan refugee problem, President Ali Hassan Mwinyi of Tanzania, wanted to consult and get the feeling of the president of Rwanda on the agenda before the conference.

The regional conference on refugees was preceded by an experts' meeting (January 17–18, 1991) and a ministerial meeting (January 19–20, 1991). It was during these two meetings that the draft declaration on the refugee problem was examined and adopted. The regional conference itself was held in Dar-es-Salaam under the chairmanship of President Mwinyi. It was attended by the presidents of Burundi, Rwanda, Uganda, and the prime minister of Zaire as the representative of the mediator, President Mobutu. At its conclusion, the Dar-es-Salaam Declaration on the Rwandan Refugees Problem was adopted.

The Declaration was a usual diplomatic litany that apportioned responsibilities and commitments to everyone but lacked specific decisions pertaining to the immediate problem. The government of Rwanda recognized the legitimate rights of the refugees to voluntary repatriation and committed itself to finding a definitive and durable solution to the problem by removing all the obstacles that impeded their return. The four neighboring countries—Burundi, Uganda, Tanzania, and Zaire—undertook to facilitate the naturalization of the Rwandans who may have desired to become nationals of the host countries, and the international community and international organizations were called upon to facilitate the naturalization.

The little that the Declaration touched on regarding the immediate conflict thanked President Mobutu "for his efforts in instituting a dialogue between the Rwandan government and the armed opposition" and urged him to maintain the momentum of the dialogue.[24] The regional leaders realized that their mediation efforts had failed to stop the military conflict, and it must have dawned on them that the failure had much to do with their mediation approach. This realization necessitated changes in both their perceptions of the conflict and the approach to its mediation. It is obvious that at that juncture, nobody among the regional leaders, apart from Habyarimana, believed the argument that the conflict was between Rwanda and Uganda. Hence, this perception was dropped.

By dropping the interstate perception, the regional leaders automatically confirmed that the RPF was a party to the conflict regardless of its legal status. And the RPF's effectiveness at the war front forced the regional leaders to realize that they would not be able to make a significant move in their efforts to mediate the conflict without seriously engaging it. It was obvious, subsequently, that if there was anybody that the regional leaders were supposed to deliver, it was not the RPF but their colleague, President Habyarimana. They had to convince him that whatever his perception of the conflict, a mediated resolution was impossible without negotiating directly with the RPF. It appears that these realities were brought home to Habyarimana during the Zanzibar and Dar-es-Salaam summits, and he was convinced to accept them in order to facilitate the mediation process.

Inspired by the Dar-es-Salaam Declaration, which, among other things, committed Habyarimana to "find a definitive and durable solution to the problem" and asked Mobutu to "maintain the momentum of the dialogue," the first direct negotiations between the government of Rwanda and the RPF took place in March under Mobutu's mediation and resulted, on March 16, in a cease-fire agreement that was formally signed on March 29 at N'sele by Rwandan foreign minister Casimir Bizimungu and RPF vice-chairman Paul Kagame. The signing ceremony was presided over by the mediator, President Mobutu, and was witnessed by the OAU secretary-general, the foreign ministers of Uganda and Zaire, the deputy foreign minister of Tanzania, and a representative of Burundi.[25] The N'sele cease-fire agreement contained provisions for a continued dialogue between the parties and instituted a Neutral Military Observer Group (NMOG) to monitor the cease-fire. The NMOG was composed of five military officers each from the government of Rwanda, the RPF, Burundi, Uganda, and Zaire, under the supervision of the OAU secretary-general's representative.[26] It took more than a month to assemble the NMOG before it was deployed on May 7, 1991. Immediately following its deployment, the government broke the cease-fire by attacking the RPF.

There are two reasons the N'sele cease-fire agreement was not respected. The first was that although Habyarimana had agreed to negotiate directly with the RPF, the decision seemed not to have been made with a genuine commitment to a compromise settlement. The fact that the government was the first to violate the N'sele agreement attested to this sentiment. The second reason was that neither of the parties had faith in the cease-fire's monitoring mechanism, the NMOG. Both the government and the RPF had problems with its composition. The government did not trust the impartiality of the NMOG's Ugandan and Burundian officials, while the RPF, for its part, did not trust the officials from Zaire. As a result, the cease-fire was deliberately violated partly in order to prevent the effective deployment of the NMOG.

From the signing of the N'sele agreement to the Gbadolite summit of September 7, 1991, there were no triggers from the war front to push the regional initiative forward. The stalemate at the front during this period contributed to the diplomatic slowdown. The question was how the region could come out of this diplomatic slumber and reactivate the mediation efforts.

It took another summitry framework to reactivate the regional process—specifically, the OAU's annual summit of June 1991. Meeting in Abuja, the OAU directed the secretary-general to organize another regional summit that would continue the mediation efforts to end the conflict. The resulting summit of September 7, 1991, was preceded by a series of talks between the parties under the chairmanship of the mediator. Many of the sessions were on the problem of striking a deal on a new cease-fire agreement. When the parties agreed on the new terms of the cease-fire, it was signed under the supervision of President Mobutu. Nigeria's president Ibrahim Babangida, the chairman of the OAU at the time, also witnessed the signing ceremony.

The Gbadolite cease-fire agreement was a revised version of the N'sele agreement. The most significant change was the reconstitution of the NMOG. Instead of having its members from Rwanda, the RPF, Uganda, Burundi, and Zaire, this time the NMOG was exclusively composed of officers from Nigeria and Zaire; Nigeria was also to provide the overall commanding officer. This decision was intended to address some of the problems that had undermined the N'sele cease-fire agreement. However, once more, the Gbadolite cease-fire agreement, like the N'sele agreement, was not respected. Military skirmishes continued and the NMOG had in effect no cease-fire to monitor. The failure of the Gbadolite cease-fire agreement could again be attributed specifically to the government's lack of a firm commitment to a compromise solution.

A Postmortem of the Summitry Phase

The Gbadolite summit of September 7, 1991, was the climax to both the summitry approach and Mobutu's role as the mediator for the Rwandan conflict. It is obvious that the summitry approach failed to mediate the conflict. The first major contributing factor to the failure was the multiplicity of perceptions in the region concerning the nature and character of the conflict. Some regional leaders still saw it as an interstate conflict and others as a refugee problem, although the perception of a civil war was growing. Second, the summitry approach contributed to the failure. The high-profile nature of the mediation failed to do the job. Third, the regional initiative at this phase did not deal effectively with all the parties to the conflict and all the issues involved. Although the RPF was invited to some of the summits, it was not involved in direct talks with the government before the N'sele meeting. Although the conflict had various demands, the summits concentrated more on the problem of the refugees. Although other groups inside Rwanda had interests in the talks, no internal group had ever been invited. Fourth, the summits were spontaneous events, each responding to particular triggers. Accordingly, they lacked consistence and continuity, which are crucial components of an effective mediation process. And last, it is doubtful whether at this stage all the parties to the conflict were ready for and fully committed to a compromise solution.

Zeroing in on the Mediator: September 1991–June 1992

By September 1991 the conflict had transformed a great deal; it was already tested both at the war front and at the negotiating table. From the battlefield the conflict had changed from its earlier conventional framework to a potentially protracted guerrilla war. From the negotiating table it was clear that the conflict no longer needed the kind of initial "fire brigade" types of responses for its resolution. It now required a well-thought-out strategy that would be complemented by both technical expertise and an expanded and effectively reliable support system. More important, from both the battlefield and the negotiating table, the parties to the conflict had a better chance to make a cost-benefit assessment of their goals and the means at their disposal to attain them. These realities also helped the interested external parties to readjust their positions. It was under these conditions that the conflict had paved its road to Arusha.

After the failure of the initial phase of the regional initiative, it was obvious that external supplementary efforts would be necessary to keep the process going. The initiative's support system was therefore expanded from the exclusively regional to the international level, involving the active participation of the United States and France. There was also a significant change of approach as well. Instead of a collective high-profile diplomacy, a low-profile and one-on-one contact strategy was adopted. Senior officials of the U.S. State Department and French officials had various contacts with the officials of the parties to the conflict, along with regional heads of state and other relevant senior officials.[27]

These efforts were complemented by the internal political developments in Rwanda. On March 4, 1992, Habyarimana compromised with the internal opposition by agreeing to form a coalition government. The new government, sworn in on April 7, was mandated to conduct peace negotiations with the RPF and made its first direct contact with the RPF on May 24, when Foreign Minister Boniface Ngulinzira met RPF vice-chairman Patrick Mazimpaka in Kampala. The meeting was an outcome of earlier separate high-level contacts between U.S. assistant secretary of state for Africa Herman Cohen and the presidents of Uganda and Rwanda. Following this meeting, it was announced that there would be direct negotiations between the two parties in Paris in June.[28] Parallel to the Paris meeting between the government and the RPF, the latter also met with a delegation of the opposition parties, composed of the representatives of the MDR, PSD, and PL, on June 6 in Brussels. The government and the RPF met again in Dakar, Senegal, in June, immediately before the OAU's annual summit, and reaffirmed their resolve to hold comprehensive negotiations as agreed upon in the Paris meeting. After three days of deliberations in Paris, the government and the RPF finally agreed on June 6 to hold comprehensive political negotiations under Tanzania's mediation. Arusha, Tanzania, was picked as the venue for the negotiations that were scheduled to begin on July 10, 1992.[29]

There were disagreements between the parties on the issues of the mediator and the venue. The government wanted the negotiations to be held in Paris under the French mediation, but the RPF insisted on holding the negotiations in Africa under African mediation. Tanzania was chosen as the mediator and Arusha as the venue. The selection of Tanzania as the mediator replaced Zaire as the initial mediator. To avoid bad feelings with Mobutu personally and the region as a whole, a compromise was reached to maintain both countries' involvement but with different responsibilities. President Ali Hassan Mwinyi of Tanzania was designated to be the "Official Facilitator," while President Mobutu was designated as the "Official Mediator." Mobutu's retention was to serve a number of purposes. It was a face-saving mechanism: it prevented Mobutu's personal ego from interfering with the mediation process. It also preserved the link between the initial regional premediation and the more internationalized second phase.

Four factors contributed to the success of this premediation phase. First, there was a change in the perception of the nature and character of the conflict. It was clear by this time that, regardless of its external characteristics, the conflict was an internal matter. The change in perception in turn allowed the real parties to the conflict to be engaged. Direct contacts were therefore concentrated on the three major contenders: the government, the RPF, and the internal opposition. Glamorous and high-profile diplomacy was replaced by a low-profile and cutting-edge quiet diplomacy. And the regional support system for the initiative was expanded to include other major actors outside the region.

Explaining the Outcome

The immediate regional response in trying to mediate the Rwandan conflict prevented a rush of other aspiring interveners. Although a number of actors became involved in the process, the region succeeded in claiming and formalizing the ownership of the mediation initiative. The only option open to other prospective mediators was to contribute to and support the regional efforts. The equally immediate Belgian diplomatic response was a good example of such support and contribution; it was not intended to create a parallel initiative but to encourage the regional leaders to take up the responsibility.

The delayed intervention of the U.S. and the French mixed position (of sending troops and encouraging dialogue) was also crucial and supportive to the region, particularly during the second phase of the premeditation process. Hence, at the end of the day, after almost two years of trying, the selection of Tanzania as the mediator became the consensus not only of the parties to the conflict but also of the other states in the region and the international community as a whole.

The stampede within Africa, and at the international level, was restrained by the firm support of the OAU, under whose auspices the regional summits took place. The OAU was very instrumental throughout the process in both arranging the regional summits and drafting the various communiqués and agreements. Equally important among its contribution was its role in the establishment and the supervision of the NMOG.

The OAU's active role in the regional initiative was explained by a number of factors. During this period, OAU secretary-general Salim Ahmed Salim was steering the organization toward a redefinition of its vision and mission at a time when the world was undergoing a fundamental transformation. The organization was discussing the relevance of having a new mechanism for conflict management and resolution, and its active involvement in the Rwandan conflict was a practical part of that objective and was an expression of Africa's commitment to find its own solutions to its problems.

UN involvement was indirect, mostly supporting the efforts of the region and the regional organization, the OAU. Its direct role was exercised by its agency, the United Nations High Commissioner for Refugees, which was active throughout, especially during the first phase of the regional process, in organizing the regional summits that addressed the refugee problem.

Zaire's replacement by Tanzania as the mediator needs to be explained as well. Zaire's president was, at that time, losing his moral authority to command events and his respect in the region. Even his initial mediating role in the Rwanda conflict was translated as his personal attempt to revive his regional status. Mobutu's declining prestige (and health) was mirrored by his country's political status, as it gradually collapsed as a political entity.[30] Hence the political decline of the leader and the country called into question Zaire's effectiveness in handling the rigors of a mediation process.

At the same time, mediators need adequate resources—facilities, logistics, influence, incentives, and sanctions—for a successful mediation. It was doubtful whether Zaire had any of these. Yet another factor was Mobutu's bias, stemming from his good relations with the Habyarimana regime. His partiality implied an ability to deliver the Rwandan regime's agreement in the mediation, which he proved unable to do.

Regardless of these factors, it is important to recognize both Zaire's and Mobutu's positive contributions to the regional initiative. It was Zaire and Tanzania that initiated the regional response, and it was from this early response that, later on, the region and the OAU endorsed Mobutu as the mediator for the conflict. It was from Mobutu's personal efforts that the parties had agreed to meet face-to-face for the first time at N'sele and concluded the N'sele and Gbadolite cease-fire agreements. The fact that the two cease-fire agreements were not respected does not diminish Mobutu's contribution in mediating the cease-fires.

Tanzania's availability as the mediator for the Arusha peace negotiations was achieved through a process of elimination. Along with Zaire, the other concerned countries in the region were tarnished in one way or another. The bitter personal hostilities then between Presidents Moi and Museveni would not have allowed the latter to convince the RPF to accept Kenya as the mediator. Burundi's similarities to Rwanda, in both history and the nature of their ethnic conflicts, were strong reasons for its elimination. Tanzania therefore remained the clear choice.

However, Tanzania also possessed other important qualifications. Apart from providing the venue for the negotiations, it was among the first countries to respond to the conflict. Furthermore, the country commanded political respect in the region as a result of its domestic political stability, as well as its contribution to the decolonization process, particularly in southern Africa. Its fights against human injustices at international forums gave the country good political standing in the region. The fact that Rwanda depended on Tanzanian ports for 80 percent of its imports and exports was also an added factor.

Tanzania's acceptance of the challenge had been influenced by human, national, and regional considerations. A peaceful resolution of the Rwandan conflict would have stopped the human tragedies associated with the conflict. The war in Rwanda had a direct impact on Tanzania in terms of economic and security reasons. A stream of refugees fleeing the war in Rwanda had ecological, economic, security, and social effects on Tanzania. Instability in Rwanda affected regional stability and, consequently, regional trade.

Why the Parties Accepted Mediation and the Mediator

The government's acceptance of mediation went through three fluctuating phases. At the initial stage of the conflict, the government readily accepted the regional intervention because it believed that the region shared its perception that the conflict was between Rwanda and Uganda. The initial acceptance had nothing to do with accepting either direct negotiation with the RPF or a compromise settlement. It was aimed at impressing upon regional leaders the need to condemn or to force Museveni to withdraw his "invading" troops. In a way, the initial acceptance was used as bait to attract sympathy and external assistance.

Although the government succeeded in getting sympathy and assistance from Zaire, Belgium, and France, it had problems in selling the idea of a Ugandan invasion to the international community at large. When the government was forced to accept the realities of the domestic sources of the conflict, it adopted the traditional "government-versus-rebels" perception. At this second phase, the government accepted the regional mediation for two reasons: It was faced with a fait accompli; the region was keen in intervening whether the parties liked it or not. And it seemed to have responded to the premise that "collective intervention is generally regarded as more legitimate than unilateral intervention."[31] However, while it endorsed the regional peace initiative, it refused to negotiate directly with the RPF because of the latter's illegitimacy. As for its acceptance of Mobutu's mediation during the initial stage of the regional initiative, the reason was the very good relationship between Rwanda and Zaire and between Habyarimana and Mobutu.

In the third phase, in June 1992, the government accepted mediation specifically because of the conflict's political and economic impact. On the political front, the government was forced to share power with an internal opposition that was keen on getting a negotiated settlement with the RPF. On the war front, the RPF was steadily gaining ground. In spite of the military assistance from France in terms of both logistics and personnel, the FAR was nowhere near defeating the guerrillas.

At the economic front, the war was badly affecting the already shaky economy. By mid-1992, while export revenue remained steady at 8.9 billion Rwandan francs, imports had increased from 23 to 38 billion francs. Public debt increased from 6,678 to 13,702 million francs. During the same period, the Ministry of Defense budget had increased from 3,155 to 8,885 million francs. The increase corresponded with that of the army, which grew from 5,200 men when the war started to 50,000 men by mid-1992.[32] The government finally accepted mediation because it was clear that it could not succeed in achieving a military victory over the RPF. And, second, it was economically too costly to continue to pursue the military option. It alone was in a hurting stalemate.

If the RPF was relatively stronger on the war front than the government, why did it accept mediation? In spite of the fact that the RPF had started the military confrontation, it appears that its objective from the outset was a political rather than a military victory. The RPF's behavior on the battlefield was the most illustrative indication of its preference for a political solution. Responding to the mass killings of Tutsi by Hutu extremists, the RPF withdrew from the Arusha talks and, on February 8, 1993, broke the cease-fire with a serious offensive against the FAR. In less than two weeks it had covered such an extensive territory that it was just thirty kilometers north of Kigali when it proclaimed a unilateral cease-fire on February 20 and withdrew to its previous positions.[33]

Regardless of the reasons that had forced it not to advance to Kigali, the mere fact that the RPF voluntarily decided to relinquish territory that it had conquered was unusual in guerrilla warfare. The action—an "escalation to call" in poker terms—was demonstrative enough to show that the RPF did not seek an outright military victory but, rather, a political settlement.[34] Not only would the majority Hutu not have accepted the total Tutsi domination of an outright victory, but military victory also would have made it difficult for the RPF to implement its political agenda. The war was intended to serve two short-term objectives: to speed up the return of the refugees and to serve as a bargaining chip for Tutsi participation in the county's politics.

Accordingly, the RPF accepted mediation because a mediated solution was consistent with its political objectives spelled out in its eight-point program. Apart from the return of refugees, the remaining points in the program made up a favorable recipe for a compromise solution. Hence, the RPF accepted the regional intervention, first and foremost because it badly wanted international recognition, sympathy, and support. Second, it wanted a quick political solution because its supporters could not afford to sustain the armed insurgency for a long time. Obviously, its stalemate did not hurt as much as the government's, but it saw that it might be if the war continued, producing the same effect subjectively. The RPF accepted Mobutu's mediation because it wanted to go along with the regional initiative and its choice of the mediator. It was also a tactical move to prevent Mobutu from undermining the regional efforts if he were not accepted as mediator.

There are two reasons the opposition parties accepted mediation. Viewed individually, each had an opportunity to advance its individual agenda through mediation. After all, dialogue is the domain of politicians; it provided them with an opening for recognition and integration into the political process. Viewed as part of the coalition government, they shared the same reasons that forced the government to accept mediation. But, frankly, the merger between the MRND and the opposition parties was in form only; each party continued to pursue its own political agenda.

CONCLUSION

The Rwandan conflict did not attract as many prospective mediators as one would have expected of a conflict of such magnitude. One of the obvious explanations for such low enthusiasm for playing an intermediary role was the risk associated with trying to resolve such a challenge in another country's internal strife. But most important, the early and effective regional response was a key factor in locking the door for the direct involvement of other prospective intermediaries. The following specific theoretical and practical conclusions can be drawn from the Rwandan experience:

1. Self-interest is basic to prospective mediators and their motivation to get involved in internal conflicts. This was shown not only in the immediate response of the neighboring countries but also in the distant interested parties such as France and Belgium. The swift regional response of specific countries in the region, and that of France and Belgium were in sharp contrast with the lukewarm response of the rest of the international community, which appeared to have been less interested in Rwanda.

2. Once access has been gained by one mediator to perform a particular mediating role, it is absolutely necessary that there should be no competitors for the same role, but this does not rule out the involvement of other actors. Other actors can either play other intermediary roles or act as part of the support system. But competitive involvement creates chaos in mediation and subsequently undermines the whole process. Gaining control provides legitimacy and creates a sense of ownership of the mediation process. The most significant contribution of control is that it establishes order in the intermediary process. In Rwanda, order had been created by the effective regional involvement. While the regional intervention did not rule out the involvement of other actors, the other actors did not compete with but complemented the regional initiative.

3. The Rwandan case demonstrated a direct relationship between perceptions, positions, and policy options. The conflict demonstrated that the three variables are not constant, they change as the conflict evolves. The change impacts both the parties and the mediator. Rwanda was a central-

ist conflict that could be defined in several ways. When the government initially perceived the conflict as an invasion from another state, it adopted an uncompromising position. A military response was the preferred policy option. The military option was directed toward the RPF as well as Uganda, which was perceived as the real culprit. The border incursions between the two countries were a clear indication that Rwanda was willing to go to war with Uganda. Although the government had accepted the regional intervention at the initial stage of the conflict, it did so within the context of its "interstate conflict" perception. The government had hoped that its acceptance of the regional intervention would have exposed Uganda.

When the government was forced to appreciate the realities of the domestic causes of the conflict, its perception of the nature of conflict changed from the original "interstate conflict" to a "government-versus-rebels" perception. Its position continued to be uncompromising and it pursued the military track as the preferred policy option, now directed not at Uganda but to the defeat of the RPF within Rwanda.

When the war began to hurt the government seriously, it was forced to adopt a compromise stance. This stance was what finally committed the government to a policy of mediated settlement. The regional initiative also experienced the same perceptual, positional, and policy transformation. Perceptually, the regional initiative shifted from an "interstate conflict" to a "government-versus-rebels" to a "refugees problem" position. Its policy options shifted from summitry to a serious mediated engagement of the parties through Tanzania's facilitation, which was mandated by the region.

3

BURUNDI, 1993–1998

Since its independence in 1962, Burundi has been a land of political chaos. Save for a few moments of political tranquility the country has undergone prolonged cycles of ethnic violence, marked by the assassinations of prominent politicians, coups, countercoups, attempted coups, massacres, political exiles, hundreds of thousands of refugees and displaced persons, and, subsequently, lack of development. From 1966 to 1993, Burundi's politics was dominated by a military oligarchy. Coups have been the vehicle of leadership change.

All the heads of state during this period came from the army. All Tutsis were from the same region and the same clan. The first successful coup was initiated by Michel Micombero, a Tutsi army captain from Bururi, a southern province of Burundi, on November 28, 1966. He abolished the constitutional monarchy and declared Burundi a republic, with himself as the president. Micombero was overthrown in another bloodless coup a decade later, on November 1, 1976, by Lieutenant Colonel Jean-Baptiste Bagaza, a Tutsi also from Bururi and a relative of Micombero. This was followed by another coup another decade later, on September 3, 1987, led by Bagaza's nephew, Major Pierre Buyoya.

This chapter focuses on the mediation entry initiatives of the Burundian conflict that erupted on October 21, 1993, following yet another military coup and the assassination of the first Hutu and first democratically elected president. It also examines the Great Lakes Region's June 1998 initiative that succeeded in bringing the principal conflicting parties to the negotiating table, although leaving out some major extremists.

This phase of the conflict is interesting for what it can tell us about the circumstances in which prospective intervenors gain access to internal conflicts. In line with that objective, the following theoretical questions are pertinent: What has been the nature of Burundi's conflict in this period? Who were the parties to the conflict? Did the nature of the conflict have any effect on the type of entry initiatives? Who tried to intervene and what were their motives? Was the conflict ripe enough to warrant the mediation initiatives? What were the perceptions of the aspiring mediators about the nature of the conflict? Were these perceptions in line with those of the parties to the conflict? Were the perceptions constant between the parties and the intervenors throughout the evolution of the conflict? If not, what caused the change and how did it affect the entry initiatives?

Did the entry initiatives have any impact on the dynamic evolution of the conflict? Did the dynamic evolution of the conflict in turn have any effect on the type of entry initiatives and their sustenance or exit? In other words, was sustenance or exit a function of a certain level of the conflict's evolution? Who among the prospective intervenors were successful and who were not, and why? Why did those who succeeded get accepted? Among the parties who committed to a compromise settlement, how genuine were their commitments?

These questions provide the analytical framework in which the conflict is presented. Theoretical and practical lessons from the answers to these questions will be drawn out to form the conclusion of the chapter.

The Nature of the Conflict

The Burundi conflict is another typical example of a centralist internal conflict whose main contention is state control. Its major causes are both political and economic. Its sporadic phases have always been triggered by a fierce struggle for political power and scarce economic resources between the elites of the two dominant ethnic groups, the majority Hutu and the minority Tutsi.[1] Ethnicity is thus used as a vehicle for political and economic competition. By being political, the conflict becomes not just about who is in control but more about governance in general, legitimacy, the country's political system, its political institutions, and political stability.

This characterization simply means that the conflict is about who is in political control at a particular point in time, how legitimate that control is, under what political system the control is based, under what political institutions it is operated, and how stable the political institutions are. In economic terms, the conflict is more than a mere issue of resource scarcity. It is about how scarce resources are mobilized and distributed. Essentially, it is about how economic demands are met, and it becomes more viciously driven and existential as the conflict itself reduces the resources available for distribution.

The current phase of the conflict was triggered by the political events of October 21, 1993, which were the latest link in a chain of other triggers that had sparked off other related political events. The October 21 coup was followed by a process of political reform that had been initiated by President Buyoya in late 1988, less than a year after coming to power through a military coup. The launching of the political reforms was not voluntary; it was done mainly under external pressures, which were in turn a reaction to the 1988 massacre in the central communes of Ntega and Marangara. The massacre was sparked by the savage, pre-emptive Hutu killing of the Tutsi in response to premonitions of a repeat of the 1972 Hutu massacre by the Tutsi.[2] Following the massacre, Western powers pressured Buyoya to introduce political reforms as a way to end the vicious cycle of ethnic violence. The role of the U.S. Congress in these pressures was critical. It encouraged President Reagan to reassess U.S. relations with Burundi and called for the suspension of U.S. aid unless ethnic discrimination was eliminated and democratic political reforms were initiated.[3] It was partly under these pressures that Buyoya was forced to introduce the democratic reforms.

Apart from the external pressures, internal political realities also called for such a move. The ideology of ethnic exclusion practiced by the Tutsi-dominated military regime was increasingly pushing the country to the brink of ethnic civil war. In the late 1980s, the African wave of demands for political transformation was gaining momentum. Burundi was not able to build a wall against the wind of political change sweeping across the continent. The three factors that had helped in the introduction of the political reforms show that the reforms were partly indigenous and partly exogenous; that is, they were domestically and externally induced.

In late 1988, as a result of these domestic, regional, and international pressures for political reforms, Major Pierre Buyoya made a number of significant political decisions that were aimed at steering the country toward a democratic political system. These efforts started with the creation of a bi-ethnic Consultative Commission on National Unity, whose objective was, inter alia,[4] to "conduct a sustained investigation into the historical and socio-cultural foundations of Burundi unity, to trace its evolution, and identify the reasons and manifestations of the divisions so as to propose appropriate solutions."[5]

The commission's assignment ended in the production of two important reports: "On the Question of National Unity" in 1989 and "On the Democratization of Institutions and Political Life" in 1991. Out of the two reports a Charter of National Unity was formulated. It proposed a new constitution that called for the establishment of a democratic multiparty political system. Both the charter and the constitution were overwhelmingly approved by the people through national referendums. One of the most significant aspects of the new constitution was that it prohibited political organizations that advocated tribalism, division, and violence. Political parties were required to be national—that is, to recruit their membership from all ethnic groups.

The new democratic multiparty political system was tested on June 1, 1993, during the first free presidential elections. Of twelve registered parties, only three put up candidates: the incumbent party, the Party of National Union and Progress (UPRONA), whose candidate was the incumbent president, Major Pierre Buyoya; the Burundi Democratic Front (FRODEBU), which put up a Hutu candidate, Melchior Ndadaye; and the monarchist and, predominantly Tutsi People's Reconciliation Party (PRP), whose candidate was a Hutu, Pierre Claver Sendegeya. The elections resulted in the victory of Melchior Ndadaye of FRODEBU, who got 65 percent of the votes, against the incumbent, Pierre Buyoya of UPRONA, who received 33 percent of the votes, and Sendegeya of the PRP who received a little more than 1 percent.

The presidential elections were followed by the legislative ones on June 29, 1993. Ndadaye's party won sixty-five of the eighty-one seats in the National Assembly. With a clear victory in both elections, Ndadaye was sworn in on July 10, 1993, as the first democratically elected president, as well as the first Hutu and the first civilian to hold that office. Likewise, FRODEBU became the first opposition party to replace the incumbent state party, UPRONA, which had been in power since independence.

The outcome of the political reforms symbolized a regime change, a transformation from an authoritarian to a new, democratic political system. The ushering in of the new political system represented an introduction of a new set of political norms and values—a major departure from the old regime, whereby the country's political stability was, according to Rene Lemarchand, based not on "a broad consensus of opinion among different ethnic groups" but on "the sheer capacity of the regime to ensure its own survival regardless of the means employed to achieve this goal."[6] Henceforth, the country's political stability would depend on how much the new values would be respected.

The political reforms not only restored political legitimacy but also changed the basis of governance. Instead of depending on force, governance in the new political system would depend on the new norms on national political consensus. The effectiveness of governance would now be measured on the basis of how much the new leadership would respect the national consensus: "Effective governance depends on the establishment of a national consensus on norms, the reinforcement of those norms and values as a legitimizing regime, and the establishment of new institutions and principles as a replacement regime if the former values and institutions prove inadequate."[7]

Another significance of the outcome of the political reforms was that they changed the mode of political organization and mobilization. The establishment of political parties, which were required to be national in character (drawing membership from all ethnic groups), was designed to ensure that politics would no longer be organized on the basis of ethnicity. Political mobilization was to be on the platform of constructive ideas and social issues and not on ethnic sentiments. A political party voted into office democratically through free and fair elections would exercise power.

The fact that for the first time in the country's history a civilian—and most important, a Hutu—became president was another remarkable significance of the political reforms. And taking into consideration the country's unfortunate history of ethnic rivalries and violence, the political reforms put Burundians into the untested waters of both ethnic and political tolerance and reconciliation.

Immediately after the presidential election, however, thousands of Tutsi youth, mobilized by UPRONA, protested the elections' results. And on July 2, following the legislative elections but before the president-elect was sworn in, Tutsi soldiers of the Second Commando Battalion tried unsuccessfully to seize power by force. Among the officers who commanded them was Lieutenant Sylvestre Ningaba, Buyoya's cabinet director.[8] As Leonce Ndikumana explains:

In Burundi, the military, members of the ruling party, and the elite from the south have regularly accused leaders of "selling out the nation" every time the latter made a move toward power sharing. In June 1993, members of the military stormed the residence of the late Melchior Ndadaye; backed by the elements of the civilian elite, they attempted to stage a coup d'etat against the FRODEBU regime before it was even inaugurated. The events were a signal that the military and the southern Tutsi oligarchy were not ready to share power.[9]

These events and subsequent pronouncements of the Tutsi politicians indicated that the Tutsi were not happy with the election results. Interestingly enough, their argument was not that the elections were not free and fair in terms of the way they had been conducted, rather that they were considered not free and fair in terms of their outcome. They interpreted FRODEBU's victory, in both the presidential and the legislative elections, on the basis of ethnic lines—that is, as a Hutu victory—in keeping with the "Savimbi scenario," whereby the elections would have been considered free and fair, as far as the Tutsi were concerned, only if UPRONA won them. Lemarchand provides an exact appreciation of the Tutsi perception of the elections' results: "The victory of the FRODEBU is not a democratic victory but a Hutu victory; what is now emerging is the institutionalization of the tyranny of an ethnic majority, in short, a Jacobine state under Hutu control."[10]

Burundi's first encounter with democracy did not last very long. Three months after the inauguration of President Ndadaye, he and four other top government officials were assassinated on October 21, 1993, in an attempted coup engineered by the extremist elements within the Tutsi-dominated army. The coup and the death of the president spelled the end of the brief democratic experiment and returned Burundi to yet another sad phase of violent ethnic conflict. Thousands of Tutsi were massacred by Hutu, and thousands of Hutu were massacred by the Tutsi-dominated army and militia in retaliation, leaving more than 50,000 dead, 400,000 internally displaced, and 800,000 refugees—nearly a quarter of the population.

The coup was significant because it was a watershed in Burundi's political evolution.[11] It did not affect merely the government of the day but, more important, an infant political system. As such, it posed a major challenge to the country's future political process and ethnic relations. Hence, the October attempted coup was significantly different from the previous ones, with the exception of that of 1966. The 1993 coup and that of 1966 were about regime change. The 1966 coup changed the nature of an authoritarian rule from a monarchy to a military oligarchy, and the military oligarchy formalized an ethnic exclusionist ideology in all spheres of public life, pursuing a skewed-development strategy based on regional favoritism whose outcome was a national socio-economic imbalance. The 1993 coup swept aside a legitimately elected government. It revived not only authoritarian rule but also the issue of legitimacy in governance; it also revived the ethnic exclusionist ideology in favor of the Tutsi. Burundi returned to the status quo ante of the past three decades. The ensuing Hutu violent reaction was not only a function of the death of a Hutu president but also, more fundamentally, the demise of a new political system that, for the first time, had given them hope in and respect for their political future.

The Parties to the Conflict

One of the most significant aspects of the brief democratic experiment was that it elevated those involved in the Tutsi-Hutu ethnic conflict from crude mob-like organizations to official and well-organized political parties. Regardless of the constitutional inhibitions, the parties were organized mainly along ethnic lines. Hence, from the October 21, 1993, coup attempt, when President Ndadaye was assassinated, to the July 25, 1996 coup, when the civilian government was overthrown, the major protagonists to the conflict were the army and UPRONA, representing the Tutsi, and FRODEBU and the National Council for the Defense of Democracy and its military organ, the Forces for the Defense of Democracy (CNDD/FDD), representing the Hutu; an additional extremist Hutu group, the Party for the Liberation of the Hutu People (Palepehutu), and its National Liberation Front were still not brought into the growing agreement a decade later.

It is interesting to note that each ethnic group had a dominant political party and a military wing. UPRONA was the Tutsi-dominant political party and the army was its major military wing. On the other hand, FRODEBU was the Hutu-dominant political party, with the CNDD/FDD established in the first half of 1994 as its military wing. The dominant political and military wings of each ethnic group were supported by a network of other political parties and military groups. These various groups constituted a continuum that ranged from weak moderates to powerful extremists. After the coup, a clear line of battle was drawn between the two antagonistic ethnic camps and the country sank into a prolonged, low-intensity civil war.

A party's stakes in a conflict depend on its perception of the conflict and in turn determine the means of their realization. Any change in one variable carries a potential change in the other two. If a party modifies its perception of a conflict, this may harden or soften its position in the conflict and may as well have an impact on the policy options for its resolution. What were the parties' perceptions in Burundi's conflict?

The Army and UPRONA

These two actors have perceived the conflict in ethnic terms throughout its entire cycle. What is at issue for the Tutsi is the fear of Hutu numerical strength. Coupled with the myth of Tutsi ethnic superiority, this fear has been driven with yet another mythical notion of the Tutsi being victims of the Hutu conspiracy of trying to wipe them completely from the face of the earth. The Tutsi then are in an existential struggle and are required to be always on guard to make sure that the Hutu do not get a chance to realize their sinister motives. The solution to this problem is set in zero-sum terms: The Tutsi numerical weakness must be counterbalanced by their dominance in all spheres of public life as the only way to guarantee their survival.

In relation to the current phase of the conflict, the Tutsi perception has been that the unexpected outcome of the June 1993 elections was the first-ever serious threat to their monopoly on power. It appeared as if, for the first time, the Hutu caught them napping. As far as they were concerned the culprit was not only the FRODEBU party that had won the elections, but also, and more important, those who created the political environment that enabled it to grab power from them—mainly President Buyoya. The FRODEBU victory was therefore perceived as a "sell-out" and a "national betrayal," as well as, and more significant to their paranoia, a stepping-stone toward the Hutus' long-term genocidal intentions. This perception was the basis of the army's justification for initiating the October 21 coup and the subsequent assassination of President Ndadaye. The coup and the assassination constituted a pre-emptive move to prevent the "impending" Tutsi genocide by the Hutu and to return power to the Tutsi.

FRODEBU and the CNDD/FDD

These actors perceived the prolonged conflict as a problem of "ethnic apartheid" practiced by the Tutsi in order to exclude them from all spheres of public life. They are Burundians but they do not feel a sense of national belonging. They are treated like second-class citizens in their own country, and, as in apartheid South Africa, their efforts to change this intolerable situation have always been met with violent responses.

Throughout the cycle of the conflict, the Hutu never perceived the solution to their plight in zero-sum terms but, rather, in inclusive or participatory terms. In their perception, justice would prevail only if they would be allowed to participate equally in the affairs of their country. This perception entailed the opening up of all national institutions to all Burundians. The political reforms, which culminated in the June 1993 elections, were perceived as a window of opportunity to realize this dream. FRODEBU's victory in the elections epitomized the realization of the dream.[12]

The events of October 21 were, therefore, perceived as an indication that the Tutsi were not ready to share power with them, that the Tutsi were bent on continuing their apartheid ideology. The events of October were also interpreted as an effort to wipe them physically off the map. Hence their killing of Tutsi triggered by the death of Ndadaye constituted a pre-emptive move to prevent the repeat of the 1972 massacre of Hutu.[13]

THE MEDIATION INITIATIVES: OCTOBER 21, 1993–JULY 20, 1996

The coup and the assassination of the president evoked an instant worldwide indignation and condemnation. There was a general concern within the international community that if these events did not receive immediate attention, there would be a real danger that the country would plunge into another outright genocidal civil war. This fear ignited a flurry of international and regional initiatives at the state, international organization, and nongovernmental organization levels to prevent another spiral of ethnic violence. No other country on the continent received more attention from so many conflict resolution experts than did Burundi between October 1993 and July 1996. Particularly striking in the entry of mediators was the direct intervention of external parties that seized the initiative from the outside with only vague acquiescence of a government that was decapitated and awkwardly reconstructed.

Out of the international frenzy of responses to the conflict, a distinction should be made between those who intervened because of humanitarian concerns and those whose objective was to try to mediate the conflict.[14] It is the second category with which this chapter is concerned. Those who tried to mediate the conflict between October 21, 1993, and July 20, 1996, were France, the UN Security Council and the special representative of the secretary-general (SRSG), the regional states, the Organization of African Unity, and one NGO—the Carter Center. The initiatives consisted of a political and a military track. It is important to analyze the initiatives sequentially in order to observe how the conflict evolved and how the mediation efforts affected each other.

The first reaction, and sudden entry, came from France, which offered asylum in its embassy to the decapitated government and then swiftly flew in twenty *gendarmes* to guard its members as they were moved to a nearby hotel. While France took no further lead actions in the subsequent mediations, it supported others' moves, and its initial reflex preserved both the Burundian government and the French position.

The second reaction came from the UN secretary-general. Immediately after the coup, Secretary-General Boutros-Ghali dispatched James Jonah, the UN undersecretary-general for Africa, to Bujumbura on a fact-finding mission. On his arrival, he was confronted with a request for international military protection from Prime Minister Sylvie Kinigi. The Security Council rejected a call for peacekeeping forces but authorized sending an SRSG, and Ahmedou Ould-Abdallah arrived little more than a month after the assassination.[15] Ould-Abdallah had been foreign minister of Mauritania and was serving in a senior position with the United Nations in New York when he was called.

His mandate included facilitating contact between the parties to the conflict, restoring the legal institutions, conducting an investigation of the coup and the massacre that followed, and linking up with the OAU. He was instrumental in helping to quell the violence and in reviving the country's tattered political institutions. His actions included reassembling the members of the National Assembly and helping to revive and amend the constitution to facilitate an indirect election of the president.

These efforts facilitated the election of another Hutu president, Cyprian Ntaryamira, in January 1994, and the installation of a coalition government in February. As Burundians were trying to sort out their political mess, fate seemed not to be in their favor. Hardly four months after the election of President Ntaryamira, they were plunged, once more, into another situation of political uncertainty following the plane crash in Kigali that killed the presidents of Rwanda and Burundi, who were returning from Dar-es-Salaam after an emergency regional summit on the situation in the two countries.

Ould-Abdallah's role in renegotiating another agreement was crucial. By September, he had succeeded in helping the political parties strike another deal that culminated in the Convention of Government, which spelled out the modalities through which both Hutu and Tutsi would participate in a coalition government. It provided for a Hutu president from FRODEBU and a Tutsi Prime Minister from UPRONA. It was from this agreement that President Sylvestre Ntibantunganya was elected in September 1994, to succeed the late Ntaryamira.

Ould-Abdallah's mission achieved entry by dint of personality and perseverance, armed with the authority of the United Nations. That authority has been used in various ways by SRSGs around the world, and its successful use in Burundi depended above all on personally grasping the initiative and exercising it with tact and conviction. At salient moments, he played a crucial role in preventing Burundi from becoming another Rwanda; for example, he amended the constitution and dissolved the constitutional court in order to elect a successor to assassinated President Ndadaye and maintained calm and order upon the death of President Ntaryamira.

The regional and the OAU response to the events of October 21 was also immediate and firm. They perceived the conflict in terms of legitimacy and democracy, that the coup toppled a legitimate democratic government and replaced it with an illegitimate one. In addition, it was likely that the conflict would increase the problem of regional security. Their intervention was motivated by three aims: to discourage the role of the military in African politics, to encourage democratic rule in Africa, and to address regional security concerns. The initial objective of their intervention was therefore to restore the democratically elected government to power, and they intended to pursue this through political dialogue or, if necessary, even through military intervention.

The regional leaders strongly condemned the assassination of President Ndadaye and the derailment of Burundi's nascent democracy. They called for an immediate reaffirmation of the democratically elected government and an international military intervention to stop ethnic killings and to restore order. They called on the international community, especially the OAU and the United Nations, to come up with an internationally supported African force that could help to restore trust and the rule of law. The call for the military intervention was influenced by a similar call from the deposed government: The Tutsi prime minister, Sylvie Kinigi, who was hiding in the French embassy with some of her ministers, had requested one thousand foreign troops, from either the United Nations or the OAU, to protect the remaining government leaders and key installations.

For the OAU, the conflict and the military request served as a litmus test for the organization's newly established Mechanism for Conflict Prevention, Management, and Resolution. Not only did the organization have the new mechanism but it also had a request from the legitimate government of Burundi to intervene militarily. Although the OAU decided to send troops to Burundi and the OAU representative, Papa Louis Fall, announced the arrival of five hundred soldiers by December, the Burundian army rejected the decision, and it was finally agreed that an unarmed OAU Observer Mission in Burundi (OMIB), divided equally between civilians and military personnel, be dispatched to Bujumbura. The initial complement was to be seventy, then forty-six, and when they appeared in February 1994, they numbered only eighteen.

Among the various NGOs that were involved in the Burundi crisis during this period, the Carter Center can be singled out as one of the few to be directly involved in the political process, and it took former U.S. president Jimmy Carter to get the regional mediation process started, upon invitation by the presidents of Zaire and Uganda. Rather than consider the conflict as distinctly Burundian, the Carter Center initiative perceived it in a holistic regional context—that is, as a mixture of socio-economic and cultural problems played out on the basis of ethnic politics that had deluged the whole region. Treating the whole of the Great Lakes Region as one big conflict area, the Carter Center adopted a linkage approach, and its role was more of facilitation than of mediation. It did not engage the parties to the conflict directly but dealt with the regional leaders. Between November 1995 and

March 1996, it succeeded in organizing two summits that brought together the leaders of the region to discuss the security problems of the area.

After detailed consultations with the regional leaders, which included visits by Carter to some of the regional capitals, the first summit took place in Cairo on November 29, 1995. It was attended by the presidents of Zaire, Uganda, Burundi, and Rwanda, and a special presidential envoy from the new government of Tanzania. Carter and South African archbishop Desmond Tutu served as facilitators.

Condemning the ideologies of political genocide and exclusion, the leaders pledged to take joint concrete actions to advance peace, justice, reconciliation, stability, and development in the region. They also requested that former presidents Julius Nyerere of Tanzania, Amani Toumani Toure of Mali, and Jimmy Carter of the United States, and Archbishop Desmond Tutu of South Africa, analyze in depth the results of the meeting and the continuing problems of the region and prepare recommendations for consideration by the five governments at a second meeting in early 1996. They opened the doors for the invitation of other participants and observers during the next meeting.[16]

The second summit took place in Tunis, March 16–18, 1996. This time all the presidents of the five countries attended. Former presidents Carter, Nyerere, and Toure served as facilitators. More extensive than the first meeting in terms of duration and depth of discussions, the Tunis Summit reviewed the progress made toward the achievement of the commitments undertaken during the first summit. Among its important decisions, the summit committed the regional leaders to reduce tension, hostility, insecurity, and distrust in the region. Tanzanian president Benjamin Mkapa stressed that refugees in his country received neither arms nor military training.

The regional leaders finally requested that former presidents Carter, Nyerere, and Toure, and Archbishop Tutu, continue their efforts to facilitate contact and actions by their five governments, monitor the achievements made at the two summits, and prepare recommendations for consideration at the next meeting.[17] Unfortunately, no other summit was organized under the Carter initiative.

The Mwanza peace process began with the courting of the former president of Tanzania, Julius Nyerere, to play the mediating role on behalf of the region and the OAU. The regional leaders, Ethiopian prime minister Meles Zenawi, who was then the OAU chairman, and the OAU secretary-general sounded out the idea to Nyerere. Nyerere did not accept the offer outright;

he wanted time to reflect on it and consult with other African leaders and major powers, as well as relevant international institutions. He also wanted to make his own assessment of the viability and prospects of the assignment after consulting with the Burundian parties to the conflict. His personal contacts took him to Burundi twice, to the United Nations in New York, and to various capitals of the member states of the European Union, as well as to Canada.

A consensus emerged that Nyerere should represent not only the region and the OAU but the United Nations as well; this meant that he would be the "international envoy" to Burundi. After the two Carter-sponsored summits in Cairo and Tunis, Nyerere finally agreed to be the facilitator for the Burundi peace talks. However, he refused to be an official representative of either the OAU or the United Nations, preferring instead to adopt a "freelancing" approach. After consulting with the major parties to the conflict in April, including the armed groups, Nyerere convened two meetings in Mwanza, a town at the shores of Lake Victoria in northern Tanzania, in May and early June 1996.

When Mwanza showed a lack of progress and the security situation in Burundi began to deteriorate, the first regional summit on Burundi was convened in Arusha on June 25, 1996. Apart from the regional leaders, the prime minister of Ethiopia also attended the meeting in his capacity as the immediate past chairman of the OAU, along with the organization's secretary-general, Salim Ahmed Salim. The meeting was presented with an official request from the government of Burundi for military assistance to help reverse the deteriorating security situation in the country. Hutu president Sylvestre Ntibantunganya and Tutsi prime minister Antoine Nduwayo presented the request jointly.

This request came at the very moment that discussions were going on within the United Nations regarding a contingency plan for a humanitarian force for the Great Lakes Region. The summit endorsed the request and formed a technical committee to study the modalities of constituting the force. The request for a regional peacekeeping force and its subsequent endorsement quickly ignited protest in Burundi: Once again, the army and Tutsi radical parties believed that such a force would work against their security guarantees and interests. The political impasse and the unrest that followed were part of the contributing factors that led to the July 25 coup that returned former president Pierre Buyoya to power and brought the Mwanza peace process to an abrupt end.

Unlike in Rwanda, the United Nations was prompt in responding to the crisis in Burundi. The swift response was motivated by the United Nations' experience from its involvement in the Rwandan and the Somali conflicts. The Somali experience was instrumental in shaping the UN's role in Burundi, particularly because of the scathing attacks on the organization by its own SRSG in Somalia, Mohamed Sahnoun, for the unsatisfactory manner the United Nations had responded to the Somali conflict.[18] Burundi was also one of the fresh conflicts that had confronted the new UN secretary-general, Boutros Boutros-Ghali. Being an African himself (specifically, from Egypt), he had to act fast lest he be accused of letting the continent down.

The United Nations' perception of the conflict did not differ much from that of the region and the OAU. Perceiving the conflict as a power struggle among politicians, the United Nations also adopted a two-track approach in its response. The political track was aimed at engaging all the political parties in order to get a compromise political settlement. The military track was for humanitarian concerns and to guarantee a peaceful environment for political negotiation.

EXPLAINING THE OUTCOME

The military track of the regional, OAU, and UN initiatives was motivated by three basic objectives. For external powers, military intervention was necessary to reinstate constitutional legality and to prevent genocide. For the deposed government, military intervention was requested to provide protection. But in fact there was no actual deployment; instead, the region, the OAU, and the United Nations ended up sending a small OAU observer mission (and representative) and a small SRSG mission. Given their size, and the fact that their members were not armed, the missions were in no way capable of either protecting the deposed leaders or preventing the killings, let alone reinstating constitutional legality other than through clever diplomacy. But they ended up being very useful, nevertheless. Their physical presence in Burundi provided the international community with a respectable presence whose moral authority made its opinion credible.

Actually, their small size and harmless nature were the very reasons that the missions managed entry. All parties accepted them because they were perceived as harmless as far as the parties' interests were concerned. But more significant, the missions served as a cushion for the pressures for military intervention. This was a relief to both the internal parties that opposed external military intervention and the external actors that were requested to intervene militarily. The ones who lost were those who requested and supported the military intervention.[19] The military option failed to gain entry mainly because of the problems associated with its justification, objectives, capabilities, and, more important, acceptability.

In regard to justification and objectives, after the regional, the OAU, and UN Security Council leaders had recovered from the shock of the events of October 21, they asked themselves whether their reasons were strong enough to justify a military intervention into an African state, whether they were ready to face all the implications of such a move, how clear were the objectives of a military intervention, and what its costs would be. It was actually surprising for the OAU and the United Nations to have even considered a military action at a time when the continent had just publicly expressed its weakness in this area through the OAU's new Mechanism for Conflict Prevention, Management, and Resolution, and the United Nations was still reeling from the impact of the Somali venture.[20] Neither the region nor the OAU had the logistical capability for such a mission. Rather, their rhetoric may have been intended to take the lead in mobilizing international public opinion against the October 21 coup and to encourage the United Nations to take the military action. But, apart from all these other constraints, key to the failure of the military track was the problem of acceptability. Both the Burundian army and the Tutsi-dominated political parties refused to accept entry of any external military force in the country.

As the conflict evolved, the United Nations re-evaluated its policy options. By the end of 1995, as Ould-Abdallah was leaving the UN assignment, it was clear that political diplomacy alone was not sufficient to stop the fratricidal war. Although the UN secretary-general had called for a preventive multinational force for Burundi since August 1994, the military option had been put in the back seat. It was only in the beginning of 1996 that the secretary-general started seriously looking for a military option. In his report to the Security Council on February 15, he proposed a United

Nations–authorized contingency plan for the deployment of a humanitarian multinational force for Burundi.[21]

The military option was not conceived as an alternative but as a complement to the political dialogue. It was motivated by the fear of an ethnic genocide like the one of 1972. The Rwandan genocide two years earlier increased the fear. The military option was motivated as well by what Glynne Evans called "alibi building."[22] With the United Nations' experience in Somalia and Rwanda, the initiative was intended to protect the organization from being blamed for not having done enough to prevent genocide. Informed by the 1994 Rwandan genocidal experience, the contingency planning was proposed on the premise of preparedness to deal with a worst-case scenario. Composed of between 25,000 and 50,000, the force was supposed to be credible and strong enough to prevent mass killings and protect refugees and displaced persons, civilians at risk, and key installations.

Informed also by the experiences of previous similar peace enforcement missions, the secretary-general proposed that the plan should follow the "contracting out" approach similar to the United Nations–approved "coalitions of the willing" missions to Korea, Iraq, Somalia, Haiti, and the French Operation Turquoise in Rwanda. The choice of this approach was based on the appreciation and acknowledgment of the United Nations' inherent institutional constraints in the area of peace enforcement.[23]

The proposal did not take off the ground simply because Boutros-Ghali failed to find a coalition that was willing to lead the force. As Stephen Weissman correctly puts it, "the key determinant of success or failure of any risky UN military initiative is the political will of the five permanent members of the Security Council."[24] In Burundi, the two most interested members of the Security Council, the United States and France, did not support the plan wholeheartedly. The United States was still nagged by the questions of the clarity of the mission's objectives, its mandate, contribution of troops and funding, security of the troops, and its duration—and most of all, by attacks from U.S. Senator Jesse Helms (R-NC), head of the Senate Foreign Relations Committee at the time. Smarting from the humiliating experiences of the Somali expedition, defending its current international commitments in Haiti and Bosnia, and facing imminent presidential elections, the Clinton administration did not want to find itself caught up in the uncertainties of another messy foreign ethnic conflict. The French also had reservations. Although they opposed it publicly, they informally indicated a willingness to provide financial and logistical support for such a force. Like the Americans, they were afraid of the uncertainties of the project. After the experiences of Operation Turquoise in Rwanda, they were reluctant to go it alone. If the risks were worth taking, they would have to be borne by a coalition of credible and formidable partners, which the American reticence put into doubt. Finally, they had much faith in the political track instead. Without the support of the United States and the French, no other powers were willing to rescue the plan.

On the political track, the Convention of Government was an appropriate framework through which the international community could support Burundi's peace efforts, although it involved the registered political parties only; it left out not only other political forces, which emerged out of the recent political chaos, but also the armed groups. The Convention was firmly based on the principle of power sharing and shifted the balance of power between the two antagonistic ethnic groups and among the government institutions. It provided that 55 percent of cabinet posts and civil service positions would go to the Hutu-dominated group, the Forces for Democratic Change under FRODEBU, and 45 percent to the Tutsi group, the Coalition of Opposition Political Parties under UPRONA. Decision-making powers were shifted from the president to a National Security Council that had a FRODEBU majority.[25]

Nonetheless, the government institutions failed to function, and the government paralysis increased political uncertainty. Political militancy increased among the Hutu groups; the mass desertion of the militant Hutu from FRODEBU and the creation of the CNDD/FDD in 1995 further exacerbated the group and personality rivalries that undermined the Convention's formula.

The Carter initiative was useful for regional confidence building and contributed to the process of formalizing the regional search for a prospective mediator by endorsing and supporting Nyerere for that role. Likewise, the forum helped Nyerere to make a critical assessment of the Burundian conflict and get a feeling of the regional leaders' perceptions on the nature of the conflict and how to resolve it.

One may wonder why, in spite of the early regional and the OAU's response to the events of October 21, that an effective mediation process began so late. The Mwanza peace process started in earnest in May 1996, almost thirty-two months after the October 21 coup. There were two major reasons for the delay. First, both the region and the OAU had initially given prominence to the military track. Accordingly, when the military option ended with the symbolic OMIB, they then turned their support to the United Nations' political initiative under Ould-Abdallah. The Mwanza process began when it was realized that the United Nations–brokered Convention of Government did not work.

Nyerere's acceptance of the mediating role was motivated by humanitarian and regional security concerns. He strongly believed that trying to help in the Burundian conflict would bring not only peace to the country but also security and political stability to the region. His knowledge of and experience in the Burundian conflict made him a better candidate for the job. In addition, he accepted the job in order to live up to the confidence and expectations of the international community. Also, he was convinced that he could succeed after his own one-year personal assessment of the conflict and consultations.

The major factor that made the Mwanza peace process fail to achieve immediate results was its abrupt ending by the July 25 coup. As a process, it was not given enough time to unfold. Its life span was confined to only two sessions—not enough time to achieve much for a conflict with the complexity of Burundi's. The differences between the major political parties, UPRONA and FRODEBU, also contributed to the lack of positive results. Their biggest point of contention was who should be included in the list of participants. UPRONA was adamant against accepting some of FRODEBU's participants on the pretext that they had committed acts of genocide. UPRONA was likewise not happy with Nyerere's efforts to include the armed groups in the talks. In other words, the conflict was stronger than the peace process and was obdurately against its attempts to achieve full entry into a mediation process.

THE SECOND PHASE INITIATIVES: JULY 25, 1996–JUNE 15, 1998

The July 25 coup was motivated by the political stasis in Burundi resulting from deteriorating security and the failure of the Convention of Government. The army was worried by the advances made by the armed groups, particularly the CNDD/FDD. To many Burundians the coup appeared to be déjà vu. It was the usual way Burundi changed its leaders, and the people were accustomed to it, but, analytically, the coup was more than just business as usual. The first thing the coup makers did was to reinstate Major Pierre Buyoya as the head of state. In his first public address, Buyoya announced the suspension of all the political parties, the National Assembly, and the 1992 Constitution, replacing it with a three-year Transitional Decree. In the October 21, 1993, coup attempt, these institutions had not been suspended. Suspending these democratic institutions made the 1996 coup more than just an act targeted at President Ntibantunganya. More significant, it symbolized the completion of the regime change that began in the autumn of 1993.

Structural change of the conflict actually began before the July coup, and it was one of the factors that had hastened it. By the time the country was facing difficulties in implementing the Convention of Government in 1995, the conflict's intensity shifted from the political to the military arena, from the political parties to the armed groups. Although the major antagonistic political parties, UPRONA and FRODEBU, were still in the picture, the effective movers of the conflict were the army and the major militant armed group, the CNDD/FDD.

Realizing that the conflict was advancing at the war front and not at the negotiating table, Buyoya made it his policy priority to restore security rather than to achieve political dialogue. In his first public address, Buyoya expressed his intentions to reorganize and re-equip the security forces and the army in order to deal effectively with the country's security problems. This military buildup resulted in a drastic enlargement of the army from 15,000 at the time of the July coup to more than 60,000 by the beginning of 1998. The military option was accompanied by the "regroupment" policy, whereby hundreds of thousands of Hutu were forced into army-protected camps after their houses had been burned down in order to isolate the militant armed groups from the population, from which they drew their support.

At the time of the July 25 coup, only the regional/OAU initiative, among the prospective intervention agents, was still trying to mediate the conflict. The UN exit came with the breakdown of the Convention of Government and the subsequent withdrawal of Ould-Abdallah. The exit of the Carter Center initiative came as a result of the amicable formalization of Nyerere as the "international envoy" for Burundi. From July 25, 1996, when the coup took place, to June 15, 1998, when substantive peace talks began in Arusha under Nyerere's facilitation, only one new serious prospective mediator tried entry into the process—the Rome-based Catholic group, the Community of Sant'Egidio. The entry of Sant'Egidio at this stage of the conflict was not intended to complement the regional initiative but to substitute for it; thus its entry became more competitive than complementary.

The region's and the OAU's responses to the July 25 coup were firmer and swifter than their response to the events of October 21, 1993. The OAU's Mechanism for Conflict Prevention, Management, and Resolution met at an ambassadorial level at an extraordinary session in Addis Ababa the day after the coup took place. The meeting strongly condemned the coup and reiterated the organization's and the continent's resolve to oppose strongly any illegal change of power in Burundi and promised to impose sanctions and isolate the regime.

The region responded by holding a summit in Arusha on July 31, 1996, during which economic sanctions were imposed on Burundi, to be lifted only when Buyoya reinstituted constitutional order and restored the political parties and the National Assembly. Another key condition was to immediately and unconditionally undertake negotiations with all the parties to the conflict, including the armed groups inside and outside the country.[26]

The imposition of the sanctions was a precedent-breaking act, the first time African states took a punitive measure against one of their own. The sanctions were intended to force the military regime to not only restore constitutional legality but also come to the negotiating table. The harsh regional response had serious implications for the regional mediation efforts, for the international support to the regional peace initiative, and for Burundi's bilateral relations with the region, particularly with Tanzania.

The imposition of the sanctions was indeed an unfriendly act. The perception of the regional leaders was that the punitive measure would motivate Buyoya to cooperate in finding a lasting political solution. But instead of bringing him closer to the region, the sanctions had an unintended effect of further isolating Burundi. Initially, doubtful of the sanctions' effectiveness, Buyoya simply refused to negotiate under duress. Furthermore, a political solution was not one of his urgent priorities. Faced with the immediate problem of insecurity, he made a military solution his priority. He was therefore convinced that he could temporarily afford to ignore the regional pressures while pursuing his military option. In addition, he believed, correctly, that the Western powers had a soft heart for him personally; with the major powers' support, he believed that the regional isolation would not hurt him much.

The sanctions indeed affected Burundi's bilateral relations with Tanzania. Buyoya believed that Tanzania and Nyerere were instrumental in the imposition of the sanctions and so naturally questioned Nyerere's impartiality as a mediator and Tanzania's appropriateness as the host country for the peace talks. The movement of the CNDD/FDD's headquarters from eastern Zaire to Tanzania, following the breakout of fighting between the Banyamulenge and Mobutu's forces in late 1996, increased the animosity between the two leaders and their countries to the extent of threatening to regionalize the Burundi conflict.

The major powers did not fully support the regional sanctions, which they saw as a liability rather than as an asset to the peace initiative. Their lack of support in turn helped to reduce the international pressure on the Burundian military regime and helped Buyoya to buy time. The difference in perceptions between the region and the major powers on the issue of the sanctions was an outcome of the differences in their perceptions of Buyoya as a leader. To the Western powers, Buyoya was moderate enough to deserve a second chance. In a chaotic and volatile situation like Burundi's, Buyoya was perceived as the only man capable of re-establishing order and political stability. The regional sanctions would therefore not be helpful for such a difficult task. For the regional leaders, Buyoya was just an outmoded dictator who would respond only to negative incentives.

The resolute regional pressures on Buyoya and his negative response toward them made the regional peace initiative somewhat futile. In fact, the sanctions had an unintended effect of shifting the regional and international focus from dealing effectively with the conflict to discussing the merits and demerits of lifting the sanctions. With each party holding its ground, it was impossible to continue with the peace process under Nyerere's facilitation, and that is what gave the impetus to the Sant'Egidio initiative. The major powers' opposition to the sanctions also helped the search for an alternative to the regional initiative.

The Sant'Egidio initiative had three more advantages for Buyoya. First, it dovetailed with his military option by giving him an opportunity to engage the strongest and the most serious armed group, the CNDD/FDD. Second, unlike in the regional initiative, where Buyoya was required to deal with all the parties at the same time, Sant'Egidio provided him with a window of opportunity to tackle one group at a time, and at his own order of priority. And third, Sant'Egidio provided an aura of freedom, whereby Buyoya could negotiate from a position of strength, unlike in Arusha, where he was supposed to face the pressure of the regional leaders.

Hence, while slowly responding to the regional pressures, Buyoya, with the support of Western powers, shifted his peace initiative to Rome in September 1996. Rome was motivated by a desire to achieve a suspension of hostilities between the government and the CNDD/FDD. As for the CNDD/FDD, their acceptance of Rome was part of their resolve to get a fair political deal. Their resorting to the bush was aimed at putting pressure on their protagonists to negotiate an equitable political settlement. Being courted first gave them an international recognition they did not want to pass up.

After four rounds of talks, the two sides succeeded in coming up with a written agreement on a framework of general principles of a political settlement and an agenda for further talks. The agenda covered seven crucial items:

1. Restoration of constitutional and institutional order.

2. Status of the security forces and the army.

3. Suspension of hostilities.

4. Justice, including setting up an internal criminal tribunal.

5. Involvement of other parties in the political process.

6. Cease-fire.

7. Guarantees on the means of carrying through an overall agreement.

The talks dragged on for two more months before they broke down in May 1997. The two parties were deadlocked on the first agenda item. Whereas the CNDD/FDD demanded the reinstatement of the 1992 constitution, the government insisted on a new one. The failure of the talks could be attributed largely to this disagreement, and with it, the government succeeded in imposing its political framework on the country. The organizers of the talks and their supporters had wrongly assumed that the CNDD/FDD would be willing to join the government in exchange for an agreement on the general principles of a political settlement.[27] They also assumed that the privacy of the talks could be preserved over a relatively long period; when the talks became known, the excluded parties became suspicious. And they assumed that the CNDD/FDD would continue to tolerate a situation in which "progress" in the secret talks was frequently invoked by the organizers, their supporters, and African observers as a justification for regional decisions to relax sanctions against the Burundian government. As these assumptions proved to be wrong, the Sant'Egidio initiative collapsed.

With the exit of the Community of Sant'Egidio, only the region and the OAU still remained in the picture. Another brief entry initiative was attempted by the UN Educational, Scientific, and Cultural Organization (UNESCO), which organized a peace conference on Burundi in Paris in October 1997. The conference was attended by all the political parties (with the exception of FRODEBU), the armed groups, and the government. Nothing substantive came out of it.

Not buying the Western characterization of Buyoya as the "lesser evil," the region and the OAU believed that he was not seriously committed to negotiation. His procrastination and his attempts to find alternative forums like Sant'Egidio and UNESCO were viewed as diversionary tactics. His questioning Nyerere's impartiality and Arusha's appropriateness as the venue for the talks were also perceived in the same vein. So when Nyerere volunteered to step down as the facilitator and Tanzania offered to withdraw Arusha as a venue for the talks, the presidents attending the fifth regional summit in Arusha on September 4, 1997, turned down their offers. They urged Nyerere to continue and decided that the next session of the talks would be in Arusha.

Considering that mediation requires parties to accept the mediator and to agree on a venue, it was odd for the regional leaders to insist that Nyerere should continue to be the mediator and Arusha the venue regardless of the fact that one of the major parties—the crucial one for that matter—seemed to have reservations. However, the regional leaders wanted to send a strong message to Buyoya that they were the ones running the show and not he. Accepting the offers would have weakened their position and strengthened Buyoya's. A change of venue would have made the regional initiative slip away from them. Accepting Nyerere's resignation would have been humiliating both to him personally and to the regional leaders because they had great respect and confidence in Nyerere's statesmanship.

Hence, instead of yielding to Buyoya, they responded firmly by tightening the noose: more conditions were added. They called upon the Burundian government to halt the trials it was currently conducting until a negotiated solution was in place and to release unconditionally the speaker of the National Assembly, Leonce Ngendakumana, and to allow him, together with former presidents Bagaza and Ntibantunganya, to travel freely and participate in the talks.

After exhausting all other external avenues Buyoya was left with no other choice but to respond positively to the regional pressures. In fact, it did not take long before the sanctions began to bite. Regardless of their implementational flaws and adverse humanitarian effects, the sanctions regime as a policy tool did work. Political parties and the National Assembly were reinstated on September 4, 1996. While insisting on continuing with the sanctions until there was a substantive movement in the negotiations, the regional leaders at the fourth regional summit in Arusha on September 4, 1997, decided to ease some of their conditions for humanitarian reasons.

Faced with the regional initiative and its sanctions regime, Buyoya decided to work for an internal political solution. This approach presented a number of advantages. After the failure of the Rome talks, an internal political solution seemed to be the only rational choice. Despite its failure, the Rome engagement with the CNDD/FDD from September 1996 to May 1997 provided the government with an opportune bracing period to improve security in the country. Complemented by the "regroupment" policy and the destabilization effects on the CNDD/FDD of the fighting in eastern Zaire, the security situation had improved enough to warrant a shift from a military to a political option. If an internal political deal could be struck, it would help Buyoya get the regional pressures off his back, and the sanctions would be lifted. Hence, because of his failure to strike a deal with the CNDD/FDD and the lack of support from his own party, UPRONA, Buyoya decided to work with FRODEBU. He found in it a ready partner because the partnership helped FRODEBU come out of its political isolation. He did not engage the regional leaders seriously until the Internal Partnership Agreement between the government and the FRODEBU-dominated National Assembly was formally adopted in June 1998.

By February 1998 Buyoya was not yet fully committed to the Arusha Process. He was still insisting that additional mediators should assist the facilitator and that the venue should be changed. Since the regional leaders were not satisfied with his internal peace plan, they decided during the sixth regional summit in Kampala on February 21, 1998, to continue the sanctions. Confident that an internal political deal was imminent, Buyoya dropped charges against Ngendakumana, who, together with former presi-

dents Bagaza and Ntibantunganya, was allowed to travel freely in the first
half of March 1998.

In light of these positive developments, Nyerere embarked on a series of
consultations with all the parties between the months of March and April.
It was formally agreed that peace talks be held in Arusha under Nyerere's
facilitation, with effect from June 15, 1998.

It took almost five years, eight regional summits, and a sanctions
regime for the region to exert itself in facilitating mediation in the
Burundi conflict, indicating not only the complexity of the conflict but
also the intricacy of gaining entry into the mediation process itself. The
regional initiative was finally accepted by Buyoya because he believed
that the regional leaders would appreciate his efforts toward a political
settlement and would support the Internal Partnership deal. He strongly
believed that Arusha was an ideal place to market the Internal Partnership
to the other Burundian parties: He was convinced that with the endorsement of the regional leaders the other parties would be tempted to come
aboard. The regional endorsement would therefore lead to the lifting of
the sanctions. But even if the Internal Partnership could not be sold to
the regional leaders and the other Burundian parties, participating in the
Arusha talks would give the government enough time to implement the
Internal Partnership agreement.

CONCLUSION

A number of important theoretical and practical lessons can be drawn from
the Burundian mediation:

1. A swift and resolute response is key to entry. France, the United
Nations, and the regional leaders acted fast and got a foot in the door. The
consideration of a military intervention and the imposition of sanctions
were a clear demonstration of their determination not only to take the lead
in dealing with the conflict but also to use all the means available to fulfill
such a commitment. From a foot in the door to a full-fledged mediation
process at Arusha was a long step, however.

2. When parties define a conflict in terms of high stakes, it affects the
entry initiatives and mediated compromise solutions become hard to
achieve. Ould-Abdallah's intervention, for example, ended up almost in
a parity mode of power-sharing instead of a proportional mode in nego-

tiation of the hard position of the Tutsi-dominated group. As a result, the Convention of Government took hold only slowly, needing the Arusha process to make it part of the solution. The hard positions of the government and the CNDD/FDD in the Rome talks is another demonstrative case in point.

3. As Rwanda also showed, perceptions, positions, and policy options in a conflict are not constant; they change as the conflict evolves. The change affects both the parties to the conflict and the prospective intervenors. The political reforms that had been initiated in 1989, for example, were perceived by the Tutsi as a means of confirming and legitimizing their political dominance. When they lost the elections, their perception changed. They saw the elections' outcome as a loss of power. This new perception, in turn, changed their position from that of supporting the reforms to opposing them. The change of their position also changed their policy option from normal politics to military measures that culminated in the October 21 coup, taking the conflict to another level.

Among all the intervenors, the only one who managed to gain entry between October 21, 1993, and July 25, 1996, was Ould-Abdallah, who did not try to enter the new level of the conflict in order to reinstate the democratic results of June 1993 elections, but to negotiate a power-sharing deal. This position was influenced by the United Nations' perception of this new level of the conflict as primarily an issue of political instability rather than that of democracy. Ould-Abdallah's brokered Convention of Government did not hold because of factional infighting as much as some parties' perception of it as unfair. The change of their position moved the conflict from political dialogue to military confrontation.

4. A conflict needs an incremental intensity and drastic triggers to attract intervenors. The 1988 massacre induced the external pressure that forced Buyoya to initiate political reforms. The October 21 coup and the death of President Ndadaye attracted a full harvest of humanitarian intervenors and prospective mediators, including the region, the OAU, the United Nations, and the Carter Center. The July 25 coup brought in the region, the OAU, the Community of Sant'Egidio, and UNESCO. This response stands in contrast with that of Rwanda, whose one major trigger, the October 1990 RPF invasion, attracted just a seasonal crop of intervenors.

5. The proximity approach has its limits in initiating mediation, particularly in the instances where the positive and negative incentives are simul-

taneously applied by the very actors who try to mediate the conflict. There is something to be learned as well from the Burundian government's initial reluctance to accept Nyerere as the mediator and Arusha as the venue for the talks. The important theoretical and practical issues for consideration here are as follows: How appropriate is the proximity approach in mediating an internal conflict? What are the potential constraints to be considered and how could they be overcome? How useful are the positive and negative incentives in the proximity approach to mediation?

6. For sanctions to be effective, there must be total solidarity and strict coordination among the imposers of the sanctions, as well as unwavering international support for the sanctions. Buyoya took quite some time to respond to the impact of the sanctions, primarily because the enforcers' solidarity was quickly broken down following individual states' economic interests. The impact of the sanctions was also reduced because of flagging international support. The western countries' ambivalence on the sanctions contributed to Buyoya's procrastination on the regional initiative.

7. The two requests for regional military intervention from the legitimate governments of Burundi in October 1993 and in June 1996 were turning points in that they were the first and second time a sovereign country in Africa had voluntarily sought such assistance. The significance was not only in the requests but also in the response to the requests. The lesson from the Burundian experience is that the failure to respond to such a policy option is not necessarily a function of legal barriers of sovereignty but can also be a function of exogenous factors. For Africa and the African Union, the OAU's successor, the lesson is that there is an urgent need for the continent to start thinking seriously about beefing up its capacity in the area of peacekeeping.

8. Though more difficult, the inclusive approach of engaging all the parties to the conflict is key to success. This approach differed from the conventional one that usually favors the central authority and moderate parties in negotiations aimed at striking a deal in a compromise political settlement. The experience of the exclusive approach adopted for the Arusha process for Rwanda is a very instructive contrast to this innovation. The extremist groups that were excluded in the Rwandan negotiations in Arusha contributed not only to the failure of implementing the negotiated agreement but also to the 1994 genocide. While engaging all the parties might appear to be the right approach, however, such an approach may be its own undoing, taking so long to get the hold-outs' agreement that the early compromise falls apart.

4

CONGO-BRAZZAVILLE, 1993–1999

M ediation became a regular occurrence in Congo-Brazzaville in the 1990s, as the country's attempts to emerge from single-party rule and enter the world of democracies brought only bitter, bloody conflict. Since before its independence in 1960, the Republic of the Congo knew only the rule of one political party, growing first out of the nationalist movement and then out of the increasingly Marxist praetorian rule of the military. Yet underneath this centralized power monopoly lay a social pluralism in the country's tribal structure, in which no one ethnic group could claim more than 20 percent of the population. Thus the country was held together by a combination of authoritarianism and ethnic alliances. When the authoritarian rule was overthrown by the democratizing movement sweeping through Africa in 1990, new rules had to be established for conducting the ethnic alliance process. That process did not come easily. Nor did the nostalgia for the enjoyment of power disappear, even under the new system of selection.

Congo in the 1990s underwent a series of centralist conflicts for power. After initial political instability quickly degenerated into violence in 1993, the country righted itself under vigorous domestic and international mediation, again broke down into civil war in 1997, again regained equilibrium under reasserted authoritarian control, and again erupted in violence in 1999, until finally the original despot of the previous decades prevailed in violence and restored single-party rule.[1] Yet violence is never far below the surface, and after his appropriation of the democratic practices and adjustment of them to his authoritarian system, in 2002, violence again broke out in protest.

In each of the three rounds of violence, many prospective mediators rushed in to be of help. The first period, 1993–1994, contained five domestic and three international attempts at conflict management negotiations. The second period, 1997, involved two domestic and three international attempts. In the third period, 1999, at least four international mediators pressed their services. In all of the cases, potential mediators stood at the edge of entry, trying their hand at producing an agreement to end the conflict. All were given a chance—often repeatedly—to try, but, paradoxically, full entry was obtained only at the moment of success: If the mediator was able to elicit terms judged preferable to the amount of pain the parties were suffering, he or she was accorded entry to achieve agreement on those terms. Only a mutually hurting stalemate guaranteed initiation of negotiations, and only a sustained mutually hurting stalemate throughout the negotiations produced an equitable agreement.

Under the general question about the way in which entry was achieved by the prospective mediators, a number of subsidiary questions arise in the Congolese context. How was selection made among the many suitors? Did the fact of gaining entry in a previous round facilitate—or ensure—entry in a later round? What particular traits or conditions favored entry and selection? How did the process of escalating mediation, from the domestic to the international level, operate to secure entry? What were the interests of the prospective mediators, and how did these interests affect their entry and selection? How were the interests of the conflicting parties served by mediation and by the choice of a particular mediator? Finally, what lessons can be drawn from the Congolese experience?

The Parties

The country is divided into four ethnic groupings, bringing together diverse tribes in the north, southwest, southeast, and south around their leading politicians and, after 1990, in their respective political parties. These ethnic constituencies had formed the basis of continually fluctuating political coalitions even under the single, Afro-Marxist party and immediately became the basis of the new multiparty system. The rules of the game indicated that alliances were made to defeat an opponent and then remade to defeat the former ally, a continual recipe for instability. As time (and the conflict) went on, each leader/region developed its own militia, fueled by unemployed youths and then by remnants of militias from the other Congo and its neighbors (notably Rwanda) across the river.

The Congolese Labor Party (PCT), founded in 1970, is the sole Afro-Marxist party of the authoritarian period of the 1970s and 1980s. Its leader since 1979 has been Denis Sassou Nguesso, spokesman of the Mbochi north, the least populated part of the country. Sassou was able to take power militarily, but because of the size of his ethnic constituency he was unable to rely on the party to win power democratically. In the single-party period, the party was the patronage and support organization of the whole regime, whereas in the democratic period it was simply a minority ethnic party like the others, winning nine of eleven seats in 1993 in the only free and fair legislative elections, with Sassou winning 17 percent of the vote in the 1992 presidential elections, mainly from the north.[2] A rival Mbochi politician from the north was General Joachim Yhombi Opango, Sassou's predecessor as head of state in 1977–1979. Sassou's militia are the Cobras, composed of PCT youth and unemployed young people in general, plus refugees from the wars of the Great Lakes Region, including soldiers of fortune from neighboring Congo-Kinshasa (Zaire, now the Democratic Republic of the Congo), ex-soldiers from the Rwandan Army under Habriyamana, and his militiamen in the *interahamwe* (the *genocidaires* of 1994), among others. They benefited from French support and training.

The Pan-African Union for Social Democracy (UPADS) was the slightly left-of-center party of Pascal Lissouba, a biology professor and former prime minister of the mid-1960s. It represented the "Nibolek" (Niari, Bouenza, and Lekoumou people of the southwest), who elected forty-five deputies in 1993 and gave Lissouba—a Ndjabi from Niari—36 percent of the vote in 1992, with support also from the south around Pointe Noire and from Brazzaville. UPADS, PCT, and other smaller parties were allies in the National Alliance for Democracy in the presidential runoff, after which the PCT withdrew its support.

Lissouba's militias were the Zulus (also known as the Aubervillois) or Cacoyas, drawing on local Congolese unemployed youth from his region, some of whom served in his presidential guard when he was in office and received Israeli training.

The Congolese Movement for Development and Integral Democracy (MCDDI) was the party of the perennial anticommunist militant, Bernard Kolelas, the hero of the Lari, Bakongo, and Bateke from the Stanley Pool around (and including the southern part of) Brazzaville. Kolelas carried the Pool and won 20 percent of the presidential vote in 1992; his party won twenty-six seats from Brazzaville and the Pool. MCDDI was the core party of the other major alliance in the 1990s, the Union for Democratic Renewal (URD), which the PCT joined when it left UPADS in pique; however, an alliance between Sassou and his longtime enemy, Kolelas, was unnatural and soon fell apart. A competing Lari politician was former World Bank official and prime minister during the Sovereign National Conference (CNS) transition, Andre Milongo, who won 10 percent of the presidential vote, also from the Pool and Brazzaville. Kolelas's militia was called the Ninjas, formerly created by Milongo from Lari and Bakongo youth and officers from the Pool, Israeli trained and South African armed. After Milongo's defeat in 1992, the militia passed over to Kolelas as the leading Lari politician.

The Rally for Democracy and Social Progress was the party of the south (Kouilou region) on the Atlantic around the port and oil capital of Pointe Noire, which held a quarter of the country's population. Its leader was Jean-Pierre Thystere-Tchicaya, formerly of the PCT and then the URD alliance with the MCDDI. The party was a lesser player than were the other three and did not have an important militia.

THE CONFLICT I

The political conflict of the 1990s in Congo-Brazzaville burst out of the CNS movement, which seized sovereignty from the hands of the single-party autocrat in a dozen countries of Africa at the beginning of the decade and returned it, for a heady moment, to the hands of the people organized as civil society. In Congo-Brazzaville, the CNS lasted three months (from mid-March to mid-June 1991), appointed a one-year transitional government, wrote a new liberal constitution that was adopted by referendum in March 1992, and then held five rounds of elections—internationally judged to be progressively freer and fairer—beginning at the municipal level in May. The last two, for president in August 1992, saw first the ousted autocrat Sassou Nguesso defeated and then Lissouba elected over perennial opponent Kolelas.

In December 1991, a group of independent politicians called a meeting of their colleagues to declare a political truce and lower tensions, but the truce was soon broken by rising acrimony. Again during the presidential campaign, the moderator and the president of the CNS mediated adherence to the electoral rules of competition among the candidates. In both cases, the mediator's position of authority guaranteed entry but not success.[3]

In the second round of the presidential elections, Sassou's PCT made an alliance with Lissouba against Sassou's perennial critic, Kolelas. But when the cabinet posts were allocated, Sassou felt shortchanged and shifted his alliance to Kolelas, giving the opposition a majority in parliament. Following parliamentary practice, the president dissolved parliament and called for new elections in May 1993. The opposition (the new parliamentary majority) cried foul and called for civil disobedience, as is allowable under the constitution. Barricades, demonstrations, and clashes with security forces erupted in November 1992. The army chief of staff responded with the threat of a military takeover if the parties did not agree on an interim government, but disagreement continued over the allocation of seats. An escalation was needed in the mediation process.

In stepped neighboring Gabonese president, Omar Bongo, son-in-law of Sassou (although his senior) and a Bateke akin to Lissouba. Bongo mediated an agreement on the new government, not by presenting a special formula (he adopted the previously proposed formula of a 40–60 distribution of ministries in favor of the opposition) but by working out its detailed application and by appealing to his "family" to work together and to campaign rather than to fight. In so doing, he strengthened his own credentials as a mediator in Congolese politics.

When the new parliamentary elections gave a majority to the presidential coalition, the 40–60 formula was overtaken by events, and new violence broke out. Mediation by the CNS president brought agreement on runoff elections a month later, in June, and when the presidential majority was confirmed in the runoffs, fighting broke out in earnest. Two new CNS mediations, an intervention by the French Cooperation Ministry and coordinated efforts by the Western embassies produced much activity but no results. U.S. ambassador Daniel Phillips noted, "Neither side was convinced that they were going to be the losers, and each hoped they would still win." In other words, a mutual hurting stalemate was absent.

The prime minister then asked the OAU secretary-general to test the organization's new Mechanism for Conflict Prevention, Management, and Resolution (authorized the previous summer) by offering a mediator. Three names were submitted and the parties unanimously agreed on the Algerian diplomat Mohammed Sahnoun, former OAU assistant secretary-general, who in turn invited Bongo to work with him. After the CNS moderator (and then defense minister) secured a cease-fire, the party leaders went to Libreville, where the two mediators, aided by the French, employed shuttle diplomacy to bring about agreement on de-escalation and a judicious solution to the parliamentary contests (an international tribunal) on August 4, 1993. The mediation was successful through a combination of national and international efforts that finally convinced the parties that violence and confrontation had reached the point of diminishing returns, coupled with a satisfying formula for the electoral settlements.

Unfortunately, while the leaders agreed, the militias only geared up further for a fight. After the first round of the contested election reruns in early October, new violence broke out, producing ethnic cleansing and massive, gruesome deaths totaling some 3,000–5,000 by the end of January 1994. At that point, the tribunal rendered its verdict, a parliamentarians' committee finally established a cease-fire and a national peacekeeping force, and apparent harmony was restored.

ANALYSIS I

The entry pattern in the 1993–1994 round of the Congo-Brazzaville conflict was simple: Everyone within earshot rushed to be helpful, but then, one by one, were pushed aside as their authority proved unequal to the momentum of the conflict. The conflict provided a clear example of layered mediation, in which various levels of ever higher authority are stacked up and the conflict works its way up the pile to the level that is competent to handle it. That moment or level is determined by two elements: the degree of fatigue or mutually hurting stalemate in which the parties perceive themselves to be, and the degree of authority of the mediator before whom they are required to concede an end to their conflicting efforts. Yet even those pushed aside as mediation rose from level to level were never fully eliminated; they continued their ministrations and, in the end, contributed to the mass of efforts that finally convinced the parties of their painful, unproductive situation.

Leverage is found above all in the mediator's ability to extract a favorable position from each party and to persuade each party that reconciliation is a preferable alternative to violent conflict; leverage in this context is not found in any material gratification.[4] When all local (including ambassadorial) mediation proved incapable of providing those two elements (as well as any material gratifications), the combatants reached upstairs to the higher level offered to them by the OAU. Entry was ensured by their ability to pick the mediating individual, Ambassador Sahnoun, who then involved President Bongo, whose earlier efforts had been successful but outrun by events and whose entry in turn was ensured by his fraternal-presidential authority and his family connections.[5]

The Conflict II

Although Congo-Brazzaville appeared to have managed its conflict after 1994 by bringing it down from violence to the level of politics, the ethnic basis of the parties and the unstable coalition environment remained; so did the militias, despite agreements at Libreville and attempts thereafter to disband them. While Lissouba ruled, often with indecision at home and with snubs to Congo's international patron, France, Sassou retired to France, tended his international fences, and then returned to his home territory to tend his domestic fences. When the campaign began for the next presidential elections, scheduled for July 27, 1997, the three leaders were the prime candidates. An incident in the north resulted in deaths and in a heavy-handed attempt by Lissouba to have Sassou hand over those charged with responsibility. The second civil war broke out, on June 6, and divided the capital in half. This time, the war was between Lissouba's Zulus or Cacoyas and Sassou's Cobras; Kolelas, with alliance ties to both parties, kept his Ninjas and his district in the city out of the conflict and immediately created a National Mediation Committee. The effort was active but ultimately ineffective, although it did arrive at a number of cease-fires and worked out details for a transition government that contributed much to the evolving efforts. French troops, stationed in Brazzaville to evacuate foreigners from the civil war in Kinshasa across the river if necessary, were reinforced and immediately used to evacuate foreigners from Brazzaville in Operation

Pelican. Then, instead of intervening to monitor a cease-fire, they evacuated themselves in turn. French president Jacques Chirac negotiated a cease-fire by telephone and a return to the good offices of Bongo, but the militias ignored the agreement.

Again Bongo pressed his efforts, joined by Sahnoun as special representative of the UN and OAU secretaries-general for the Great Lakes Region. A number of cease-fires were negotiated between mid-June and the end of July, punctuated by inconclusive returns to violence that did not change the battle line along the railroad through the middle of town. The mediators agreed that the stalled conflict was ripe for an interposition force to hold the cease-fires, and the European Union backed the initiative, but the UN Security Council refused to give its agreement, calling the situation not yet ready.

With the rejection of the mediation efforts, the warring parties began looking for other sources of support or mediation. Sassou began working on Angola, which was sensitive to the collaboration between Lissouba and the rebel groups fighting the Angolan government—the National Union for the Total Independence of Angola (UNITA in the Portugese acronym) and the Front for the Liberation of the Cabinda Enclave. Lissouba in turn cultivated a new mediation effort by the "new revolutionary leaders" of the region—the presidents of Uganda and Rwanda, and Laurent Kabila, newly installed in neighboring Congo—who met in mid-August to develop alternative plans for an Inter-African Force. The anti-French orientation of this group fit with Lissouba's past policies but reinforced the French interest in supporting Sassou; when Lissouba went to France two weeks later, French officials refused to receive him and Chirac advised him by telephone to take on Sassou as prime minister.[6]

Mediation by Sahnoun and Bongo, suspended on August 6 at the time of the Security Council decision, was revived, leading to a regional summit of Francophonia neighbors in Libreville on September 14. Although Lissouba signed the summit agreement, he did not attend the meeting, looking instead for more friendly mediation or support from the progressive neighbors, and he appointed Kolelas his prime minister. Fighting continued to stalemate, and the mediators continued their efforts. On September 26, 1997 (the day after a special session of the Security Council called by the United States, asking for a study of conflict in Africa), the Security Council again turned down a request for peacekeeping forces, and on October 9, an interim government plan was finally initialed by all the parties. However, the next day, the Cobras broke out of their part of Brazzaville and captured the presidential palace, and two days later, 7,000 Angolan troops invaded Congo-Brazzaville, taking Pointe Noire for Sassou and then joining in the conquest of the capital. Some 10,000 Congolese, mainly civilians, were killed in the fighting.

ANALYSIS II

The entry problem was even simpler than in the first round, in that it followed the same logic, facilitated by the fact that 1997 was a repeat performance. The fact that the prospective mediators were all actors in the first round made them known quantities and undoubtedly facilitated their entry. Whatever their preference for a particular party, their interest in mediation, across the board, was in securing an end to the conflict that was destroying the country and troubling their relations with it. Neither the ambassadors, nor the local parties, nor the Sahnoun-Bongo team had any problem getting the ear of the sides of the conflict. The mediators' only problem was in getting the sides to sign something. None of the mediators was able to persuade all the parties at the same time that a reconciliation agreement would produce a better outcome than the one that they were fighting for. The ultimate circle, or layer, of involvement was never consummated by a UN Security Council authorization of an interposition force, which would have made the difference. As the stalemate endured against repeated efforts to break out of it, the parties started looking for sources of support rather than mediation. When the hardworking African pair of mediators finally got an agreement from all the parties, Sassou's (or his Cobras') campaign was finally at the point of a breakthrough and his Angolan ally was at the point of an invasion more decisive than the diplomatic breakthrough the mediators were able to achieve.

The unusual—and unhelpful—twist of the second-round mediation was the competing availability of Laurent Kabila across the river as a potential intervenor. Kabila had just taken Kinshasa in May, was looking for support among his neighbors, and was undecided about which of the two sides in Brazzaville was of potentially greater help. Sassou had had bad relations with Mobutu Sese Sekou, but Mobutu was now defeated, Kabila was in power in Kinshasa, and Lissouba was in power, however shaky, in Brazzaville. Kabila was an unlikely mediator but was a potential alternative source of support that Lissouba cultivated. His interest in either role was strictly subsidiary to his concern for consolidating his newly won victory. Unfortunately for Lissouba, Kabila was neither a source of support equivalent to Angola for Sassou nor a source of mediation equivalent to the regional summit for any of the parties, and the attempt to reach out to him alienated both and particularly alienated the French patron of many of his neighbors.

The Conflict III

Sassou's hold on the country remained tenuous.[7] After about a year of restiveness marked by continued combat in the countryside, Kolelas's Ninjas made a major, if suicidal, foray into Brazzaville itself in December 1998 and launched attacks against the Pointe Noire–Brazzaville railroad, the country's economic lifeline. The rail line remained cut for the following year, although Sassou's forces—Cobras more or less integrated into the army—made major gains against the Ninjas. At the same time, important action took place in the south, including a major battle for Dolisie, a transportation hub and potential base for UNITA guerrillas allied to Lissouba. By mid-1999, all three sides were hurting: Sassou was recognized as president but was not in control of his country and was unable to carry out any security or development projects. Lissouba was rich in exile in London with some control over some of the fighting forces in Congo-Brazzaville. Kolelas, who it was generally thought would have won any free and fair election in 1997, was poor in exile in Washington but with loyal forces at home. Some 6,000 Congolese were estimated to have been killed in the previous year.

In spring 1999, a number of independent initiatives were launched with the aim of developing a mediation effort. All were encouraged by one or more of the Congolese parties, in all cases, including Sassou Nguesso. Boutros Boutros-Ghali, secretary-general of the International Organization of the Francophonie (OIF), saw a possible opportunity and dispatched Senegalese diplomat Mustapha Niasse to Brazzaville. Ange Patasse, president of the Central African Republic, offered himself as mediator, along with some free advice. Gabonese president Omar Bongo was contacted from time to time by his father-in-law Sassou Nguesso about the possibility of mediation. In addition, two private businessmen with occasional contacts with the Carter Center at Emory University in the United States sent similar messages from all three principals inviting mediation by the center's International Negotiation Network (INN).

Whereas the first three approaches reflect natural Congolese relations, the fourth is unusual. Only Lissouba had had previous contact with the Carter Center, and that was only a passing visit. However, Lissouba had moved to London in 1998, when France no longer agreed to honor his presidential passport, and Kolelas was located in Washington, in part because of his past anticommunist affinity and in part to look for current support. It is likely that Sassou included the Carter Center in his contacts in order to have a non-French organization on his list; it is unlikely that he knew much about the Carter Center.

The responses of the four potential mediators differed. Bongo remained vague in his responses to Sassou, unable to refuse but wary about having been burned by his experience two years earlier. Niasse made a visit to Brazzaville in early 1999, found the situation unpromising, and returned to his presidential campaign in Senegal; Boutros-Ghali, snubbed by Sassou at the meeting of the OIF in Moncton in early September, told a representative of the INN that the OIF was withdrawing from mediation in Congo and giving its blessings to the INN. Patasse's remarks were found offensive and he was not invited back. The Carter Center found the invitation—a precondition for its involvement—attractive because it specifically referred to the INN and thus presaged a preparation for a transition to a post-Carter era of institutionalization.

I. William Zartman of Johns Hopkins University, a member of the INN, traveled with Joyce Neu of the Carter Center from Washington to London and Brazzaville in August 1999 for contacts with the three principals, which were then pursued over the coming months. Their strategy was to accumulate a series of points of agreement that the principals would initial and then meet to sign. It was felt that a meeting would be fruitless without a previously agreed basis but that a meeting of the principals themselves was necessary. The plan was to establish a framework for a transition to free and fair elections, based on a jointly established independent electoral commission that would prepare the elections while Sassou would remain in power as titular head of state. Successive drafts of the points of agreement were presented to the principals as a working document that they could edit and amend. While Lissouba and Kolelas, in their various styles, accepted the process, Sassou did so only if the Carter Center initiative coordinated with the Bongo "initiative." At the same time, a number of militia leaders, not known as the most prominent, signed a cease-fire with the government at Pointe Noire on November 16, possibly through Bongo's efforts. By the end of the month, there was general agreement from the three principals on the INN eight-point document and an upcoming meeting, with various views about the venue; however, Sassou insisted that the meeting be composed of the principals' representatives rather than the principals themselves, which the INN team accepted. When pressed about a three-party meeting scheduled for December 16–18 at the Carter Center, however, Sassou responded, after weeks of delay, that the Carter Center initiative should line up with Bongo's efforts, and the meeting was cancelled.

Yet on December 18, Bongo opened a meeting of leaders of Lissouba's and other militias in Libreville, ending in an agreement signed in Brazzaville on December 29 "to end hostilities."[8] Lissouba was in contact with his militia leaders—"my youngsters" or "my kids," as he called them—and they worked long-distance on a draft of some thirty articles, including withdrawal of foreign troops and their replacement by an international peacekeeping force. The agreement was to be initialed only (as per the INN strategy), with political conditions of reconciliation and transition to be left to the signing meeting of the principals. In the end, only the provision for the militias to lay down arms and to be integrated into the Congolese armed forces was retained. A number of militia groups, mainly associated with Kolelas, remained outside the agreement, as did Kolelas and Lissouba themselves.

To the extent that mediation was involved in obtaining the agreement, it came from Bongo. Sassou's representatives claim that they sent out envoys in November or December to the militia leaders in the bush, asking whether the militias enjoyed their current life or would rather join the army and return to normalcy, at a time when the chiefs abroad were having difficulties in maintaining their arms supplies.[9] Both elements were doubtless present. Unlike the INN formula, which was for a normalization and then election among the three chiefs, who were assumed to be in charge of their troops, Bongo's and Sassou's formula was for the rewarded surrender of the troops—a "peace of the brave"—and an elimination of the competing chiefs (who were then charged with treason and condemned to death in absentia in 2000).

ANALYSIS III

Mediators' entry is a more elusive variable in this phase of the conflict. Many close observers believe that, unlike Lissouba and Kolelas, Sassou never had any intention of admitting an INN mediation but merely encouraged it to be able to show that there was an American alternative in addition to the French and African channels. The INN mediators felt that Sassou did not make this decision until late November (his letter was dated November 23 and conveyed December 7), and even then not irrevocably. They also felt that the mutual pain of the stalemate was intense and balanced enough in the summer of 1999 to produce interest in any successful mediation as an alternative to be cultivated, but that Sassou's progress in the bush and the return of both refugees and militia members in the late summer and early fall reduced his pain and made him lose interest in evenhanded mediation.

The broader point is that each party favored the mediation most favorable to it, and by the end of 1999, Sassou—perhaps under pressure from the Carter Center and in face of the withdrawal of Boutros-Ghali—was able to convince Bongo to hold a meeting without conditions in Libreville in December in place of a meeting based on a signed agreement in Atlanta, and he was also able to coerce the militia leaders into attending. Whether the INN mediation ever actually achieved entry is thus a sharper question than warranted by the facts or than is answerable with the same sharpness.

By the same token, if the INN was active without clear entry, Bongo achieved entry without clear activity. Bongo was always an option—that is, always achieved entry—if he would only be so, but his reluctance to be involved kept him standing only at the door of entry. The other two mediators would have had no trouble in achieving access if they had appeared to have any interest and chance of success. "Access" here refers not to physical contact and meetings—the INN team was received by Sassou with jovial hospitality—but to the more subtle matter of acceptability in a political process, which is much more difficult to evaluate.

Thus access was a competitive matter. Questions of cooperation, competition, and propriety pose difficult problems for multiple mediators and complicate the matter of entry, especially when the conflicting parties are resistant to mediation. Cooperation has a procedural and a substantive dimension, the first referring to the weight that multiple mediators bring to the process, and the second to the terms on which they seek an agreement. It is the second element that legitimately brings in the matter of propriety and, hence, the real complication. As the INN was told by the Francophonie that all the other mediators were in contact with only two of the three principals (Sassou plus either Lissouba or Kolelas), and as the team believed that its strategy of obtaining agreement on some basic points before a meeting was sound, it had a substantive reason for keeping control of its initiative.

None of the putative mediators had much interest in getting involved, least of all Boutros-Ghali and Patasse. Perhaps the one with the most interests was Bongo. The presence of some 500,000 Congolese refugees in Gabon increased both his concern for neighboring conditions and his fear of importing a rebellion; also, it was hard to resist the family pressures from his father-in-law, although he tried hard to do so. Beyond the institutional interest in the mediation, the INN mediators were under no inner or external compulsion to undertake the demarche. Both members of the team were busy—one in academia and the other in working on the simultaneous Carter Center effort between Sudan and Uganda, which was signed in Nairobi on December 12—and President Carter was not deeply engaged personally. Sassou urged the INN to consort with Bongo, which the INN welcomed and tried to do, without any response from Bongo to President Carter's letters. The two businessmen urged involvement of the Sant'Egidio community; the INN team was interested in obtaining a Sant'Egidio presence at the scheduled meeting in order to take over the process once the original agreement had been signed, but not as part of the process to that point, which it preferred to control under its own strategy.

The INN team received the cooperative blessing of the Francophonie. In the end, the INN initiative clearly would have benefited procedurally from cooperation with Bongo, in which it was interested, and Bongo might have benefited substantively from cooperation with the INN. Less clearly, the INN perhaps might have benefited from Sant'Egidio to create a greater pressure in favor of its demarche. It benefited from the benevolent support of the U.S. State Department, particularly when in Brazzaville, although once it returned from Congo it was on its own, with no active endorsement from Washington.

But the missing element was the ability to affect the parties' alternatives, to operate on the basis of anything but earnest persuasion. It would have been most beneficial if the mediation were able—as an official U.S. mediation could attempt to do—to call on support from Angola or France, urging the stronger party—Sassou—to take mediation seriously (or, a fortiori, from Angola, indicating that there were limits to the length of time it could keep its troops in Congo). In the absence of such assistance, any mediator had to rely on the parties themselves to distribute pain to each other in the stalemate. Sassou, in possession of the seat of power, had "nine points of the law"; his pain was caused by the limit of his writ to the main cities and not to the bush or, above all, to the railroad in between. (He had told the INN team, "I will stop at nothing to gain control of the railroad.") The other two principals suffered the pain of political homesickness: personally they were out of the arena, and their only means of involvement in Congolese politics was through their militias, which they controlled only tenuously. They faced the continuous choice of balance or bandwagon: whether to keep up pressure on Sassou in the hope of adding his pain to theirs and bringing about a mutually hurting stalemate, or to join forces with him in the hopes of being accorded some of the spoils under his control. As neither the situation nor the mediator could produce a mutually hurting stalemate, the parties (or their lieutenants) chose to bandwagon and granted final entry to the mediator that went with it.

LESSONS AND CONCLUSIONS

There were many striking characteristics about entry into mediation in Congo-Brazzaville.

1. Perhaps the most striking was the form of frequently neutral self-interest that motivated the prospective mediators. Sahnoun above all, plus the ambassadors and the Carter Center, were in it because it was their job. They had no favorites, they had no stakes—other than to defend their reputation as peacemakers. The dedication of Sahnoun to this effort cannot be overstated. Bongo, along with the domestic mediators, had a deep interest in seeing the conflict end because it hurt them, personally and professionally.

As frequently occurs, these mediators had an interest in a stable outcome so that the conflict did not continue to trouble their relations and activities in Congo. Indeed, the more the mediator was interested in a particular outcome, the less helpful was his or her efforts. France in the second and third rounds of the conflict was of no help at all, and Bongo dropped the mediator's neutral role in the third round to broker a surrender, albeit reluctantly, the terms of which the government has not lived up to.[10]

2. Another characteristic was the access ensured by the layered multi-mediation efforts. Because of both their positions and the parties' need for a solution, the prospective mediators had no problem getting the ear of the leaders. It was in getting the leaders to sign an agreement that they had difficulty.

3. The gradual dawning of mutually hurting stalemates in the three rounds had the crucial effect of focusing the parties' attention on the mediation and the terms of the evolving agreements. Indeed, the lesson works even in reverse: In the third round, the ripeness of the situation in July-August won the mediators access, but its disappearance in September produced disinterest in an evenhanded settlement of reconciliation. The terms of the settlement reflected the situation on the ground, although both the stalemates and their breakdowns were the result of the parties' efforts at conflict.

4. By the same token, there was also an escalating element to the type of solution that was capable of keeping the parties' attention and closing an agreement. In the first two rounds, there was no difficulty in arranging cease-fires. In the first round, they were observed or not observed, as the situation allowed, but in the second round, it was the stalemate that made the cease-fires hold, doubtless the reverse of what one might expect. In the third round, no one was interested in a cease-fire. However, in the second and third rounds, the mediator needed to be able to deploy some peacekeeping troops of its own to make its entry stick. The painful failure in two instances of the UN Security Council to complement the work of the mediators with an authorization for a small number of peacekeeping troops meant that the parties would start looking for external sources of support to break out of the deadlock, which they did. Similarly, the mediators in the third round were also unable to mobilize peacekeepers or, more pertinent, to elicit a warning of possible troop withdrawals from Angola. Entry into the verbal arena is often not enough; the mediator needs to be able to borrow muscle, especially in a repeating, escalating conflict.

5. The Congo conflicts show very strongly that entry is not just a function of the leaders' acceptance. Congo was plagued from the beginning by the sorcerers' apprentice quality of relations between the politicians and the militias. The leaders had only tenuous control over their troops, either because they could not physically communicate with them during the conflict or because their communications were not heeded. This phenomenon

was particularly notable in late 1993 and 1994 as the conflict continued viciously after the Libreville Accords, and in 1999, when Sassou undercut the rival leaders (both out of the country) to reach out to the lieutenants in the field and buy them off.

5

LIBERIA,
1989–1996

Initiating entry in mediation is an aspect of prenegotiation that is as complex in all regards as the bargaining process that follows it. Belligerents immerse themselves in assessing who is eligible for intervention and what their own response to a particular candidate should be. Interested third parties also engage in evaluating capacity vis-à-vis the dynamics of the mediation they wish to enter, and they decide if their interest will be best served by their intervention. A point of entry must also be considered and an entry program devised. Most of the time, all these assessments must be made against the backdrop of escalations, stalemates, and the entry (or exit) of other parties. The result is often a complex mix of perceptions, goals, actions, and events that shape entry opportunities and help determine whether interested third parties can utilize those opportunities or not.

The Liberia mediation was full of such dynamics and provides a good insight into the nature of entry initiation in internal conflict mediation. This chapter examines the process of entry in the Liberia mediation in an attempt to draw some general conclusions regarding the practice. The details of the complex negotiations that brought the Liberian conflict to an end have been extensively covered elsewhere and so will be cited here only when they illuminate the dynamics of third-party entry.[1] The nature of the conflict and the third parties involved is presented as a background to the discussion of the dynamics of entry in the mediation.

The question of why some third parties chose to mediate in the conflict is one that also draws on the reasons why other third parties elected to stay away. While the varied and complex nature of behavior exhibited by those third parties that concerned themselves with the Liberian conflict makes a generic conclusion impossible; a micro-analysis of the circumstances of entry suggests that the principal factor that determined the third-party entry into mediation was access to the armed conflict. What are the factors that shaped access? And how did they determine third-party entry in Liberia? How did a choice among different definitions of the conflict affect entry? What was the relation between availability and access?

The Phases of Mediation in the Conflict

The Liberian civil war was a centralist conflict for control of the government and all its resources. Five phases can be identified on the basis of the pattern of the conflict and the leadership of mediation. The phases show the way entry is shaped by evolutions in mediation.

Phase One (December 1989–June 1990). This phase was dominated by American mediation. It spanned the period from the outbreak of hostilities on Christmas Eve 1989 to the U.S. decision to abandon plans to whisk President Samuel Doe into exile in June 1990. It covered the invasion of Nimba County from the Ivory Coast by Charles Taylor's National Patriotic Front of Liberia (NPFL), the breakaway of the Independent NPFL from the main NPFL, contacts between the United States and both Taylor and Doe, and the Togolese agreement to grant Doe political asylum. The phase overlaps with entry preparations by two future mediators—the Inter-Faith Mediation Committee (IFMC) and the Economic Community of West African States (ECOWAS).

Phase Two (June 1990–July 1990). The second phase of the mediation was dominated by the IFMC's effort to broker an agreement between Doe and Taylor. It spanned the period from the U.S. exit to the end of the first Freetown conference of the Liberian parties. This phase also covers the first entry of the All-Africa Conference of Churches (AACC) and of the Carter Center.

Phase Three (July 1990–September 1991). This phase was the first ECOWAS–Nigeria mediation. It covers the period from the IFMC exit (at the end of Freetown I) to the beginning of the Yamoussoukro series of meetings in 1991. This period includes the loss of momentum of Taylor's assault on Monrovia, the establishment by ECOWAS of the Interim Government of National Unity (IGNU), the second Freetown conference, the two All-Liberian National Conferences, and the ECOWAS Bamako Talks. The phase also witnessed the deployment of the ECOWAS Cease-

Fire Monitoring Group (ECOMOG); the murder of Doe by Prince Johnson's Independent NPFL and the emergence of the new faction of former Doe supporters, the United Liberation Movement for Democracy in Liberia (ULIMO). The third phase also witnessed the assumption of a new role (as facilitator) by the United States and attempts by the Organization of African Unity and United Nations to play a more active role in the mediation.

Phase Four (September 1991–1993). This phase of the mediation was characterized by the temporary replacement of Nigeria by the Ivory Coast as the leadership of the ECOWAS mediation to produce the four Yamoussoukro Accords of 1991–1992, the Geneva meeting, and the Coutonou and Lome Accords. It witnessed Taylor's bloody renewed attempt to capture Monrovia (Operation Octopus), the brief entry of Senegal into the war, and a greater UN role in the mediation. New parties such as the Liberian Peace Council (LPC) and the Lofa Defense Force (LDF) also emerged as the conflict prolonged and presented the negotiation with new problems during this phase.

Phase Five (1994–August 1996). The fifth phase marks the return of Nigerian leadership to the ECOWAS mediation. It begins with the end of the Yamoussoukro series and ends with the Abuja Peace Accords of 1995 and 1996. Within its span lies the ECOMOG offensive against Taylor (leading to the capture of the cities of Harbel, Kakata, and Buchanan) and the Ghanaian mediation of the Akosombo and Accra Talks. The final phase also witnessed ECOWAS's acquisition of international legitimization, rapprochement between the NPFL and Nigeria, and the second entry of the Carter Center as election observers.

The Mediators

The Liberia mediation is often thought of as completely an ECOWAS affair; however, it was far from that. Several actors (both powerful and weak) tried their hands at brokering deals at various periods in the mediation. They ranged from NGOs and civic and religious bodies to regional and international organizations, continental organizations, great powers, and states. Several categories of such third parties participated in the mediation.

Local actors included local religious bodies, civic groups, and opposition political parties. As indigenous bodies, these parties exercised mediation roles that were shaped largely by their proximity to the conflict and a shared sense of responsibility to preserve peace and stability in their country. Their negotiating resources did not, however, match their deep commitment. Hence, they did not achieve any lasting results in their mediation efforts.

Local religious bodies included the Liberian Council of Churches (an association of Catholic and Protestant denominations) and the National Muslim Council (the principal association of Liberian Muslims). These two bodies pooled resources in 1990 to establish the IFMC, which began vigorous consultations among the contending parties. IFMC leaders such as Bishop Ronald Diggs undertook several trips to NPFL-held territory to convince Taylor to negotiate. The committee successfully organized a major peace conference in Freetown in March 1990 and was key in attracting the attention of other third parties (such as the United States, the OAU, and the AACC) to the conflict. It suffered, however, from an inaccurate assessment of its own power as well as the power and motives of the combatants. The IFMC therefore lost its rank as a major player when it became clear that it had neither the carrots nor sticks required to reach and sustain an agreement.

Several civic and interest groups were also interested in the mediation even though they too lacked the requisite tools and appreciation of the true nature of the conflict. Some of them (including the Grand Gedeh Association, which represented Doe's Krahn ethnic group) attended the Freetown talks and also the first All-Liberia Conference. They later pooled resources to form the Liberian National Conference, which attempted to seek a more active role in the mediation. They were largely ignored by the major parties, however, in part because they remained incoherent and were unable to produce a formula for resolving the conflict. Nevertheless, the civic groups, though marginalized, did not exit the mediation process completely and resorted to the provision of commentary that occasionally influenced the behavior of other parties.

The opposition parties were most visible in the early days of the conflict, when Doe was desperate for friends and therefore decided to recognize them. They comprised groups operating from both within (such as the United People's Party) and abroad. In May 1990, Doe invited some of the parties to join a delegation to Washington to urge the United States to play a more visible role in the conflict resolution and also to hold discussions with the NPFL. The parties later produced a formula for ending the conflict that heavily favored Doe (in spite of the fact that opposition leaders such as Ellen

Johnson Sirleaf were certain of a Taylor victory). The United States considered the formula for a brief period and pressured Doe to consider making the modest concessions it required of him.[2] The formula was rejected by Taylor, however, which forced the United States to abandon it. The opposition influence waned thereafter, and as the conflict progressed many of their leaders left Liberia for exile.

The major regional actor in the mediation was ECOWAS, which purported to represent the position of all of its sixteen members. However, the ECOWAS mediation effort was not a homogenous continuum but, rather, consisted of a series of initiatives and actions articulated by influential members of the organization. For most of the time, the initiative came from Nigeria (the dominant party in ECOWAS) with support from mostly anglophone West African states. However, this Nigerian-led momentum was challenged and supplanted when the Ivory Coast, with the support of several francophone West African states, took control of the mediation. Between these two forces in ECOWAS, Senegal and several other, more independent-minded members (notably Ghana, Burkina Faso, and Togo) occasionally attempted to put their own imprints on the mediation in spite of their general association with either the Ivorian or Nigerian camps. However, these actors lacked the wherewithal to sustain any independent actions and so generally fell back into endorsements of the Nigerian or Ivorian positions.

Continental actors such as the OAU, other African states (Tanzania and Uganda), and the AACC played an important supplementary role in the mediation. These actors were crucial in legitimizing the ECOWAS effort when its credibility began to slip in the aftermath of Doe's capture in the ECOMOG compound and subsequent murder. The OAU in particular also served as a guarantor of several of the agreements and helped to assuage Taylor's fear of a Nigerian conspiracy to deny him victory at all cost.

International actors such as the United States, the United Nations, and the Carter Center were also very visible in the mediation. Contrary to popular belief that the United States showed no interest in the conflict, it played a crucial (if limited) role in the initiation of the process that eventually brought the parties in the Liberian conflict to the negotiating table.[3] As the "unofficial colonial master of Liberia,"[4] the United States stood out as the mediator most preferred by both Taylor and Doe. Even though it did not always play the role anticipated, the United States nevertheless remained a major player throughout the mediation. The United Nations, for its part, helped to establish ECOWAS as the sole mediator in Liberia by endorsing the mission. It also helped ECOWAS to enforce agreements through the imposition of sanctions on recalcitrant parties and gave credence to the process through its role as independent observer.[5] This was particularly helpful in moments when ECOWAS's military attacks on Taylor cast a shadow of doubt over its ability to be a neutral mediator.

The support role of the Carter Center also contributed to this credibility-repair mission.[6] Compared with most of the other third parties, the Carter Center was less visible in the mediation. However, this enabled it to focus its attention on the resolution of deadlocks created by side issues relating to Taylor's distrust of the Nigerians. The Center also helped to implement the electoral components of the final agreement reached at Abuja II in 1996.

The Nature of the Conflict

Access to the Liberian mediation was affected by the way the conflict was defined. There were two views of the conflict: internal rebellion or regional problem. These definitions were conveniently adjusted to reflect changes in a party's motives and interests in the conflict. They influenced third-party access to the conflict by affecting the legal basis for external intervention or nonintervention.

Defining the conflict as an internal problem was favored by both contenders, incumbent Samuel Doe and rebel leader Charles Taylor, as well as by three of the third parties involved in mediation: the United States, the IFMC, and the Ivory Coast. Though each of these parties had specific reasons for this classification, there was a common tendency to see the label of internal conflict as one that established an important criterion for choosing eligible mediators. Voluntary external "interventions" were unacceptable under this definition and, hence, it was greatly favored by Taylor, who was anticipating a military victory as early as August 1990. The major Taylor-backer, the Ivory Coast, as a nonmediator also favored this definition to block the entry of its regional rival (and Doe-backer), Nigeria. The United States, on the other hand, favored this definition of the conflict because of its reluctance to commit any major resources in the resolution process. Washington projected this view even after the United States agreed to play a major but low-key role in the negotiation. This view was insurance against entrapment and guaranteed the United States a smooth exit from the process when the Bush administration decided to limit U.S. commitment to the evacuation of foreign nationals. Unlike Taylor (who was anticipating a military victory and so opposed any external intervention), Doe (the weaker party) hoped to benefit from intervention by sympathetic third parties such as Nigeria. He was nevertheless careful not to define the conflict as a regional problem and thereby grant automatic access to hostile third parties, such as the Ivory Coast and Burkina Faso. Doe therefore stuck to the internal conflict label, which closed off all uninvited third-party access and also minimized the threat of peace enforcement actions by the United Nations. This definition also promised him unilateral control as the "legitimate" ruler of Liberia (within the prevailing international legal framework) over the mediator-invitation process. Later, Doe would utilize this unilateral power of invitation to call for the mediation of ECOWAS and Nigeria, the United States, the United Nations, and the OAU. The net effect of this definition was therefore exclusionary and limited mediation access to weak local actors such as the IFMC and opposition parties in the first phase of the mediation.

Definition of the conflict as a regional problem was mainly associated with the ECOWAS mediators who began their demarche in October 1990 at Banjul, Gambia. ECOWAS member states, particularly the pro-Nigerian faction, clearly considered the Liberian conflict as having the potential to escalate into a regional security crisis. With Liberian refugees flocking to their territories and their citizens coming under attack by rebel as well as government troops in Liberia, states such as Ghana, Guinea, Sierra Leone, and Nigeria were united in their conviction of a need for a regional response to the crisis. With the exception of the Nigerians, who appeared to harbor a second agenda in their determination to save Doe, the other states, especially during phases two, three, and four, seemed to be genuinely concerned about averting a humanitarian crisis in a neighboring state. They saw their mission as one of necessity, mandated by the waning of the international interest in Africa's crises in the aftermath of the Cold War and big-power disengagement. For these states, therefore, pooling resources in response to a regional crisis that had been largely ignored by the world community was not only the right thing but also the only available option. By defining the conflict as a regional problem, the states that felt inclined to "help" Liberia were granting themselves access to the conflict. It was therefore this view of the conflict as a regional problem that enabled ECOWAS to produce the consensus among member states that made the Nigeria-led mission a success, even though for the purposes of legality, the organization based its decision to intervene partly on the invitation by Doe.

ACCESS AND INVITATION

Access to the mediation was also determined by invitation. Although definition of the conflict was an important route to instituting and blocking access by establishing jurisdictional boundaries, invitation became the actual means of entry for virtually all of the third parties. Only one third party (the IFMC) entered the mediation without an invitation. The importance of invitation is also evident in the fact that even stronger third parties such as ECOWAS-Nigeria, whose definition of the conflict as a regional problem forecast the possibility of an enforcement action requiring the approval of neither Doe nor Taylor, nevertheless proffered an invitation from Doe as proof of legality. Invitation therefore not only determined the practical means of entry, but also justified its legality and hence influenced the success of the mediation. Invitation came mainly by three routes: by the conflicting parties, by other third parties, and by consensus. Each had different situational dynamics and, hence, specific implications for the invitee's mediation effort.

Invitation by the conflicting parties was by far the most common means of gaining access to the mediation. Third parties that were offered access through this means included the United States, ECOWAS, the OAU, and the United Nations. The main motives underlying a conflicting party's decision to invite mediation were the need for power augmentation and a strategic play for time. Doe, who was by far the weaker party, saw invitation as a means to counter the power asymmetry in the conflict. His decision to invite U.S. and ECOWAS intervention was therefore based on the conviction that such intervention could halt Taylor's advance. Taylor, on the other hand, was close to winning a unilateral victory by August 1990, and thus he had no interest in inviting any external mediation. He nevertheless recognized the importance of maintaining good relations with the United States, a major player in Liberian politics, and so began sending signals to Washington about his readiness to accept American mediation. Taylor's invitation of U.S. mediation, therefore, had more to do with the desire for the legitimacy that cooperation with Washington bestows than with concerns about the outcome of the military contest. Taylor was also motivated by the need to minimize the damage to his reputation done by his rumored association with Gaddafi's Libya, a pariah state in the eyes of the United States as well as of several African states. As far as ECOWAS was concerned, Taylor regarded its intervention as a deliberate attempt by Nigeria to prop up Doe and thus opposed it. Not even the murder of Doe could assuage Taylor's distrust of Nigerian motives—hence his uncooperative stance vis-à-vis the entire ECOWAS mediation effort.

Invitation by other third parties provided access to another set of mediators. Notable among these were the AACC and the Carter Center. Each of these mediators was invited in order to enhance the negotiating power of the particular third party that invited it or to help break a deadlock in the negotiating process. The AACC, for instance, was invited by the IFMC (with assistance from the Carter Center) as part of the former's negotiating-power enhancement effort. The AACC's intervention was brief and centered around chairman Desmond Tutu's July 4–6, 1994, visit to Liberia. The visit produced few dividends for the IFMC, despite the fact that Bishop Tutu managed to meet with numerous key personalities such as David D. Kpomakpor, chairman of the Council of State of the Liberian National Transitional Government; Hezekiah Bowen of the Armed Forces of Liberia; George Boley of the LPC; François Massaquoi of the LDF; and Roosevelt Johnson of the ULIMO. He also managed to meet with a wide array of diplomats, religious leaders, and NGO workers concerned about the conflict. The highlight of the AACC intervention, however, centered on Tutu's visit to Taylor's NPFL stronghold of Gbarnga in the company of Kpomakpor. Tutu secured a commitment from Taylor for an immediate cease-fire, a person-to-person meeting with Kpomakpor as soon as possible to discuss urgent matters of state, and a "summit" meeting in the near future with all factional leaders.[7] In spite of these assurances, nothing came out of the Tutu mission and the IFMC mediation eventually folded up.

ECOWAS leaders who were troubled by the credibility deficit plaguing the Nigerian-led mediation, on the other hand, invited the Carter Center, which enters mediation only on invitation of the parties. Following cooperation between ECOWAS and the Center's International Negotiation Network beginning in Banjul, in October 1990, former President Jimmy Carter visited Monrovia in September 1992. He held talks with interim leader Amos Sawyer and traveled to the NPFL headquarters in Gbarnga to meet with Taylor. President Carter persuaded Taylor to free about 500 ECOMOG soldiers he was holding hostage and urged the rebel leader to disarm his army and also to respect the ECOWAS peace plan as outlined in the Yamoussoukro Accord that Carter Center representatives had facilitated. Even though Taylor ignored this last plea, the Carter trip won his confidence to the point that he requested the presence of the center at the Geneva Talks of July 1993, held as part of the Yamoussoukro Process.[8] The Carter Center was again invited by ECOWAS and the OAU to participate in election-monitoring activities that eventually brought the conflict to an end. There was the perception among the other parties in the mediation that Carter enjoyed the support of the U.S. government, and, because of that, Taylor (who had been denied official U.S. endorsement) considered cooperation with the Carter Center paramount to his designs for the establishment of good relations with the United States.

The United States also invited the Ivory Coast and Senegal during the fourth phase of the mediation, when it became necessary to diversify the composition of the ECOWAS team in order to dilute Nigerian influence. As members of ECOWAS, both the Ivory Coast and Senegal could have gained access to the mediation by association; yet they chose to stay out for specific reasons. For President Félix Houphouet-Boigny (who still bore Doe a grudge for the 1980 murder of his son-in-law, A. B. Tolbert), the decision not to join the ECOWAS mediation was a product of his suspicion that the mission was simply a front for Nigerian attempts to save the Doe presidency. Houphouet-Boigny therefore rejected an invitation by the Banjul sum-mit to join the ECOWAS Standing Mediation Committee[9] and failed to receive Nigerian president Ibrahim Babangida when he visited Abidjan for talks on Liberia in May 1990.[10] During the same period, the Ivorians also opposed a discussion of the conflict at the UN Security Council, stressing their view that it was an internal problem that should be left in the hands of Liberians. Ivorian opposition intensified when ECOWAS went ahead with the deployment of ECOMOG in August 1990. Foreign Minister Amara Essy urged the United Nations to replace the ECOWAS force with a UN peacekeeping force.[11] The Ivorian attitude softened only when the United States approached Houphouet-Boigny about the possibility of joining the mediation in order to repair the credibility of ECOWAS. Vice President Dan Quayle's visit to Abidjan in September 1991 also assured the Ivorians of the United States' friendship and willingness to financially support an Ivorian entry.[12] Though this assurance was a major factor in the decision to enter, Houphouet-Boigny was also aware of the need to enter the mediation in order to limit Nigerian influence in determining outcomes. His move reflects a classical defensive calculation by a mediator to limit the opportunity for a rival power (in this case, Nigeria) to increase its influence in a region through mediation and instead use the mediations to increase its own influence.[13]

The U.S. invitation to Senegal took a slightly different form. The Senegalese had stayed out of the ECOWAS mediation because of factors such as commitment in the Gulf War, its own local war against separatists in Cassamance, and also French objections.[14] The United States regarded Senegal as a neutral party useful for rebuilding trust between ECOWAS and Taylor, who was using the perceived ECOWAS bias as an excuse for noncooperation.[15] The United States was also concerned about Ivorian commitment to the process even after Houphouet-Boigny's agreement to join the mediation. Robert Mortimer has argued that the decision to invite Senegal was therefore crucial for two reasons—namely, the diluting of Taylor's excuse for noncooperation and the pressure it placed on the Ivory Coast to commit to the mediation.[16] The process of invitation began with consultations held when Senegal's President Diouf visited Washington in September 1991. President Bush and Secretary of State James Baker urged him to commit troops to the ECOWAS mission and pledged financial support. There was also talk of a $42 million debt forgiveness package that was also part of the reward for Senegalese participation in Operation Desert Storm. Diouf responded to the invitation by attending Yamoussoukro III in September 1991, where Taylor agreed to disarm Senegalese troops if they joined ECOMOG (which they did, but he did not).

The United States made good on its promises by providing some $15 million worth of equipment to Senegal and announcing an additional $3.5 million in support of "the Yamoussoukro Process."[17] The Senegalese participation, however, did not last long or live up to its high expectations. They pulled out of the mediation at the first sign of trouble from Taylor, who murdered several of their troops in spite of the warm welcome he accorded them in principle.

A third category of mediators was invited by all-party consensus reached during negotiation sessions. Such parties played a marginal role in the mediation and were brought in mainly to even out the negotiation field and provide insurance to Taylor after a deal had been struck. Third parties that gained access through such consensus included Ugandan and Tanzanian troops (who were brought in during Phase Five to further dilute the Nigerian/Ivorian domination of the process, although they were not mediators) and the UN Observer Mission in Liberia (UNOMIL), which was established to help create an atmosphere of transparency for the disarmament segment of the Cotonou Process. The Carter Center's election-monitoring entry also fell within this category. Even though all parties agreed on the need to bring in such "consensus invitees," the process of invitation often required the intervention of major players such as the United States, the United Nations, and OAU. The United States, for instance, had to bankroll the Tanzanian/Ugandan participation and did not bankroll potential Zimbabwean participation because their demands were exorbitant. This category of invitees was less visible but played a crucial stabilizing role in the final phases of the mediation.

Invitations could be deferred or declined. The Ivory Coast, for instance, turned down an invitation to mediate in Phase One, preferring instead to enter in Phase Four. The United States (which entered the mediation in Phase One and exited shortly thereafter) was the universally preferred mediator and so had access to the mediation throughout all five phases. It nevertheless elected to limit its involvement to what Reed Kramer has referred to as arms-length diplomacy and became at best an incoherent facilitator in phases of its choosing.[18] Two other third parties that had open access to the mediation but chose to stay in the background in most of the phases were the OAU and the United Nations. Two main factors accounted for the decision to defer or reject an invitation to enter: a third party's perceptions of the end game and of its mediation capacity.

Third parties' perception of how the conflict might end and how their own interests might be affected by the end game was a major determinant of the decision to accept or reject an invitation. The Ivory Coast, for instance, stayed out of the mediation in phase one because it expected the conflict to end in a unilateral victory for its protégé, Taylor. Houphouet-Boigny, therefore, did not want to complicate matters by joining a Nigerian-led mediation that was likely to alter the momentum in favor of his foe, Doe. This perception of the end game changed in the aftermath of Doe's death, which produced a proliferation of parties and a soft stalemate between ECOMOG and Taylor. As the stalemate began to shift in favor of ECOMOG, Houphouet-Boigny became pressured into getting involved in the negotiation in order to curtail Nigerian influence in shaping the outcome. There was also the desire to maintain good relations with the United States (which facilitated a face-saving entry through invitation in Phase Four). Because good relations with Washington translated into a valuable resource both in the negotiation and in Houphouet-Boigny's quest to counter Nigerian hegemony in West Africa, the Ivorians were eager to oblige the Americans. The United States, on the other hand, entered in Phase One (when Doe appeared to be willing to make the necessary concessions for a negotiated settlement) but pulled out when U.S. political leaders got cold feet about taking on a responsibility for an outcome that they did not feel to be in the United States' interest.

The second factor that influenced the decision to defer or reject an invitation to enter was the capacity of the concerned third party for mediation and its adequacy for the task at hand. This was the determining factor in the pattern of entry displayed by the OAU and the United Nations. As key international actors, both were offered access first through Doe's invitation and then by ECOWAS. They nevertheless lacked the wherewithal to play a leading role in the first three phases. The OAU in particular suffered from a lack of the basic institutional resources needed to intervene in the fluid circumstances of Phases One to Three. It has also been suggested that the members of the organization lacked the political will to intervene because of vivid memories of the OAU's perceived 1981 failure in Chad.[19] However, the organization's members appeared to be genuinely confused about what its role in Liberia should be. On the one hand, it faced a mission dilemma stemming from a general lack of focus (in the aftermath of the demise of its favorite cause, the anti-apartheid struggle), while, on the other hand, it perceived its own nonintervention norm as being put to the test in Liberia. In his endorsement of the mission, for instance, OAU secretary-general Salim Salim told *West Africa* that the intervention did not breach the norm because "there is a government in Liberia which simply cannot govern."[20] This statement contradicted (without intending to) the mandate for the ECOWAS intervention, which was very much based on the notion that an invitation had been offered by Samuel Doe, an incumbent leader of a sovereign state who alone had the right to invite intervention under OAU (and international) norms.[21] The OAU's lack of clarity and purpose in this matter made it difficult for it to become fully engaged in the mediation process at least until the later stages, when ECOWAS was able to pinpoint areas in which the organization could be of assistance.

The United Nations also appeared to be in a similar predicament as far as capacity was concerned. The organization, under Boutros-Ghali, was still struggling over its post–Cold War mandate when the Liberia crisis occurred. With its major sponsor, the United States, not really interested in a peace enforcement action and with the United States' own poor performance in Somalia as an example of what could go wrong in Liberia, the United Nations remained understandably hesitant in the first phases of the mediation. Added to this was pressure from contending parties (such as the Ivory Coast) who initially urged the organization not to endorse the Nigerian-led intervention. The UN Security Council therefore could not discuss the crisis until January 22, 1991, fourteen months after the NPFL invasion of Liberia. The United Nations' capacity was also limited by its financial burdens, particularly as the United States initially was unwilling to support international funding of any intervention because of its suspicion that Nigeria was using the Liberia mission as a new front and support network for its international drug trade. (The United States had "decertified" Nigeria for its alleged role in international narcotics trafficking.) Nevertheless, once the organization overcame its role-definition problem, it was able to play a more active part in the mediation that followed, which led to the establishment of UNOMIL.

DETERMINING RECEPTION

The reception accorded to a mediator by the conflicting parties was determined by factors such as the motives of the conflicting parties, perceptions of the resourcefulness of the mediator, the dynamics of the resolution exercise, and the mode of entry employed by the mediator. Typically, each disputant accorded a good reception to mediators whose entry it deemed beneficial to its cause and opposed those whose entry benefited the competition. Disputants' calculation of the potential benefits of a particular mediator's entry was shaped significantly by their own motives and strategies for maximizing their gains. Doe and Taylor therefore hailed the ECOWAS-Nigeria and Ivorian entries respectively. In a few instances the motives-benefits calculus also led the adversaries to react in identical fashion to a particular mediator's entry in spite of their diverse needs and motives. For instance, the United States received a great reception from both Doe and Taylor, who had very different understandings of the likely impact of the U.S. entry. Capacity relative to the mediation task was another reason that Taylor in particular welcomed the American entry. He saw the United States as the only mediator with sufficient leverage to force Doe's exit without significant concessions from the NPFL. Washington's overwhelming power and influence also made noncooperation potentially too costly for Taylor. Doe, on the other hand, saw in a Nigerian-led ECOWAS the requisite military resource for altering the power asymmetry between Taylor and himself. He therefore welcomed the entry of ECOMOG, even though he was unsure of who (either Ghana or Nigeria) held real control over ECOMOG's commander, Ghanaian General Arnold Quainoo.

The dynamics of the conflict and its resolution provided another key element in determining reception. For instance, third parties such as the Ivory Coast and Senegal, which entered at a period of stalemate (resulting from the credibility problem facing ECOWAS), were hailed by the United States and also by Taylor because they were perceived as potential agents of positive change. Another major factor in determining reception was the mode of entry employed by a third party. Mediators that entered upon invitation by both parties (such as the United States) enjoyed a better reception than did parties that entered without the blessing of one of the factions (such as ECOWAS-Nigeria). For those mediators who were invited by other third parties, reception was determined by the adversaries' perception of the invited third party's own capacity to deliver preferred outcomes, perceptions of the motives and power of the inviting party, and estimates of the cost of noncooperation to the disputants. Typically, the adversaries accorded a warm reception to mediators invited by other third parties if they perceived their entry as being beneficial to their cause. The inviting third party's own power and influence serve as a gauge to the cost of noncooperation for each of the conflicting parties. Good receptions were therefore accorded to less-endowed mediators if the inviting third party was sufficiently powerful as to make the cost of noncooperation prohibitive for the adversaries. This was seen in the case of the reception accorded to both Senegal and the Ivory Coast by Taylor and ECOMOG. Ironically, the conflicting parties also accorded good receptions to weak mediators invited by equally weak third parties, as was the case when the IFMC invited the AACC. Both of these third parties were considered too weak and, hence, irrelevant to the structure of the conflict. The warm reception from Taylor in particular was more out of respect for Bishop Tutu (leader of the AACC team) than any strategic calculation involving anticipated benefits from entry.

Reception was not a fixed attribute and often varied with the conflict dynamics. In most cases, there was no fixed correlation between the type of reception initially accorded to a third party by conflicting parties and subsequent treatment of that third party. For instance, Doe welcomed the United States and the ECOWAS-Nigeria entries but nevertheless expelled the U.S. military attaché[22] in Liberia and also launched an attack on the Nigerian embassy in July 1990.[23] Similarly, Taylor attacked Senegalese troops despite the good reception he gave to them when they were brought in to dilute Nigerian influence in ECOMOG. In much the same way, bad reception did not always cause a third party to exit the mediation. Taylor's and Ivorian opposition to the ECOWAS-Nigeria entry, for instance, did not result in a Nigerian exit. However, that bad reception created a credibility problem that lasted beyond the phase of entry and provided the excuse for the entry of other third parties.

DECIDING TO STAY OR EXIT

Parties faced three options once they entered the mediation: stay active until the end, hang around even though marginalized, or exit the process. As pointed out earlier, some of the principal third parties did not stay for the full course of the mediation. The United States, for instance, exited the process after Phase One; the IFMC and the AACC left in Phase Two after having been rapidly marginalized; and the Carter Center, the Ivorians, and the Senegalese made their exit after Phase Four, the Carter Center having been marginalized off and on in the process and exiting for a year in Phase Five when its local headquarters was looted. The ECOWAS framework (the common platform for the negotiation), however, remained intact and was present throughout the last three phases of the mediation, although the actors at its helm changed. Nigeria (which had control of the ECOWAS machinery most of the time) "exited" temporarily in favor of the Ivory Coast in Phase Four and in favor of Ghana in the early part of Phase Five, only to return at the end.

The decision to exit the mediation, either temporarily or permanently, was based largely on three factors: performance in the mediation, capacity problems, and changes in the perception of the value of the mediation vis-à-vis the third party's interests. Third parties that performed poorly in the mediation sometimes chose to exit because they became redundant when other parties took over their functions in the mediation, or they remain, marginalized but ready to return to the job if needed. For instance, the IFMC had no option other than to exit when its mediation efforts failed to yield any tangible results. The Ivorians and Senegalese had their chance but produced no lasting results, for lack of ability to pursue and implement the decision taken at Yamoussoukro and Coutonou in the first case and for loss of political will in the second.[24] Changes in the perception of the value of the mediation can also be a basis for the decision to withdraw. This was the case in the Senegalese exit after the NPFL's attacks on its troops raised the cost of the mediation beyond what Dakar considered reasonable.

Beyond Exit

When parties exit mediation, they often do so permanently or temporarily. In Liberia, parties that chose to exit permanently included the IFMC, the AACC, the opposition parties, and Senegal. Those who exited the process in one phase only to reappear in another form within a different phase include the United States, the Ivory Coast, Nigeria, and the Carter Center. Several factors shaped return after exit or marginalization, including sunk costs, capacity, and initial motivation of the third party.

The extent of a third party's involvement in the mediation often determined whether it could exit permanently or not. Parties such as the United States and Nigeria that invested substantial resources and diplomatic effort in the mediation found it more difficult to exit completely; they were always pulled back by the conflict and the parties. In another light, high sunk costs also meant that these third parties' names had also become associated with the mediation and thus any permanent withdrawal could also be interpreted as acceptance of failure. Such parties therefore exited only tactically to emphasize the extent to which the success of the process depended on them or to give other parties an opportunity to fail as alternative leaders of the process.

Another factor that determined post-exit behavior for most third parties was their capacity for mediation. More endowed parties (such as the United Sates, Nigeria, and the Ivory Coast) found it easier to rebound from losses made in previous mediations than those parties that had either few or no resources of their own. The IFMC, the AACC, and opposition parties, for instance, could not recover from the impact of failure, partly because of funding problems. Capacity also often translates into desirability, another reason that those parties with ample resources found it impossible to disengage completely. Because of its enormous capacity, the United States, for instance, remained in high demand even after it made fully clear its intention not to commit. Likewise, parties with few resources had no attraction power and so were usually not reinvited once they exited.

A third factor in determining post-exit behavior is the issue of a third party's initial motivation for entry. Parties that entered the mediation in pursuit of specific interest goals—national or professional—found it more difficult to exit permanently if those goals remained unattained. Nigeria for instance entered partly to defend a friendly regime and partly to ensure that a less friendly one did not replace it. This goal was tied to that country's quest for hegemony in the subregion, and so any failure (which a permanent exit would indicate) was considered to be out of the question. The Ivory Coast, on the other hand, defined its interests in Liberia as being closely linked to ensuring that the friendlier Taylor (whom it backed openly) replaced the unfriendly Doe regime. For the Ivory Coast, this definition also meant that as long as its rival Nigeria was still active in Liberia, Abidjan could not exit permanently. The Carter Center had a professional interest in making peace and observing elections, and it hung around in hopes of being helpful at some point—as it eventually was when Taylor was elected and then again after Taylor left. For smaller parties with no specific interests or goals in the mediation, permanent exit posed no such problems. Senegal for instance had gotten involved mostly in order to please the United States. It invested very few resources of its own in the mediation and did not really expect much from it either. At the same time, the problem in Cassamance was threatening to escalate, and its major ally, France, was quietly voicing its displeasure at Senegalese involvement in America's Liberia. Senegal therefore did not hesitate to exit for good when its troops came under attack in Liberia.

Conclusion

The Liberian mediation offers several lessons that enhance our understanding of the nature of entry decision making in internal conflict mediation.

1. The first lesson relates to the multiple ways in which various parties employ their definition of the crisis and how it affects their decision to enter. For the conflicting parties, the definition was framed to invite or reject third-party mediation; to include or exclude particular third parties once the decision is made to accept mediation; and to provide justification for specific demands, positions, or strategies adopted in contravention of previous agreements. The third parties, on the other hand, fashioned their definition of the conflict to justify their own entry into the mediation; to deny rival parties access to the mediation; and to facilitate their exit from the mediation. The import of this lesson is that when parties define a conflict, they concern themselves not only with perceptions of the status quo but also with the way their definition might help them alter that status quo in their favor by determining who gains entry.

2. Another important lesson from Liberia is the fact that invitation to mediate in a conflict does not come only from the conflicting parties but also from other third parties involved in the conflict's management. This fact suggests that in much the same way as conflicting parties may invite mediation as a power-augmentation strategy, some third parties (both weak and strong) may also view the entry of other (friendly) third parties as a source of power or means to minimize loss through burden sharing.

3. An additional lesson relates to the question of exit from mediation, emphasizing the link between a party's interest and capacity, on the one hand, and the decision to enter and exit mediation, on the other. Parties with the specific goals and the requisite resources for pursuing them seldom exit mediation permanently, even though marginalized. Such parties will often re-enter either independently or in association with other third parties to pursue those specific goals or at least to prevent an adverse change in the status quo.

The Liberian mediation, above all, emphasizes the fact that not all parties willing to enter mediation are able to gain access and that not all those who gain access can make a positive contribution to the mediation process. The fact that the Liberian mediation achieved the good results it did with Nigeria (the most endowed of the African parties in the mediation) back at the helm of ECOWAS is also evidence of the role that resources and capacity play in effective utilization of entry.

6

SUDAN,
1983–1993

Much time has passed since the Inter-Governmental Authority on Development (IGAD) entered the Sudanese conflict as a mediator. Its intermediary role was formally endorsed by the principal parties to the conflict in the second quarter of 1993. Although IGAD relentlessly tried its level best to engage the belligerent parties, nothing substantive was achieved for the rest of the decade, with results coming only at the beginning of 2005. Throughout a lengthy and frustrating process, IGAD did not exit from its intermediary role and remained the only internationally recognized and acknowledged mediator of the peace process.

This chapter attempts to trace the background through which IGAD entered the Sudanese conflict. Its time frame is from May 1983, when the second phase of the civil war began, to April 1993, when IGAD formally entered the conflict.[1] The following issues will be addressed: the nature of the conflict; the parties to the conflict and their perceptions of the nature of the conflict; the various prospective mediators who tried to enter the conflict and their perceptions of the nature of the conflict, as well as their motives of entry; and the evolution of the conflict from 1983 and its impact on the parties' and the aspiring mediators' perceptions, positions, and policy options.

An evaluation will also be made on why the various potential intermediaries exited and IGAD remained to facilitate a mediated political settlement. The chapter will conclude by drawing out theoretical and policy lessons from the mediation experiences of the Sudanese conflict.

THE NATURE OF THE CONFLICT

The root cause of the Sudanese conflict that has triggered the current civil war is not significantly different from that which had sparked the first civil war in 1955. A national identity crisis was and still is its major cause.[2] The crisis arises out of the controversy over which should be the basis of the social contract, an individual or an ethnic group, in constituting the Sudanese nation-state. Under colonial rule, the state was constituted to protect racial, cultural, and religious differences. Although the unity of Sudan was preserved as one state, geopolitically and administratively, the predominantly Arab-Islamic north and the African-Christian/animist south were governed as two distinct entities.[3]

The conflict erupted on the eve of independence, when the British and the northern Sudanese nationalist movement tried to integrate the two parts into one independent Sudan. The south initially rejected this arrangement. Given its separate national and colonial upbringing and the disadvantageous role the south played in the colonial economy, the people of the south feared that they would be treated the same way as they had before colonial rule: as a backwater for socio-economic exploitation for the benefit of the north. They assented to integration within independent Sudan only when it was agreed through the Juba Conference of 1947, the Anglo-Egyptian agreement of 1953, and the independence resolution of 1955 that the Sudan would adopt a federal system of government guaranteeing the southern Sudanese political autonomy.[4]

Yet at independence, this promise was not kept and became the major contributing factor to the first phase of the civil war, from 1955 to 1971. The war pitted the Southern Sudan Liberation Movement (SSLM) and its military wing, the Anyanya, under the leadership of Joseph Lagu, against the first four governments of independent Sudan. The nature of the conflict during the first civil war was exclusively regionalist in that the south specifically demanded a federal united Sudan that could guarantee southern political autonomy.[5] The war came to an end when the south was granted regional autonomy by the Addis Ababa Agreement of 1972, negotiated by the government of Colonel Ja'far Muhammad Numayri and the SSLM.[6] The granting of regional autonomy brought relative peace to the country for the first time since independence. However, peace could not be enjoyed for a long time because the Addis Ababa agreement was abrogated in 1983 by the very government that had negotiated it. The country was plunged, once again, into a north-south civil war.

An immediate question is why the government that had negotiated an agreement that brought relative peace to the country dared to abrogate it and jeopardize the peace dividends that accrued from it. The explanation is that the agreement was negotiated to win Numayri allies and support, but when these did not ensure full security for the regime, it was abrogated to win the support of more threatening forces in the north. Numayri's efforts toward total political control immediately after the 1969 coup had antagonized the northern political establishment. His repression of political opposition from the north was crowned by the July 1971 coup attempt by the Sudan Communist Party. The south was thus intended to serve as his new political base and as a countervailing force against the northern political establishment. But the agreement alienated growing Islamist and Arabist forces in the north, so Numayri cancelled it to win their support. Numayri saw his political survival at this time to depend more on his realignment with the northern political forces than on those in the south.

As for the abrogation itself, it was not difficult to do, regardless of its peace dividends, because the northern political elite had never accepted it in the first place, and the southern political elite fell to their own tribal rivalries when the unifying northern enemy was removed and became allies in undoing the federation. The northern politicians had actually considered the agreement as a sell out. Its abrogation was therefore mutually beneficial to Numayri and to those who had opposed it. The deteriorating economic situation was also an added factor. The economic crisis was aggravated by the impact of the war. The termination of relations with the Soviet Union, following the July 1971 coup attempt, robbed the regime of one of its major sources of arms supplies; this had a negative effect at the war front.

The current civil war was launched against the background of the 1983 abrogation. Other issues included the Jonglei Canal, which drew protests against its destruction of the southern habitat; the 1980 provincial border dispute, in which attempts were made to carve off oil-rich areas of Bentiu and the fertile mechanized agricultural lands of the northern Upper Nile in order to annex them to the northern provinces of Kordofan and White Nile, respectively; and the siting of an oil refinery in the north rather than in the south, where oil was found.[7] Numayri's political maneuvers to undermine the regional autonomy resulted in political uprisings in the south, particu-

larly within the army. The former Anyanya guerrillas, who were integrated
in the army, started to remobilize and, by May 1983, two southern bat-
talions in the army mutinied. Anyanya 2 was launched and the civil war
began. These developments led to the formation of the Sudan People's
Liberation Movement and its military wing, the Sudan People's Liberation
Army (SPLM/SPLA), in July 1983, under the leadership of Colonel John
Garang. The government completed its alliance with Arab-Islamic forces by
introducing Islamic shari'a laws in September.

The crisis of national identity remains the central issue of the conflict. Race
and religion continue to be the basis of organizing the Sudanese nation-state,
generating exploitative and discriminatory policies that aggravate the crisis
of national identity. Identity is used here not as a mere simple category of
an individual's social recognition but, according to Francis Deng, as "a starting point to understanding who gets what, occupies what position, or plays
what role in the political, economic, social, and cultural life of the country."[8]
Central to the conflict therefore are the social relations emanating from the
exploitative and discriminatory policies. Deng puts it in a clear perspective:

> In the Sudan, the mere fact that different identities, however fictitious, have
> evolved . . . would not in itself be a source of conflict if the resulting diversity
> did not affect the position of the parties in a significant way that is unaccept-
> able. The question that needs to be posed, therefore, is how identification
> symbols influence the participation of the various groups in the shaping and
> sharing of power, wealth, and other national resources. The critical issue
> here is whether differences in racial, ethnic, cultural linguistic, and religious
> identities tend to foster stratification, discrimination, or disparities in the
> way that is not tolerable to the disadvantaged groups.[9]

However, domination and discrimination originate not from the rank
and file in a society but from its apex. They are a product of state policies and are then mirrored in the population. To the extent that the state
in Sudan pursues discriminatory policies, based on identity differentials,
political leadership then becomes the real source of the conflict. This kind of
sanctioned discrimination, in the final analysis, is the problem of the failure
of governance. Governing is conflict management; peace and tranquility
prevail in an environment where a country's political leadership pursues
policies that create harmony rather than discord among its social groups.[10]
When the state fails to play a mediating and moderating role regarding the
demands of various social groups, political and social strife is inevitable.

The use of an ethnic group, rather than an individual, as the basis for constituting the nation-state has failed miserably in post-independence Sudan. Although colonialism and northern nationalism are to blame for the circumstances that led to the first civil war, the post-independence leadership is responsible for the second, primarily because it has never addressed the contentious issue in an objective and satisfactory manner.

When the civil war began again in 1983, it involved three principal parties fighting over two major issues. On one side, the government and the SPLM/SPLA were fighting a centralist conflict over the control of the state. On the other side, the Anyanya 2 was fighting a regionalist conflict for the south's autonomy. The three parties–two issues situation continued up to 1988, when the Anyanya forces were finally united with those of the SPLM/SPLA.[11] However, the transformation of the conflict's character from dyadic to triadic did not change the nature of the contentious issues. The only thing that did change was that the contest over the state and regional autonomy was merged within the SPLM/SPLA. The two parties–two issues character gave the conflict both a central and a regional dimension. Viewed from a national perspective, the conflict is not different from the Rwandan, Burundian, Liberian, and Congolese conflicts. It is an *elitist* and *centralist* internal conflict whose major contention is state control.

Viewed from a regional perspective (north-south), the conflict becomes quite different from those of Rwanda, Burundi, Liberia, and Congo-Brazzaville because it is more than just a centralist conflict that aims exclusively at state control. Although state control still forms part of the contest, it is no longer considered as an end in itself. It becomes a pivotal means through which a final decision on the political relationship between the north and the south can be determined. At this level, the nature of the conflict changes from a *centralist* to a *regionalist* conflict, whereby the political status between the north and the south becomes the central issue. It is the dual nature of the Sudanese conflict (centralist and regionalist) that not only distinguishes it from the Rwandan, Burundian, Liberian, and Congolese conflicts but also generates a dual approach (unity and autonomy/secession) in the efforts toward its final resolution. At the same time, non-Arab areas in the north also began to identify with the SPLA/SPLM vision for the nation, further complicating the regionalist/centralist nature of the conflict.

Parties' Perceptions and Policy Options

SPLM/SPLA

The SPLM/SPLA's perception of the conflict has been metamorphic. Its transformation is a function of an internal dynamism of the movement itself and that of the conflict, as well as changes at the regional and international levels. Three distinct periods of the transformation during the entry period can be identified. The first is from 1983 to 1985; the second is from 1986 to 1990; and the third is from 1991 to 1993 (and to the present). During the first few years after its founding in 1983, the SPLM/SPLA perceived the conflict in a class perspective. The crisis of national identity was construed as a cover-up for the domination and exploitation that was responsible for the country's lack of development. From this perception, the conflict became an issue between the privileged class and the underprivileged majority of all the races and all the regions. The SPLM/SPLA was created not for the specific objective of separating the south from the north, regardless of the movement's southern origins. It was established essentially in order to wage a revolutionary armed struggle with the goal of snatching state power from the privileged class on behalf of the underprivileged majority and establish a "new secular, united, and socialist Sudan."[12] The socialist state was envisaged as the lasting solution in dealing with the issues of democracy, equality, justice, and development.

By being set in centralist terms, this perception was completely different from that of the Anyanya 2 and the other southerners whose regionalist perception confined them specifically to the "southern problem." In waging an armed struggle with the sole objective of replacing the state, the perception set the SPLM/SPLA on a collision course with the military regime. The confrontational approach drew a clear line of battle and set the conflict in a zero-sum equation, ruling out the possibility of a compromise settlement.

However realistic the perception was regarding the distributive aspect of the conflict, it was not consonant with the perception of the majority in the south. The facts on the ground, and even the timing of the founding of the SPLM/SPLA itself and the launching of the civil war, can attest to the immediate issues related to the south that had triggered the civil war. However numerous and divergent the southerners' perceptions were, they did not define the conflict in ideological or centralist terms. Their understanding of the conflict was exclusively regional in nature, as Peter Nyaba certifies: "[W]hen the first bullets were fired in Bor in May 1983, South Sudan was already ripe for another military confrontation with the North, despite the fact that the political leaders had not prepared the people for it. The insurrection that ensued throughout the South was spontaneous, and every tribal grouping in the South had its own agenda for joining the insurrection."[13]

The existence of both central and regional perceptions of the conflict had a serious impact on both conflict and mediation efforts. An effective execution of the war demanded a common understanding of the problem, a common prescription for its solution, and a common approach to achieve it. Given that the southerners were not in agreement on the definition of the conflict and its final outcome, their agreement on the approach of its resolution (through a civil war) was not helpful. The dual approach had a negative impact on mediation efforts because, while those who were aspiring to regional autonomy were predisposed to a compromise political settlement, those who were fighting for control of the state were, according to the way they had defined the conflict, inhospitable to it.

As the conflict evolved and many southerners rallied behind the SPLM/SPLA as the principal party to the conflict, the two perceptions were subsumed within the movement. The SPLM/SPLA's refusal of the invitation to participate in the 1985 transitional government, following the popular uprising that led to Numayri's overthrow, reflected the dominance of the centralist class perception.[14]

However, its participation in the March 1986 Koka Dam Conference with the northern political forces, which resulted in the Koka Dam Declaration, and its direct talks with the Democratic Unionist Party (DUP) in 1988,[15] indicated the watering-down of the centralist class perception. It demonstrated that the SPLM/SPLA was moving from a zero-sum to a positive-sum posture, as the regionalist perception was gaining an upper hand within the movement.

From 1986 to 1990, as the SPLM/SPLA was trying to win over the Anyanya 2 and the other southerners who were fighting for regional autonomy, the class perspective and socialism as the goal were dropped. But they were replaced by another centralist goal, the territorial model, in Anthony Smith's terms, whereby the creation of a secular and democratic state became the goal of the fight. Consequently, as it was entering the 1990s, the SPLM/SPLA put more emphasis on democracy than on socialism and

was actually talking of cutting a deal with the government. In his response
to President Umar al-Bashir's initial peace overtures in July 1989, Garang
put forward the following conditions:

> [I]n any meetings with government emissaries, SPLM negotiators would
> not only listen to the junta's peace plan but would also stress the need to
> restore democracy. They would demand that Bashir free all political prison-
> ers, lift the ban on political parties and unions, and form a nonsectarian
> national unity government comprising democratic parties and unions,
> nonsectarian mass organizations, the SPLA, and the army. The SPLA must
> be integrated into the armed forces on a fifty-fifty ratio.[16]

A number of factors contributed to this change of perception. The first
was the aspiration of the people of the south for regional autonomy, which
was gaining momentum. They considered the SPLM/SPLA as the regional
organization that embodied that aspiration regardless of what the leaders
said about the organization's ideology and objectives. By not acknowledging
this aspiration, the SPLM/SPLA leadership seemed to be out of touch with
their reality. Thus it should not be surprising for the SPLM/SPLA to adopt
a compromise option that could, ultimately, lead to the realization of the
southerners' aspiration.

Another factor was political change at the international and regional
levels. The end of the Cold War resulted in the end of the world socialist
system and the revival of the aspirations of self-determination, especially
among oppressed minorities. These developments presented a dilemma to
the SPLM/SPLA, which was now forced to balance between its own stated
objective of fighting for socialism in an environment in which the socialist
system was dying worldwide, and suppressing the regional aspirations for
self-determination in an environment bolstered for the realization of such an
aspiration. To escape the dilemma, the SPLM/SPLA changed its aim from
socialism to democracy.

The collapse of socialism and the revival of the aspirations for self-
determination had a regional impact that affected the SPLM/SPLA. The
fall of Mengistu's socialist regime in Ethiopia, which had been the staunch-
est supporter of SPLM/SPLA, had a demoralizing effect not only on the
movement's socialist aspirations but also on its survival as an organization.
On the other side, the revival of the aspirations for self-determination
and the fall of Mengistu's regime boosted Eritrea's chances for statehood.
Eritrea was the incarnation of self-determination aspirations in Africa. After
enduring a thirty-year war and total ostracization, its struggle was finally

vindicated. Eritrea's victory in 1991 and independence in 1993 was thus a positive demonstrative event to the south Sudanese who were aspiring to their own self-determination.

Eritrea's independence seemed to have a serious impact on the sacredness of the Organization of African Unity's principle of *uti possidetis juris* (although the exception was only apparent, as Eritrea had had its own separate colonial existence). Historical and political conditions in southern Sudan were somewhat different, in that it had a different type of status than the north but under the same colonizer and never as a separate colony, but the SPLM/SPLA nevertheless felt freed from the continent's ethical restrictions on pursuing self-determination objectives. Hence, from 1991 the movement underwent its third period of perceptual transformation. In this period, the conflict was perceived more in a regionalist perspective. Democracy was relegated to an instrumental level and self-determination was elevated to the primary objective of the struggle. This position was formalized at the SPLM/SPLA's high command meeting of September 1991.[17]

Apart from the impact of the international and regional changes, the SPLM/SPLA's move from a centralist to a regionalist perception could as well be explained by the movement's own internal dynamism. The self-determination option was given a boost by the 1991 split of the movement into two major factions: the SPLM/SPLA mainstream, under the continued leadership of Garang, and the Nasir group, SPLM/SPLA United, under three dissident commanders, Riek Machar, Lam Akol, and Gordon Koang Chol.[18] Although leadership issues and rivalry rather than policy issues were the main causes of the split, the splinter group's initial policy was clear: it wanted the secession of the south.[19] This major shift of perception and position was not fully articulated into a policy statement like the 1983 Manifesto. The shift has to be observed from the movement's behavior and practical responses to the evolution of the conflict, most notably by the movement's insistence that self-determination should be one of the principal agenda items in both the unsuccessful 1992–1993 Abuja Peace Process and the stalled IGAD peace initiative.

But the split, which was promoted by encouragement from Khartoum, did not last. After ten years, some of the leaders of the Southern Sudan Independence Movement, such as Machar, returned to the SPLM fold, while others, such as Akol, moved to Khartoum to militate for their cause from within. Along with the leaders' return came the corresponding shift in policy to a regionalist ethnic model, in response to grassroots pressure for secession. By the beginning of the 2000s, the SPLM/SPLA position was to offer Khartoum one last chance for meaningful autonomy for the south, but to demand a self-determination referendum in a few years to test whether these efforts were satisfactory.

The State

There have been four administrations since the eruption of the civil war in May 1983: the last two years of Numayri's government (May 1983–April 1985), the transitional military/civilian government of General Abd al-Rahman Suwar al-Dhahab (April 1985–April 1986), an elected government of Prime Minister Sadiq Al-Mahdi (May 1986–June 1989), and the military regime of General Umar al-Bashir thereafter.

All these administrations consecutively perceived the conflict in an ethnic model, whereby Arabism and Islam form the "ethnic core"[20] of the Sudanese national identity. Operating from the ethnic nationalism perspective, the Sudanese state, since independence, identified the nation as characteristically Arab and Muslim. Armed with an ethnic (Arab) strength of 40 percent of the population—out of more than fifty different ethnic groups—and a religious (Islam) strength of more than 50 percent of the population,[21] the state believes that language and religion must be the guiding principles in the organization of Sudanese political life, especially in determining the country's political and legal systems.

Though the country's ethnic and religious diversity is appreciated, the state strongly believes that the national identity of Sudan would be realized and sustained only if the other various nationalities and religious groups are assimilated within the Arab-Islamic culture. This belief is used to justify otherwise controversial statements such as "Sudan is an Arab country, and whoever doesn't feel Arab should quit"[22] and "The Muslims are the majority among the population of the Sudan . . . [and] therefore have a legitimate right, by virtue of their religious choice, of their democratic weight and of natural justice, to practice the values and rules of their religion to their full range—in personal, familial, social, or political affairs."[23]

Since independence, the state has lived up to the Arab-Islamic aspirations in both policy and action. Hence, the conflict is consistently perceived as a sinister move to break up the unity of the Arab nation of Sudan and a blasphemous affront to Islam, led from outside and imputed to Zionism: It is a war imposed by external forces that aspire to control Sudan and run it according to their regional and international interests.[24]

Otherwise, the external factor has changed its character according to political shifts at the domestic, regional, and international levels. In the late 1970s and early 1980s, when Islamic radicalism was rising domestically, the culprit was communism. At the international level, the target was the Soviet Union, following Numayri's breakup with the Kremlin after his own brief fling with socialism. At the regional and domestic levels it was Ethiopia and the SPLM/SPLA (to which Ethiopia gave support and sanctuary), that were perceived as the Kremlin's regional and domestic communist agents, respectively.[25]

From the late 1980s to early 1990s, as a result of domestic regime changes, the attainment of the zenith of Islamic fundamentalism, and the collapse of communism in both the Soviet Union and Ethiopia, imperialism became the culprit. The target became the United States and the Sudanese neighbors, particularly the new regimes in Ethiopia, Eritrea, and Uganda. The United States characterized Sudan as a terrorist state and accused it of training international terrorists. Ethiopia, Eritrea, and Uganda considered Sudan to be a pariah state because of its unacceptable discriminatory domestic policies that contributed to the continuation of the war affecting them directly. They also feared the impact of the Sudanese radicalized brand of Islam on their own Muslim populations.

Perceived as the incarnation of the external threat bent on destroying Sudan as a nation and Islam as its religion, the SPLM/SPLA was cast in the traditional "government-versus-rebels" image. Since the beginning of the current civil war, the state's major policy option was to use military power to crush the SPLM/SPLA. Political dialogue was entertained intermittently only when the conditions for the military option were not favorable. Considering the way the state defined the conflict, it appeared that, whether through the military approach or political dialogue, the state preferred a zero-sum outcome of the conflict—that is, a united Islamic Sudan.

MEDIATION: THE ENTRY INITIATIVES

About nine substantive entry initiatives were attempted between the time the second civil war started in May 1983 until 1993, especially after 1987 and within the last two of the four Sudanese governments that have been involved in the conflict. The parties' and the prospective mediators' initial perceptions of the nature of the conflict and its prescribed solutions were instrumental in discouraging the initial mediation attempts.

Within Africa the conflict was perceived in the traditional "government-versus-rebels" context. Although individually some African countries were sympathetic to and supportive of the SPLM/SPLA's cause, collectively they were constrained by the continental organization's (that is, the OAU's) principles of noninterference in internal affairs of the organization's sovereign members and the sanctity of international borders. Thus in the African context, both objectives of the southern Sudan's rebellion seemed to be the victims of timing. Neither the regionalist nor the centralist objective could be openly supported by African governments. Ethiopia's open support to the SPLM/SPLA was an aberration based on a different context and perspective. Any mediation attempt originating from an African country would have been interpreted as recognition of a "rebel" movement—hence, an unfriendly act against Sudan and a direct violation of the OAU's principles.

Thus covert support was the policy option left for those who were sympathetic to the SPLM/SPLA, with the exception of Ethiopia and, briefly, Libya. Ethiopia's open support was based on the hostile bilateral relations between Sudan and Ethiopia. The open support was in reciprocity to Numayri's support to the Eritrean secessionists and antiregime forces of Tigray and Oromo.[26] Libya's brief open support was based on containing pro-Western Egypt and Sudan, but it shifted from the SPLM/SPLA to the government after the fall of Numayri in April 1985.[27]

The African restrictions were also a factor in discouraging prospective mediators from outside the continent. For the Western countries, the problem was more than just falling in line with the African perception. The SPLM/SPLA's initial socialist objectives ran counter to some of the Western countries' policy positions in the Horn of Africa. A successful socialist revolution in the Sudan would have put the region into the strong grip of two socialist states: Sudan and Ethiopia. In the calculus of Cold War politics, this obviously would have been detrimental to Western countries' interests in the region and beyond.

The Western countries' interests therefore lay with the Sudanese state, regardless of its embarrassing policies. This explains, for example, the United States' continued military and financial assistance to Numayri's regime even when he abrogated the Addis Ababa Agreement and introduced Islamic shari'a laws. During the Reagan administration, Numayri's regime was the biggest recipient of the United States' economic and military assistance in sub-Saharan Africa.[28] Therefore, Western countries' response was in favor of managing rather than resolving the conflict. Their financial and logistical support was a boost to the Sudanese administration's military option, and the lack of matching assistance to the SPLM/SPLA enhanced the conflict's asymmetry in favor of the state. The socialist countries could not have been prospective mediators as they were perceived by the state to be the major source of the conflict. Thus from 1983 to 1986, the international and regional environment was not conducive for prospective mediators to initiate entry. Entry attempts would have been possible only if the Sudanese governments would have taken the initiative of extending an invitation for such a role. Given the governments' own perception of the conflict, such an initiative did not materialize.

Mediation attempts were also discouraged by the Sudanese government's own peace approach of direct interparty negotiations, as opposed to mediated negotiations. Although the conflict's initial environment was not conducive for external intervention, the Sudanese developed an immense potential for direct contacts. One of the early hallmarks of the direct approach was the March 1986 Koka Dam Declaration, which called for the abrogation of shari'a laws and the holding of a national constitutional conference.

Entry initiatives started in 1987 during Sadiq Al-Mahdi's administration as a result of changed domestic, regional, and international environments. Domestically, Sudan was catching up with African aspirations for democratic transition. Al-Mahdi's civilian administration was democratically elected in 1986. The numerous direct contacts among the SPLM/SPLA, the northern political parties, and the government were an indication that political dialogue was seriously being considered by the parties to the conflict as an important policy option. The direct meeting between Garang and Al-Mahdi in July 1986 in Addis Ababa[29] demonstrated that the principal parties were ready to discuss a compromise political solution. This was also the period that the SPLM/SPLA was moving from a zero-sum to a positive-sum posture that, in a way, diluted its revolutionary rhetoric.

The changed domestic environment was an incentive to the prospective mediators. Western countries were encouraged by the SPLM/SPLA's shift from a radical to a moderate position. Socialist objectives were no longer a threat to Western interests as the system's future and prospects seemed oblique. At the continental level, the principle of sovereignty was under scrutiny, especially when it involved violations of human rights. In specific terms, the failure to honor the Koka Dam Declaration was a clear indication that the direct negotiation approach needed to be supported by external intermediaries.

With the new favorable environment for mediation, one would have expected a stampede of prospective intervenors. One of the reasons this did not happen was that the Sudanese conflict was the oldest in the continent; as Africa's spinster, it could not attract many suitors. The new generation of conflicts was more attractive for prospective mediators interested in investing resources in the fresh conflicts rather than in the old, intractable ones. The nine prospective mediators that attempted entry were no stampede. Their number was a function of the conflict's complexity, intractability, longevity (in terms of the period the interventions were attempted, from 1987 to 1993), and complementarity among the interventions. Otherwise, the interventions were orderly and almost sequential. They came in three types: through intergovernmental organizations, by eminent personalities, and by states.

From 1987 to 1991, numerous entry initiatives were attempted through the OAU framework. These included the ones initiated by Presidents Daniel Arap Moi of Kenya and Yoweri Museveni of Uganda in 1987[30] and Mobutu Sese Seko of Zaire and Hosni Mubarak of Egypt in 1990.[31] The initiatives were motivated by the OAU's position as the regional organization responsible for dealing with the continent's political conflicts. The Sudanese membership in the organization provided the legitimacy for the OAU's involvement. The Sudanese government accepted the initiatives because it perceived them to be in its favor. Rather than considering them as an infringement on its sovereignty, the government perceived the OAU's intervention as an act that would strengthen its position and reaffirm its sovereignty. The SPLM/SPLA, for its part, accepted the OAU intervention primarily because it provided recognition of and legitimacy for the movement.

The initiatives were not successful because of the way the OAU perceived the conflict. Considering that the organization was still operating through the old paradigm of conflict management, it was obvious that its initiatives would be in favor of the government. Second, the moves were neither initiated by the parties nor fully endorsed by them. They originated from the procedural arrangements of the OAU's meetings. It is customary within the

OAU that during its annual summits, the organization's secretary-general apprises the heads of state of all the political problems prevalent in the continent, among other things, and the summits pass resolutions that commit the current chairman to follow up on the problems and report any developments at the following summits.

Many of the OAU-sponsored initiatives on Sudan, with the exception of the Abuja Process, were proposed in this context. Given the short tenure of the OAU's chairmanship, nothing substantive could be accomplished within this period, especially in dealing with a conflict of such complexity as the Sudanese one.[32] Apart from the OAU-sponsored initiatives, other significant ones were the Obasanjo-Deng initiative; the Carter initiative; the U.S. initiative of 1987–1988 under Herman Cohen; the Abuja initiative of 1991–1992; and the IGAD initiative.

The Obasanjo-Deng Initiative

The Obasanjo-Deng initiative grew out of a problem-solving workshop on the Sudan held in Washington, D.C., in early 1987. The workshop was organized by Francis Deng, a former Sudanese minister of state for foreign affairs, then a senior research associate at the Woodrow Wilson International Center for Scholars.[33] The workshop was attended by scholars, policymakers, and some individuals with experience in different kinds of conflicts, both Sudanese and non-Sudanese. Among eminent personalities in attendance were the former president of Nigeria, Olusegun Obasanjo, and the former U.S. ambassador to the United Nations and mayor of Atlanta, Andrew Young.

The initiative was motivated by the moral conviction that emerged from the spirit of the workshop that individuals could contribute toward peaceful resolution of conflicts. In his introductory remarks in the workshop's proceedings, Deng underscores this conviction: "[I]ndividual and collective efforts in the cause of peace, national unity, and the task of nation-building cannot be halted by lack of visible progress. The final goal can only be attained by the determined efforts of individuals propelled, supported, and reinforced by the national will to bring an end to this costly war."[34]

Apart from the moral conviction, Obasanjo and Deng were motivated by their own individual status. By being one of very few benevolent former heads of state in Africa, Obasanjo commanded international respect. He was also very much involved at that time in the efforts of creating an appropriate collective security mechanism for the continent through the African Leadership Forum.[35] Being a Sudanese national and someone who was involved in the country's politics, Deng was motivated by national patriotism and his vast knowledge and experience in the complexities of the conflict. His respectable academic and diplomatic credentials were additional advantages. Both of them were inspired by the spirit of the workshop, which indicated that points of convergence among the conflicting parties could be exploited for a compromise political settlement. Deng noted:

> Except for the small but vocal minority in the north that is prone to place religious beliefs above national unity, or those elements in the south that still quietly relish the dream of separatism, there now appears to be a national consensus on the quest for unity as an overriding objective. The next logical question should be: What divides and what can be done about it? If unity is a principle on which everyone agrees, it ought to be possible to agree on what can bring the country together and what threatens to tear it apart.[36]

From the above quotation and the final outcome of the workshop, it is clear that Obasanjo and Deng perceived the conflict in a centralist and pluralist model in which the Sudanese state failed to appreciate and accommodate the country's cultural and religious diversity. The objective of their intervention therefore was to help the parties agree on a formula that could "redefine the country's national identity so as to be genuinely uniting and to foster full equality of opportunity in the political, economic, social, and cultural life."[37]

The Mahdi government accepted the Obasanjo-Deng initiative because it was seriously hurting at this period, and efforts to solicit enough external logistical support for the war were not paying off. The government also accepted the initiative because the intervenors' perception of the conflict and the objective of their intervention posed no serious threat to the government's position. On its side, the SPLM/SPLA was very strong in the battlefield, so strong that it even dared to venture into northern towns such as Kurmuk and Geissan in the Blue Nile province in late 1987.[38] It accepted the intervention to enhance its recognition and legitimacy. Furthermore, at this period, dialogue was the movement's preferred policy option, and the intervenors' perception and desired outcome of the conflict resonated with that of their own.

Obasanjo and Deng adopted a behind-the-scenes, shuttle-diplomacy approach to engage the parties separately on a one-on-one basis. After several contacts with the two principal parties to the conflict, the initiative was interrupted by General al-Bashir's coup of June 30, 1989, before it achieved any positive outcome. Its negative outcome could be explained by four major factors. The most important was the Islamic shari'a laws. There was no way that a compromise outcome could be agreed upon with the shari'a laws in place, and given the sectarian nature of the political parties in the government and their positions on this issue, there was no way that the government could compromise on the shari'a itself. The only room for government compromise was to revise the shari'a laws rather than to annul them, on the basis of the perception that the problem was not so much the laws themselves as their application.[39]

The second factor emerged from the first. Having failed to prevail over the parties on a centralist outcome, the government had only one viable alternative: to opt for a regionalist outcome. It appeared that there was potential for an agreement that would have allowed the SPLM/SPLA to assume the administration of the south until a final decision on the structure of national unity could be determined by an envisaged national conference. Because this alternative was contrary to its centralist position, the SPLM/SPLA rejected it.[40] The third factor was the absence of tangible leverage to back up the initiative. Moral and sentimental appeals were not strong incentives to compel the parties to strike a compromise deal and guarantee its implementation.

Last, the internal direct negotiation track undermined the initiative. While Obasanjo and Deng were engaging the two parties, the SPLM/SPLA was at the same time negotiating directly with the DUP, the junior partner in the government. Their interaction was dictated by the political realities prevailing at that time. Both were disappointed by Mahdi. The SPLM/SPLA's frustration was a result of Mahdi's failure to implement the Koka Dam Declaration and to annul the shari'a laws. The DUP was terrified of the growing relationship of Mahdi's Umma Party with the fundamentalist National Islamic Front (NIF) and feared that the NIF would replace it in the government. The DUP needed a new strategy to attract new support.[41] The DUP–SPLM/SPLA negotiations culminated in the November 1988 agreement, whose main features included the convening of a national constitutional conference and abrogation of military pacts.[42] It appeared to the SPLM/SPLA that this track had better prospects than did the Obasanjo-Deng mediation track. The first half of 1989 was the earliest that the government and the SPLM/SPLA could have struck a peace deal through the internal and direct contact approach. This possibility was aborted by General al-Bashir's coup of June 30, 1989.

The Carter Initiative

The Carter initiative took place in November, some four months after the coup. It may appear surprising that the initiative was launched on such an uncompromising background and at a time when Islamic radicalization was at its peak. Nonetheless, regardless of the uncompromising signals, there were also some indications that Bashir was open for negotiations. On the peace issue, he hinted at a clean-slate approach by saying that the DUP–SPLM/SPLA Accord of November 1988 had no place in his government's plan for resolving the southern problem. Rather, he would have preferred that each party come up with its own peace plan that could form the basis of discussion at an all-party meeting. Another promising signal was the contact that the government made with the SPLM/SPLA just two weeks after the coup, although the subsequent bilateral talks in August stalemated. The new government also organized a National Dialogue Conference in September to build a national consensus on a new federal government structure. The conference was attended by the supporters of the new regime but not by the SPLM/SPLA, which broke the cease-fire at the close of the conference in October.

The Carter initiative was influenced by these mixed signals. The former U.S. president had a particular interest in Sudan because of his Guinea worm eradication campaign, and he realized that if there was a willingness to talk among the parties, intermediary assistance would be necessary to help them narrow their differences in order to achieve a positive outcome. The major concern was the impact of the war on peace in general and human life in particular. The initiative was therefore motivated by a desire to "lend Carter's prestige and influence to reassuring the parties of the seriousness of the endeavor, the benefits of participation, and the likelihood of some measure of success."[43]

Thus, he generated an invitation from both leaders and they accepted the initiative because they both had indicated a prior willingness to talk. They also recognized the importance and impact of a former U.S. president's role on the peace process in particular and on U.S. policy on the Sudan in general, and built on the ongoing work of the Carter Center in eradicating river blindness.

The initiative was conceived as "act two" of the groundwork done by the Obasanjo-Deng initiative. Deng's services were instrumental not only in linking the two initiatives but, more important, in facilitating lines of communication between Carter and the parties. After some serious consultations, the two parties were brought together in Nairobi on December 1, 1989.[44] The negotiations deadlocked on two items: the government's agreement to exempt non-Muslim regions from some, but not all, Islamic laws in a federal system, and the SPLM/SPLA insistence on a secular and broad-based national unity government.

Carter tried to move the parties from their uncompromising positions by proposing that the government suspend the Islamic laws for three months until the national conference, when a final position could be reached.[45] The proposal was not accepted by the government and the Carter initiative rapidly reached an impasse.

The U.S. Mediation Attempt

The U.S. mediation attempt was initiated by Assistant Secretary of State for African Affairs Herman Cohen immediately after the collapse of the Carter initiative. It was based on the spirit of the Obasanjo-Deng and Carter initiatives. Although the negotiations were deadlocked in December, there were areas of agreement. The parties agreed to hold a popular referendum after the constitutional conference. They also agreed to meet again as soon as possible on the basis of the resolutions of the September 1989 National Dialogue Conference. However, when Kenyan president Daniel Arap Moi invited both leaders to his retreat at the end of February 1990, both accepted, but only Bashir showed up. Cohen based his initiative on these mixed aspects.

The initiative perceived the conflict in the same manner as Obasanjo-Deng. Motivated by the same peace and humanitarian concerns as Carter, Cohen hoped that bringing the influence of the U.S. government to the peace initiative could be a strong incentive for the parties to agree on a peace deal. More important, the Sudanese government itself took the initiative in March 1990 to request the United States to play the intermediary role. This action could be explained by the military imbalance, which continued to be in favor of the SPLM/SPLA at the time. Cohen not only adopted Obasanjo and Deng's approach of both shuttle- and behind-the-scenes diplomacy, but he also actually used the two African diplomats as informed conduits in his engagement with the parties.

Cohen's concrete proposal had two important components.[46] The first involved separating the belligerent forces by mutual withdrawal and establishing a civilian administration in the south under the SPLM/SPLA. The second component was to negotiate a comprehensive settlement based on a federal arrangement. The proposal was predicated on the practical situation on the ground. The SPLM/SPLA was by then in almost total control of the whole of the south, and the idea of a federal arrangement had already been endorsed by the government and reaffirmed during the Carter-mediated talks.

After numerous and complicated consultations among Obasanjo, Deng, and Cohen on one side, and between the three and the parties on the other, the proposal was not endorsed by the parties, then was watered down by Washington, and then was rejected by both parties, who wanted the original proposal to be presented by the United States, not by intermediaries. The failure of the initiative could be explained by some serious complications intrinsic to the proposal itself. Separating combatants would have created a buffer zone that would have demanded some kind of a monitoring mechanism to guarantee its effectiveness. Any involvement of external personnel in such a mechanism would have been very difficult for the government to accept as it would be an affront to its sovereignty. Also, the SPLM/SPLA centralist objective was a stumbling block for the movement to go along with the regionalist arrangements for the south's self-rule. In the same vein, a comprehensive settlement based on autonomy for the south would have complicated matters between the SPLM/SPLA and its principal backer, Ethiopia. It would seem illogical and embarrassing for Ethiopia to have sacrificed so much just to help the SPLM/SPLA attain secessionist objectives while fighting an internecine war at home to suppress the same objectives. And if the SPLM/SPLA were also fighting an "Ethiopian war" in the Sudan, as the government always believed, the regionalist outcome would not have been acceptable because it would have left the Khartoum government intact and its support to the Ethiopian rebels uninterrupted.

Another explanation for the failure of the Cohen initiative was the SPLM/SPLA's alternative prospects for a centralist outcome from the internal direct interaction track. Parallel to the Cohen initiative, the SPLM/SPLA was coordinating with other political forces, in both the south and north, under the umbrella of the newly created opposition group, the National Democratic Alliance (NDA). The NDA's single objective was to overthrow the military government in the style of the 1964 and 1985 popular uprisings and restore old-time democracy. As far as its centralist objectives were concerned, it was more advantageous for the SPLM/SPLA to invest in this track than in the Cohen peace initiative, particularly considering the movement's favorable military situation on the battlefield at the time.

Although marginalized as relations with Sudan deteriorated, the United States continued to probe for possible entry as a mediator in the conflict over the next year. After the Gulf War, Sudan again invited the United States to return to mediation, but Cohen indicated that renewal of peace initiatives would depend on improved passage for U.S. relief efforts, among other things, and the support of the United States for new OAU efforts to achieve entry into the conflict mediation. Soon after, Sudan notified the United States that its efforts would not be needed, now that the OAU was involved.[47]

The Abuja Initiative

The OAU effort was launched in completely transformed international, regional, and domestic environments. At the international level there, was a rise of the aspirations of self-determination that accompanied the collapse of the Soviet Union, socialism, and the Cold War. At the continental level, the inveterate Sudanese conflict was joined by a new generation of internal conflicts that raised serious concerns about regional peace and security. These concerns placed conflict resolution at the center of the continental organization's urgent priorities.

At the domestic level, the situation on the ground was quite different from the one experienced by the previous entry initiatives. After the failure of the U.S. peace initiative, the Sudanese government radicalized its religious ideological position by formally reconfirming Islamic law in January 1991; Mengistu's regime in Ethiopia fell in May; the SPLM/SPLA split in two in August, followed by fratricidal, interfactional bloodletting; and in September, the SPLM/SPLA mainstream endorsed self-determination as one of its demands in any future peace talks with the government.

The fall of Mengistu and the split within the SPLM/SPLA changed the conflict's structure fundamentally. Its new power balance favored the government both politically and militarily, a situation not conducive to a compromise settlement. The shift in the power balance created a feeling within the government that it could resolve the conflict militarily. At this time, the SPLM/SPLA mainstream was fighting not only to hold on to its previous military gains but also for its soul. It was indeed one of the worst moments in its history.

Although launched within the OAU framework, the Abuja initiative was characteristically different from the previous OAU attempts. It was attempted at a time when the OAU was redefining its perspective on dealing with the growing number of internal conflicts and was responding to the government's invitation. The OAU chairman in 1991, Nigerian president Ibrahim Babangida, who had been supportive of the Obasanjo-Deng initiative, accepted the challenge only after both parties expressed their willingness regarding the Nigerian involvement. Preparations began in June 1991, after the SPLM/SPLA formally accepted Babangida's mediation. After consultations with all the parties, it was agreed that talks should begin on October 28, 1991, in Abuja, the Nigerian capital.

Babangida accepted the challenge because of his role as chairman of the continental organization. His acceptance was in line with the OAU's new commitment of trying to find "African solutions to African problems."[48] His acceptance also had to do with Nigeria's own national image as one of the continent's powerhouses. Babangida was likewise convinced that because of some similarities between the two countries, Sudan would benefit from Nigeria's own political experience in its efforts toward resolving its conflict.

Babangida's OAU chairmanship was of course one of the factors in the government's and the SPLM/SPLA's acceptance of Nigeria's intervention. But more important, they both wanted to learn how Nigeria overcame divisive politics regardless of its similar regional, cultural, and religious diversities. As in Sudan, northern and southern Nigeria were ruled separately by the British. Apart from having alternating civilian and military administrations after independence, both countries also have a Muslim majority in the north and a Christian minority in the south. Both have had similar experiences of civil wars. Despite these similarities, Nigeria has been able to forge a relatively stable national identity based not on ethnicity, geographical location, or religion, but on individuals' equality before the law. This was the important experience from which the Sudanese were expected to benefit in Nigeria's intervention. From its own experience Nigeria perceived the conflict as an inability of the Sudanese leadership to appreciate the country's cultural and religious diversities. Thus its major objective was to help the parties resolve their political differences without compromising the unity of Sudan.

The peace talks did not start at the end of October as planned, because of the split within the SPLM/SPLA.[49] The talks were delayed in order to give the SPLM/SPLA factions time to sort out their differences. The Sudanese government worked hard during the delay to weaken the opposition militarily and diplomatically by playing the two SPLM/SPLA factions against each other. At the war front, the government benefited from its collaboration with the Nasir faction by providing it with military logistics in order to fight the mainstream Torit faction. At the political front, the government engaged the Nasir faction in secret peace talks, which culminated in the January 25, 1992, Frankfurt Agreement.[50]

The government's divisive tactics were a stumbling block in the efforts to reconcile the SPLM/SPLA factions undertaken by a Nairobi-based religious NGO group, People for Peace in Africa, and the New Sudan Council of Churches.[51] The factions' own intense hostility and the government's efforts to widen the rift between them prevented the possibility of a rapprochement. As a result, when the talks finally began in May 1992, the SPLM/SPLA was in reality represented by two different delegations, although they portrayed a resemblance of one united delegation.[52]

The Abuja Process went through two major sessions. The first (Abuja I) lasted from May 26 to June 4, 1991, and the second (Abuja II) from April 26 to May 18, 1993. During the talks, the government presented its federal position with a commitment to respect religious, linguistic, and cultural diversities of the country, on the one hand, and the primacy of the principle of majority rights, on the other. The SPLM/SPLA delegates rejected this position. Their biggest problem was with the principle of majority rights that seemed to have packaged the controversial religious issue. Taken to its extreme, the principle meant that the Muslim majority would have the leeway to decide whatever was in its interest without regard to the interests of other groups. This was interpreted by the SPLM/SPLA as the government's maneuver to maintain Islamic shari'a laws through the back door.

The SPLM/SPLA's initial position favored the establishment of a secular democratic system based on the principle of equality before the law.[53] The government rejected this position because it contained demands for reviving multiparty politics, to which the military regime was vehemently opposed. Following the government's continued insistence on its position, the SPLM/SPLA delegation changed its position from the centralist, secular democratic system to regionalist self-determination.

To avoid a deadlock, the mediators tried to steer the parties toward a gradual approach by encouraging them to tackle urgent security issues of cease-fire and secession of hostilities first; move to political, economic, and social structures for the interim period; then deal with the constitutional issues. The government rejected this approach and refused to discuss security issues, claiming that Sudanese security was the government's exclusive domain and, as such, was not open for discussion.[54] The talks were adjourned when it was clear that neither party was ready to compromise. However, they agreed to meet again soon. This was the official culmination of Abuja I.

Given the uncompromising and inconclusive nature of the Abuja I talks, it was unlikely that another session would be convened soon. It took a direct intervention by Presidents Moi and Museveni to convince the parties to revive the Abuja Peace Process.[55] During the preparations for Abuja II, Nigeria wanted to extend the Kenyan and Ugandan positive role by proposing a collective mediation. The Sudanese government rejected the proposal as both neighbors were viewed as being SPLA supporters.[56]

When Abuja II started on April 26, 1993, both parties presented their proposals on the political structures of the interim period and beyond. The government's proposals contained the contentious issue of shari'a laws, with an allowance of exempting the south from certain shari'a provisions. The SPLM/SPLA proposals also did not drop the demand for self-determination, although it was presented as an alternative to its principled objective of a secular democratic Sudan.

For more than twenty days the parties stood by their positions. When the mediators failed to move them toward a compromise, the talks were considered a failure. The Abuja Peace Process was thus concluded amid acrimonious statements, with the government swearing that self-determination "will come through the 'mouth' of the gun" and not from debates in Abuja, and the SPLM/SPLA vowing that the south "will be part of an Islamic state only if it will be defeated militarily."[57] The relationship between state and religion remained the single most important factor that could explain the failure of the Abuja Peace Process.

The Inter-Governmental Authority on Development

IGAD entered the Sudanese conflict immediately following the Abuja initiative. As with the Abuja Process, IGAD's entry was an outcome of the Sudanese government's invitation. The government's continued desire for mediation was dictated by the difficulties associated with pursuing the military track. Although IGAD entered the conflict while the power balance was in the government's favor, it was extremely costly for the government to sustain. The deteriorating economic situation could not support the war, and the impact of the war on the economy enhanced military and civilian opposition to the regime.

More than three military coups had been attempted between 1991 and 1993. The government's harsh response to the coup attempts had isolated it further from the military's rank and file. On April 15, 1991, the regime executed twenty-six serving officers for participation in a coup attempt. On August 20, it arrested fifteen serving officers and ten retired officers for another alleged coup attempt. In February 1992, nineteen officers were cashiered and forty-one more arrested for planning yet another coup.[58]

The civilian opposition took two major fronts. There had been increased political solidarity between the SPLM/SPLA and the northern political forces under the NDA umbrella, which posed a serious challenge to the military regime's survival. On another front, the opposition had taken the form of unions and women's and students' protests. The unions' and students' protests in 1992–1993 were so serious that security officials warned Bashir that spiraling inflation and food shortages might trigger a popular revolt.[59] The government responded by arresting hundreds of union members, students, and women.

At the war front, military victories came at a higher cost of human life. The 1992–1993 military offensive, which the government called "a jihad against the infidels and traitors in order to consolidate the Islamic state," cost the government more than 15 percent of its fighting forces in the south.[60] Hence, immense casualties, logistical problems, and inability to pay the salaries of a bloated military led to intensified military opposition to both the war and the government.

The government preferred mediation in order to extricate itself from regional and international isolation. Its neighbors isolated Sudan because of its fundamentalist and discriminatory policies, and Sudanese isolation was championed by the United States, which placed Sudan on the list of terrorist countries.[61] Sudan was also isolated by some of its traditional Arab allies because of its support of Iraq during the Gulf War. Isolation had a serious impact on both Sudan's economy and the war. The U.S. isolation led to a ban on bilateral trade and assistance, while the Arab states' isolation denied the country financial and logistical support that would have been instrumental in prosecuting the war. As if this were not enough, Sudan also faced isolation from the international financial institutions. The International Monetary Fund suspended Sudan's membership in August 1993 for failing to honor its debt obligations.[62]

There were a number of explanations for the parties' preference of IGAD over other prospective mediators. One was that IGAD resonated with the new African perspective of searching for African solutions to African problems. The basis of this new thinking was not only the African realization of the conflicts' impact on regional peace and security but, more important, a sober realization of the reluctance and inability of other external actors to act. As IGAD noted:

> [I]n a world in which the international community appears reluctant to invest in preventing, managing, and resolving regional conflicts, preferring instead regional and subregional arrangements, the IGAD peace initiative is a timely move. . . . [T]he four members of the IGAD mediation committee see the Sudanese conflict not merely as a national problem, but also as one with implications that impact directly on the peace, security, and stability of the region, and is therefore of great interest and concern to them.[63]

Even within Africa, the preference for IGAD was in line with the "layered-responsibility" framework. After the failure of the OAU-sponsored initiatives, including the Abuja Process, the choice of IGAD was natural.[64]

Another explanation was the neutrality factor, which, though theoretically insignificant, the parties still considered important. It was assumed, especially by the SPLM/SPLA, that IGAD's neutrality would help the parties reach a compromise solution. Sudanese membership in IGAD was another important factor; contrary to existing neutrality, the government actually banked on IGAD's support for its position. The government's hope was that its fellow members in an organization of sovereign states would in no way support a rebel movement bent on challenging its sovereignty. This hope for support was expected to come from Ethiopia and Eritrea because Sudan had helped their new governments overthrow Mengistu's regime. Yet the very experience of these two new regimes led them to sympathy for the southern cause as a national liberation movement, even though they were perplexed by the dual centralist and regionalist nature of the cause. For the SPLM/SPLA, in addition to the above reasons, it was hoped that IGAD's collective pressure would be instrumental in moving the government from its rigid position.

IGAD's acceptance of the challenge was based more on the fact that it was an interested party to the conflict. Although individually its members might have perceived the conflict differently, collectively they perceived the conflict more on regional security terms. They were concerned not only with the conflict's impact on regional security but equally with its spillover effects on their own individual countries' political stability. Their objective therefore was to help fellow members in order to help themselves. They hoped that their collective political will and pressure would help them prevail over the parties.

CONCLUSION

The Sudanese case study offers useful theoretical and practical lessons about entry:

1. A conflict does not always attract potential mediators at all stages of its evolution. The unattractiveness could be a function of factors intrinsic to the conflict itself: how long the conflict has been around, direct efforts by the parties themselves to resolve the conflict, uncompromising positions of the parties. It can also be a function of factors exogenous to it: potential mediators' interests in the conflict, their perceptions of the conflict's tractability, their priority among conflicts in terms of generation and location.

The intractability and duration of the Sudanese conflict caused it to lose its attractiveness to prospective mediators. The shifting alliances among political forces demonstrated a potential for direct interparty negotiation, but this direct peace track has been a discouraging factor to potential mediators. Prospective mediators have at the same time been discouraged by the initial zero-sum positions of the parties. Entry initiatives have been attempted mainly during the periods that the parties demonstrated a willingness to move toward positive-sum positions. Prospective mediators also had a range of choices among an ancient conflict such as the Sudan, a fresh one such as Burundi, or a leftover Cold War one such as Angola.

2. Entry, like ripeness, is not a guarantee of success. In contrast to Burundi, which initially resisted the regional entry, the Sudanese government, uncharacteristically, not only readily accepted many entry attempts but also took the initiative to shop around for prospective intervenors. The U.S. initiative, the Abuja Process, and the IGAD initiative were all the outcomes of governments' invitations.

However, neither an easy acceptability nor an invitation is necessarily an adequate measure of an entry's effectiveness in attaining a mediated settlement. Sudan amply showed that a party's commitment to mediated negotiation is not equal to a commitment to a compromise settlement. It appears, for example, that the government accepted mediators' entry not necessarily for a compromise settlement but only to solve its short-term or immediate logistical problems with the military option.

3. Timing matters in initiating entry. If the main objective of entry is to help the parties attain a positive mediated outcome, it is absolutely essential that entry should be attempted at a time when there is a possibility for such an outcome. Such entry points depend on the structure of the conflict at a given period. Many of the initiatives in Sudan gained access at a time when the conflict's structure was not favorable for a positive mediated outcome because one side was too strong or too weak and the two were not equally at a painful impasse. The Obasanjo-Deng initiative, for example, entered at a time when the government was receiving a steady flow of financial and logistical assistance in support of its military track. Although the power balance was still in favor of the SPLM/SPLA, the government could not compromise at a time of weakness. The Cohen initiative faced similar structural impediments to a positive mediated outcome. The Carter initiative entered almost simultaneously with the arrival of al-Bashir's regime, sometimes during periods of heightened Islamic radicalization, and other times during periods not propitious for compromise. From Abuja to IGAD, the structure of the conflict had changed to being in the government's favor, again one of the factors responsible for the failure of the Abuja Process that needed mitigation before there could be a real opportunity for IGAD. The tragedy of Sudan in regard to mediation has been that the parties never felt that they were in a hurting stalemate at the same time.

4. Entry does not always permeate the whole spectrum of the conflict. This is one of the factors that explains an initiative's quick exit or ineffectiveness of its mediated outcome. The initiatives in Sudan engaged only the principal protagonists, leaving out a large group of political forces. This was in contrast with Burundi, where all the major political forces were engaged. Peace agreements that do not have the support of all the political forces in the country run the risk of not being sustainable. The 1972 Addis Ababa Agreement during the first phase of the Sudanese civil war and the 1993 Arusha Peace Agreement on Rwanda are clear examples; even the IGAD initiative, which ultimately managed to arrive at a peace agreement, initially engaged only some of the parties and collapsed prematurely.

5. Problem-solving workshops can be helpful to conflict management. There is no doubt that the Woodrow Wilson International Center for Scholars–sponsored workshop on the Sudan played a useful diagnostic and facilitative role. A series of serious mediation initiatives took place after the conclusion of the workshop.

7

ETHIOPIA-ERITREA, 1998–2000

A border dispute between Ethiopia and Eritrea that broke into violence in May 1998, startling unperceptive observers who had celebrated the latter's painless emergence as a new independent state, provides a case of interstate mediation, a residue of the thirty-year Ethiopian civil war. A minor border incident on May 6 escalated into a battle by May 12 when Eritrean forces occupied the towns of Badme and Shiraro in the Yirga Triangle and overran the local civilian administration. After Eritrea's action, Ethiopian forces retaliated, terming the invasion an act of territorial aggression and demanding unconditional withdrawal, but Eritrea accused Ethiopia of having crept into its territory since October 1997. Over the course of two years, the conventional war spread to three separate fronts: Merib-Setit in the west, Zalambessa in the center, and Bure on the eastern side of the border. The war resulted in the death of about 100,000 Ethiopians and Eritreans, and many more were displaced by the vengeful expulsions. As part of the war effort, each side bought weaponry on an extraordinary scale, pouring more than $300 million a year into rearmament. From the start of the conflict, a variety of mediators shuttled between Addis Ababa, Ethiopia, and Asmara, Eritrea, in attempts to resolve it. Broadly motivated by the desire to de-escalate the conflict and restore stability to the volatile Horn of Africa, these mediators succeeded in crafting a number of agreements that finally led to the end of the war in June 2000.

This chapter examines the entry of mediators in the conflict, illuminating broader themes such as the points of entry for mediators, their access to parties, and the outcomes of intervention. Although the Eritrean-Ethiopian

War was an interstate conflict, it was the continuation of an intrastate regionalist conflict that had—paradoxically—reached a conclusion by becoming a centralist conflict. Eritrea broke away from Ethiopia by first overthrowing the Ethiopian government. This situation immediately raises questions, as seen in the previous cases, of the definition of the changing nature of the conflict. Other concepts are equally pertinent. Dominant conceptions of mediation are anchored in notions of hurting stalemates, ripe moments, invitation, motivation, and leverage. These analytical categories both capture the structural and process components of mediation and furnish insights into the entry and durability of mediators in all types of conflict. From this view, successful mediation hinges on the interplay between the structure of the conflict and the interests and leverage of mediators converging on the conflict.

Most of the literature on intermediary intervention conceives of mediation as a coordinated and sequenced process along a clear conflict resolution continuum. Mitchell, for instance, has proposed that mediation be viewed as a number of interlocking and complementary roles played by a variety of actors: "Such process conception of mediation seems not only an analytically more fruitful way of understanding the essential nature of 'mediation' but is, in many cases, a more accurate reflection of an empirical reality than the 'single mediator model,' in which the same entity attempts to carry out every single task."[1]

Conceptions of the utility of multiple intermediaries in conflicts tend to obscure the problem of "crowdedness" (particularly the obstacles of coordination and sequencing of roles) that characterizes entry. This chapter argues that in conflicts where multiple actors vie for mediation roles, entry is an exclusionary process of keeping many out to establish a credible and orderly negotiating framework. Mediation is a process, but entry is often a decisive event, a moment of disaggregating parties with intervention proclivities. In such a competitive environment, marginalization of mediators is most significant at the initial point of entry because it helps determine the parties with the leverage to contribute to conflict de-escalation. Although the winnowing process in the formative stages overcomes some of the problems of multiple intermediaries, competing and marginalized mediators do not necessarily fade away, hence the continuing importance of order to the evolution of the mediation. In the Ethiopia-Eritrea conflict, order was created by the intervention of the United States from the outset, the institutional ownership of the mediation by the Organization of African Unity, and the international partnership established in the latter phase of the conflict among special envoys from the United States, the European Union (EU), the OAU, and the United Nations.

THE NATURE OF THE CONFLICT AND THE PARTIES

The Ethiopia-Eritrea border conflict needs to be understood as a post-colonial conflict in which weighty questions of political and geographical identity were compounded by the unique transition from a provincial to a state boundary.[2] The outbreak of the border conflict occurred within the larger context of a host of unresolved questions stemming from Eritrean independence in 1993. The conflict manifested fundamental issues of redefining the bilateral relationship, issues that had been postponed in the euphoria of independence. Overselling the idea of an amicable split that created Eritrea had postponed a serious reflection on future institutional arrangements. Although a secondary source of the conflict, the border war compounded the primary political and economic areas of contention, exposing outstanding hostilities and igniting new ones.

The guerrilla war for Eritrean independence against the Ethiopian empire of Haile Selassie and then the dictatorship of Mengistu Haile Mariam forged a close military and political alliance between the Eritrean People's Liberation Front (EPLF) and the Tigray People's Liberation Front (TPLF). After the fall of Mengistu, this alliance enabled a peaceful transition to Eritrea's statehood. Under President Isaias Afwerki, the EPLF (now called the People's Front for Democracy and Justice) took the leadership in Asmara while the TPLF, led by Prime Minister Meles Zenawi, formed the core of the governing alliance of the Ethiopian People's Revolutionary Democratic Front government.

Although Eritrea and Ethiopia signed wide-ranging agreements that pledged economic, political, and military cooperation, the decisive glue in the bilateral relationship was military camaraderie and cultural consanguinity. Moreover, even as Zenawi and Afwerki basked in the glory of the previous alliance, the camaraderie of the war of liberation concealed historic rivalries based on ideology and personality within their parties. As was characteristic of postcolonial states, Zenawi and Afwerki came to embody the image of their nations. In stamping their individual styles and leadership onto otherwise weak institutions, however, they guaranteed that the resurgence of conflicts over identity and stature would have enormous consequences for their countries. It is in this respect that the border conflict (widely posed in populist terms as a war among "brothers" and "cousins") exhibited an inability to structure rule in impersonal institutions. Soon after the border hostilities broke out in May 1998, Afwerki suggested that settlement would be illusive because "we might be more concerned about pride, integrity, respect, trust, confidence, and all those kinds of things. When you lose them, it becomes a big problem for us in this region—it is not always money or resources."

From the outset, both nations began to forge diverse political identities, which strained the relationship. To manage ethnic divisions that had bedeviled Ethiopian politics, Zenawi adopted a new system of ethnic federations that potentially gave each group the right to self-determination. In contrast to Ethiopia's federalism, the Eritrean government created a unitary, one-party state informed by the pattern of postcolonial consolidation with emphasis on a charismatic leader. At the core of the National Charter for Eritrea, approved in February 1994, was the principle of enhancing nationhood as the means to postwar reconstruction. Although Eritrean nationalism initially focused on the domestic front, it gradually assumed regional dimensions. Endowed with a battle-hardened military and self-confidence, President Afwerki seemed ready, in the words of one commentator, to "boost Eritrea's identity at every opportunity." As part of its regional assertiveness, Eritrea was embroiled in border conflicts with Sudan, Djibouti, and Yemen before the conflict with Ethiopia began.

The promise of close economic cooperation and integration initially mitigated Ethiopia's loss of ports along the Eritrean coast. Agreements reached in 1991 and 1993 allowed for reciprocal rights of citizens; Eritrea's use of the Ethiopian currency, the birr; and Ethiopian access to the Red Sea ports of Assab and Massawa. In addition, Ethiopia was to remain the principal market and supplier of Eritrean food, the source of revenues from transshipment duties, and the provider of jobs to almost 300,000 Eritreans. Yet differences in economic policy surfaced early on when Eritrea abruptly expelled 150,000 Ethiopians, fueling Ethiopian resentment that there was no real reciprocity regarding access to employment. Other strains developed after Ethiopia complained about mounting costs of fuel supplied by Eritrean refineries and doubling of port charges.

These economic conflicts culminated in Eritrea's decision to introduce its own national currency, the nakfa, in November 1997 to solve its shortage of currency reserves. Although the Asmara authorities requested that the nakfa and the birr be legal tender in both countries, Ethiopia rejected this move and instead insisted on the use of letters of credit and hard currency in all commercial transactions. The currency crisis caused considerable economic hardships for both states as the hard currency transactions raised the costs of Eritrean ports for Ethiopians and food supplies for Eritreans. After the outbreak of border hostilities, a report in the *Addis Tribune* described the economic arrangements as unfavorable to Ethiopia:

> Under pressure, the Ethiopian government was made to sign several unequal economic treaties with Eritrea, including those related to the use of the Ethiopian birr as a common currency, the establishment of the free trade area, the utilization of the port of Assab and the Assab oil refinery, nearly all of which violated internationally accepted principles and norms pertaining to such bilateral monetary, economic, and other arrangements. . . . These benefits were exacted from Ethiopia as a result of Eritrea's hitherto hegemonic relationship with Ethiopia.[3]

Heightening the contests over political identity and economic relations were the uncertainties in the demarcation of the boundary that had previously been a provincial line. In normal circumstances, boundaries require certainty, predictability, and a modicum of fixity. In the special circumstance of a history of relatively unimpeded border mobility and migration, clarity becomes even more critical. The political temperature raised by the core geostrategic and political conflicts boiled into a showdown over the border.

ENTER THE MEDIATORS

Phase One: The Washington-Kigali Intervention

Once the clashes began in May 1998, the United States and Rwanda quickly intervened as "Friends of the Belligerents," a role that the two parties accepted. The diplomatic efforts of U.S. assistant secretary of state for African affairs Susan Rice and Rwanda's minister in the presidency, Patrick Mazimhaka, were pertinent as the war threatened to destabilize the Horn of Africa and destroy the reputations of allies at the center of the "African renaissance."[4] Their intervention surmounted the issues of acceptability and lent some clarity to the peace initiatives. As the conflict seemed to cross a dangerous psychological threshold in which the military logic clouded peaceful entreaties, the United States–Rwanda initiative focused on de-escalation. In addition, with the parties locked into a war of words about who invaded first, the mediators committed them to a peaceful solution.

In almost two weeks of shuttle diplomacy, Rice and Mazimhaka produced a Four-Point Plan, which was publicly unveiled on June 5, 1998, before agreement from the Eritrean side. The plan required the parties to resolve the dispute by peaceful means, to reduce current tensions by agreeing to a small observer mission to be deployed to Badme to oversee the Eritrean withdrawal to positions held before May 6, to agree to a lasting resolution of the underlying dispute through a swift and binding delimitation and demarcation of the border, and to demilitarize the entire common border as soon as possible. In announcing the plan, the mediators indicated that they had presented both sides "with a detailed implementation plan and recommended that each party convey, in a legal and binding manner, their acceptance of the recommendations and implementation plan to the facilitators."

Ethiopia readily accepted the plan on June 6 because it fulfilled the requirement for Eritrean withdrawal and the return of Ethiopian administration. But Eritrea objected to major provisions of the plan, claiming that withdrawal "as a precondition would unlikely win local support. Why should we withdraw from our own territory?" Instead, Eritrea suggested the recognition and adherence to colonial borders, the demarcation of the boundary by the UN Cartographic Unit, and the demilitarization of the border to be monitored by an observer team acceptable to both sides. As Asmara dithered on some of the provisions, Assistant Secretary Rice warned: "Half an agreement is less than 50 percent if you're talking about war and peace. . . . We hope that Eritrea will also accept this package of recommendations in toto. Piecemeal acceptance of one part or another is not the way forward."[5] Despite its rejection, however, the plan became the primary formula for subsequent initiatives.

The Friends of the Belligerents created a credible initiative that, in turn, kept other competitors at bay. To be effective, entry must be exclusive at critical moments, but other mediators cannot be kept out permanently. The biggest obstacle in dealing with those waiting in the wings is to establish their specific contribution to the peace process. Do competitors supplant, supplement, or subvert ongoing efforts? Soon after the entry of the United States and Rwanda, Libya's Moammar Gaddafi launched a parallel initiative as president of the Common Market of Sahel and Saharan States (COMESSA), comprising Libya, Chad, Niger, Mali, Burkina Faso, and Sudan. Seeking to use the war as a means to expand his influence in the Horn, Gaddafi argued that the conflict needed to be resolved within a "friendly African framework." He thus sent COMESSA's Assistant Secretary-General Adam Togoe to propose a Three-Point Plan that would require the end of hostilities, the deployment of COMESSA troops along the disputed border, and international arbitration. Without the key provision of Eritrean withdrawal from Badme, Asmara embraced the Libyan plan on June 8, 1998. According to an Ethiopian official, the competing Libyan plan helped "Eritrea to be even more stubborn." Over the course of the conflict, Eritrea moved closer to Libya, which culminated in military collaboration and Asmara's membership in COMESSA.

Following Eritrean rejection of the United States–Rwanda plan, Ethiopia mounted retaliatory air raids on military targets on the outskirts of Asmara. In response, Eritrea bombed the provincial capital of Tigray, causing civilian deaths. The air strikes occurred alongside the reinforcement of ground forces in the other contested border fronts.[6] As the air strikes continued, Eritrea claimed that Ethiopia had imposed a virtual blockade of its air space and ports by threatening to attack commercial aircraft and civilian vessels. President Afwerki threatened further military strikes if Ethiopia did not lift the air and sea embargo: "We will make it very difficult for Ethiopia to enjoy the luxury of closing our ports and airports while at the same time enjoying free air space. . . . They have overestimated their power, and leaders believe their own propaganda."[7]

On June 14, U.S. president Bill Clinton intervened to put pressure on both countries to suspend the air strikes.[8] Consistent with the role of a close ally to both parties, U.S. presidential intervention helped reduce the escalation of the air war, leading to a moratorium on air strikes. According to a U.S. government statement, "[The] moratorium will continue indefinitely or until such time as either party concludes that any prospect for a peace process has come to an end and provides formal, advance notice to the United States Government that it will no longer respect this moratorium."[9] Although both sides continued to beef up their ground forces along the 630-mile-long frontier, the lull in the shooting allowed the resumption of new talks building on the United States–Rwanda Plan.

Phase Two: The OAU Mediates

The entry of the Friends of the Belligerents pre-empted the crowdedness of mediators that mars most African conflicts. Rather than establishing an orderly framework for negotiation, multiple mediators, infused with mixed motives, often create confusion. In addition to the Libyan initiative, the Inter-Governmental Authority on Development and other emissaries had already coalesced around the conflict without a clear sense of purpose. More critical, as the Libyan plan revealed, multiple mediators spawn competing expectations by promising different rewards. But once the United States and Rwanda had established negotiations that engaged both parties, one way to undercut the Libyan initiative and build momentum for the original plan was to anchor the mediation in a broader African multilateral initiative. Thus, to prevent the subversion of the United States–Rwandan effort in the name of African solutions to African problems, the OAU had to enter the conflict in a supplementary role. Furthermore, as an institutional compromise between multiple African mediators and the Friends of the Belligerents, the OAU intervention reinforced the need for order that had undergirded initial entry. Marginalized but never exiting, Libya waited for an opportunity to re-enter.

The outbreak of the war in the OAU's backyard had embarrassed its leaders and raised doubts about the efforts of Secretary-General Salim Ahmed Salim to strengthen the capacity of the OAU in matters of conflict prevention, management, and resolution. To reclaim its sagging image, the OAU formally entered the mediation on June 4, 1998, at the summit of foreign ministers in Ouagadougou, Burkina Faso. Urging Eritrea and Ethiopia to observe a cease-fire and explore avenues for a peaceful resolution to the dispute, Salim told the foreign ministers "to put the entire weight of our continent in support of a peaceful resolution and avoid the widening of the conflict whose catastrophic consequences are self evident."[10] At a later summit of heads of state on June 10, the OAU adopted a resolution appealing to both parties to accept the United States–Rwanda plan. During the summit, Ethiopia stated its desire for restraint and willingness to cooperate with mediators. But Foreign Minister Seyoum warned that Eritrea's bid to create facts on the ground before negotiations constituted a dangerous precedent in Africa: "Eritrea's arrogance and its disdain for Africa . . . and of all principles governing interstate relations has now reached a stage where Eritrea has become, not only a source of shame for Africa and for its neighbors, but also a menace to peace."[11]

Eritrea expressed interest in more talks, insisting that it would withdraw from the contested areas only in the framework of a general demilitarization of the border. It also noted that it had rejected the United States–Rwanda plan because of the "premature announcement of the recommendations before discussions on these outstanding issues were exhausted." The stumbling block to a genuine solution, its delegate argued, was "not differences over general principles or the temporary authority over civilian centers in the demilitarized areas [but instead it is] Ethiopia's logic of force and spiral of measures that have begun by blowing the problem out of proportion and have ended up escalating the conflict to the brink of full-scale war." To restart the talks, Eritrea made three proposals: full demilitarization of the border areas to ensure that hostilities would not recur, direct talks between Eritrea and Ethiopia in the presence of high-level mediators, and appointment of high-level African mediators.[12]

Responding to Eritrea's request, the OAU appointed a Mediation Committee of Burkina Faso, Rwanda, Djibouti, and Zimbabwe to negotiate the implementation of the peace plan. The OAU initiative occurred against the backdrop of mutual recriminations stemming from continued mass population expulsions. At the same time, Eritrea charged that Addis Ababa was reimposing the air and sea blockade in violation of the moratorium on air strikes.[13] The OAU Mediation Committee initially read its mandate in the modest terms of winning acceptance of the United States–Rwanda plan, but it soon found itself in the awkward position of either strengthening the plan and risking Ethiopian rejection or maintaining it and risking Eritrean rejection. This dilemma was captured in contrasting positions on the eve of the OAU mission. To Eritrea: "If the OAU delegation brings a dead package, there will be no solution." To Ethiopia: "The OAU delegation should prevail upon Eritrea to comply with the peace proposal."[14]

Shuttling between Asmara and Addis Ababa on June 18 and 19, 1998, the presidents of the OAU Mediation Committee secured concessions from the Ethiopian government on cessation of hostilities and a negotiated settlement after Eritrean withdrawal from Badme, but Asmara remained firm in its rejection. In the words of Secretary-General Salim, "Eritrea made it categorically clear that the United States–Rwanda facilitation process was over."[15] Operating within the strictures of the United States–Rwanda plan, the African team was unable to advance any new ideas without fundamentally altering its terms. As an Eritrean official remarked: "The OAU team did not present any new proposals. . . ."[16] In the face of disagreements about the ownership of Badme prior to the May 1998 hostilities, the OAU committee opted to change its approach to the mediation into a ministerial investigation body, a task that entailed a review of maps and other government documents about the disputed area. As Sam Ibok, head of OAU's Conflict Management Unit, acknowledged: "When the committee was set up, it soon became clear the issues were complex and needed on-the-ground fact-finding investigation."

As the ministerial committee began its investigations, new mediators from countries such as Uganda, Egypt, Libya, the Democratic Republic of Congo, Sudan, and Italy launched separate initiatives. Central to the invitation of these mediators was Eritrea, whose president, Isaias Afwerki, suggested that the OAU act merely as an umbrella organization for all the mediation efforts:

> I do not think it is a matter of who should take the lead or not, this is not a competition for anyone. We are striving to find a peaceful solution to the problem and we would like to see a process put in place that would guarantee that we are on the right track. Yes, the OAU has its limitations and no one can exaggerate the capabilities of the OAU. We have always talked about a consolidation of efforts. It is not that some have the influence and capability. We would like to see all efforts combined to bring an effect and I think the OAU can be one element. The OAU on its own could not come up with miracles and find a solution to the problem.[17]

With the OAU convinced that some of these initiatives complemented its own process, Ethiopia called for an end to parallel mediators. Worried that they would only distract from the United States–Rwanda plan and provide more time for Eritrea to procrastinate, Prime Minister Zenawi, on a visit to Nairobi in July 1998, warned that further initiatives outside ongoing efforts by the OAU would impede peacemaking.[18]

As the OAU frantically reinvigorated the peace process, both sides began to seek new sources of arms after the Clinton administration suspended sales of weapons and war materiel in July. In an aggressive buying spree they acquired small rifles, grenades, and ammunition, as well as fighter-bombers and helicopters from China and the former Soviet Bloc nations.[19] At the same time, marking a departure from the era of cutbacks in defense spending, the Ethiopian parliament approved a 9 percent increase in the defense budget for the 1998–1999 fiscal year, the first increase in seven years.[20]

After two months of investigations, the OAU committee drew up a draft report that was presented to the foreign ministers meeting in Burkina Faso in October 1998, and later to Eritrean and Ethiopian leaders. In early November, Afwerki and Zenawi met separately with the leaders of Burkina Faso, Djibouti, and Zimbabwe and assessed the draft proposals. In a nutshell, the OAU proposals did not substantially differ from the United States–Rwanda peace plan, except for ascertaining the status of the Badme area before the onset of the conflict: "With regard to the authority which was administering Badme before 12 May 1998 and on the basis of the information at our disposal, we have reached the conclusion that Badme town and its environs were administered by the Ethiopian authorities before 12 May 1998. This conclusion obviously does not prejudge the final status of that area which will be determined at the end of the delimitation and demarcation process." On the basis of this conclusion, the report recommended that pending UN arbitration on ownership, Eritrean forces would withdraw from Badme and its environs, allowing the return of the Ethiopian civilian administration and the deployment of a United Nations–supervised African peacekeeping force. The OAU also recommended that ultimate sovereign jurisdiction over the contested areas be exercised by the legitimate authority once the entire border had been demilitarized and demarcated, a process that would be completed in six months. Finally, the plan asked both parties to address the negative socio-economic impact of the crisis on the civilian population, particularly the displaced and deported people.[21]

During a meeting of the sixteen-nation summit of the OAU Central Organ for Conflict Resolution in mid-December in Ouagadougou, Ethiopia accepted the recommendations, stating that they met its primary concerns. In his submission to the OAU summit, Isaias requested amendments to the core proposals requiring withdrawal from the disputed areas. The summit, however, rejected this request and adopted the proposals, the OAU Peace Proposal Framework Agreement, as the basis for a settlement. In addition to the key provisions in the previous plan, the framework contained new elements: redeployment of forces along all contested border areas supervised by a group of military observers, deployment of human rights monitors in both countries, and creation of a follow-up committee of the two nations to work with the OAU and United Nations on implementation of the framework agreement. Replacing the United States–Rwanda plan, the framework agreement encompassed eleven provisions. Subsequently, the

European Union and the UN Security Council backed the OAU framework and appealed for Eritrean compliance.[22]

In January 1999, Ethiopian foreign minister Seyoum Mesfin told diplomats that the border dispute has reached "a critical turning period of the
eight-month-old crisis" and urged sanctions against Eritrea for frustrating
diplomatic efforts to end the dispute.[23] Blunt language coincided with
massive troop reinforcements along the border and a new round of expulsions. In February 1999, Ethiopia broke both the long lull in war and the
United States–mediated moratorium on air strikes by retaking Badme,
forcing Eritrean withdrawal. Employing fighter-bombers, helicopter gunships, and reconfigured transport aircraft in tactical support of ground
operations, Operation Sunset reversed Eritrea's nine-month-long occupation. Following this decisive victory for Ethiopian forces, Eritrea accepted
in principle the OAU framework agreement.[24]

Phase Three: Enter Special Envoys

The capture of Badme and Eritrean concessions were important victories for
Ethiopia, taking a tremendous load off the government that was increasingly under pressure from domestic critics of its soft line. Yet, as the acrimony over the details of the agreement revealed, the change in the power
balance did not improve the prospects of reaching a cease-fire as a prelude
to implementing the agreement. While the OAU and United Nations
lauded Eritrean acceptance, Ethiopia made it clear that any cease-fire and
subsequent negotiations would depend upon its recovery of all its territory,
whether by military action or by diplomacy. In light of the ensuing stalemate, the mediators had to scramble to broaden the terms of the OAU
framework to make them acceptable to Ethiopia without further alienating
the Eritreans.

The OAU's institutional ownership of the mediation process, in particular the active involvement of the secretariat, had whittled the relevance
of other competing African mediators. With the subsequent appointment
of OAU special envoy Ahmed Ouyahia, the mediation process gained
additional credence and legitimacy. The order created by the pre-emption
of parallel bids in turn led to a sustained OAU mediation effort that could
draw support from external mediators with considerable clout, notably
the United States, the European Union, and the United Nations. As the

mediation process continued, special envoys from these institutions furnished diverse pressures and leverage on the parties.

The United States re-entered the mediation process when President Clinton dispatched former U.S. national security adviser Anthony Lake and an interagency team from the State Department, the National Security Council, and the Department of Defense on missions to Ethiopia and Eritrea. Similarly, UN secretary-general Kofi Annan appointed Mohamed Sahnoun to assist the OAU's efforts. Both Lake and Sahnoun sought to reinvigorate the international presence in the peace process in ways that would supplement the OAU initiative. Between the final phases of the negotiations for the framework agreement and the onset of February hostilities, Lake and Sahnoun traveled to both countries, putting forth numerous proposals consistent with the OAU framework.[25] Rather than moving in with a new initiative, Lake and Sahnoun preferred to complement the OAU's priority for a cease-fire.

With the sticking points to implementation hinging on the withdrawal of troops and questions about the administration of the other disputed areas during the demarcation process, Prime Minister Zenawi of Ethiopia offered a cease-fire in return for an explicit commitment by Eritrea to remove its forces unilaterally from all contested areas. Meeting with Sahnoun in April 1999, he proposed a short time frame for Eritrean withdrawal because "as long as Ethiopian territory remains under Eritrean occupation, it is impossible to discuss a cease-fire and negotiate a resolution to the border conflict. Ethiopia believes that aggression cannot and must not be rewarded."[26] Eritrea, however, rejected this offer, demanding implementation without tampering with the framework agreement: "Adulteration or tampering of the framework agreement would bear no fruit other than throttling the agreement itself and bringing the OAU initiative to a dead end. The OAU should work for the implementation of the framework agreement and not to open the door for another round of fruitless wrangling."

The impasse led to another spate of military confrontations in May and June 1999 as both sides sought to win a strategic advantage before the start of the rainy season in July. In a large-scale battle in May, Ethiopia repulsed an Eritrean advance across the Mereb-Setit sector of the western battlefront. At the same time, as Eritrea made renewed efforts to recapture Badme, Ethiopia retaliated by using its formidable air power. At the end of the skirmishes in June 1999, Eritrea suffered heavy loses, estimated to be at least 30,000 troops.[27] The fighting eased only when the World Bank warned that both countries could not expect new lending and the UN Security Council threatened to impose economic sanctions against them.

In a fresh diplomatic effort in June 1999, the Italian secretary of state for foreign affairs Rino Serri intervened wearing the hats of the EU special envoy to the Horn of Africa and a "friend of both nations." On a visit to both countries, Serri held the carrot of economic assistance in return for a commitment to implement the OAU Framework Agreement. But even with the new external entrant, old local faces reappeared on the mediation scene, bent on parallel initiatives. In June 1999, Uganda, Rwanda, Libya, and Egypt proposed alternative negotiating tracks, but the OAU Mediation Committee in a session in Harare rebuffed these offers and reaffirmed its standing as the official mediator.[28]

The special envoys from the United States, the UN, and the EU converged at Algiers, Algeria, during the OAU summit in July 1999 to attempt a creative revision of the OAU Framework Agreement that would appeal to both sides. As Lake, Sahnoun, and Serri coalesced to exert multilateral pressures on the parties, experts from the OAU, United Nations, and United States worked to clarify and strengthen the technical arrangements of the agreement. As a result, the mediators broadened the agreement by adding a new clause on the modalities for the implementation of the agreement. Under the modalities, both sides agreed to sign a formal cease-fire agreement before the start of redeployment of troops; Eritrea would commit to withdrawing its forces from territory it occupied after May 6, 1998; Ethiopia would pull back its forces from positions taken after February 7, 1999; and Eritrea and Ethiopia would accept OAU military observers, working with the United Nations, to supervise troop redeployment.

Although both sides agreed to the revised modalities after the Algiers summit, wide differences remained over the interpretation. In particular, Ethiopia dismissed Eritrean acceptance as "meaningless," contending that the new OAU proposals lacked guarantees of Asmara's intention to withdraw its forces from all occupied territories.[29] As one diplomat commented after Algiers: "They do not even seem able to agree on what they have agreed to. . . . They are both likely to interpret the fine print of the plan in very different ways." Amid these differences, the OAU mediators, under the leadership of Algeria's Ahmed Ouyahia, launched new shuttle diplomacy to obtain Ethiopian consent to the amended agreement.

Throughout most of August 1999, the mediators tried to narrow the differences over interpretation of the framework and the modalities. These efforts culminated in a third document, the technical arrangements providing a detailed implementation plan of the peace package on the basis of the framework agreement and the modalities.[30] Ethiopia, however, rejected the technical arrangements, questioning the timetable, the details for restoring Ethiopian administration in the disputed areas, the compensation for property, and the details of the proposed demarcation and monitoring missions. In a late October 1999 meeting with the mediators, Zenawi informed them that the technical arrangement contained numerous points that were inconsistent with the OAU Framework Agreement and the modalities. Moreover, he continued to reiterate the Ethiopian position that the technical arrangements failed to guarantee a return to the territorial and administrative status quo that existed before war first broke out in May 1998: "Ethiopia has genuine interest to give peace a chance, but nothing short of the restitution of previous Ethiopian administration in occupied areas is unthinkable [sic]."[31]

By the end of 1999, the OAU and special envoys had broadened the initial agreement but in the direction that was less palatable to the strong party, Ethiopia. Thus the euphoria that had greeted Eritrea's acceptance of the original agreement in February 1999 was dissipated by Ethiopia's recalcitrance. Cumulatively, the diplomatic efforts had engendered an uneasy peace that stopped the fighting during the rainy seasons and allowed both sides to resupply already massive stocks of armaments and raise new forces.

After an eight-month lull, fighting broke out again in February 2000, on the eastern Bure front, near the Eritrean port of Assab. The clashes coincided with a new diplomatic effort to break the stalemate since the release of the technical arrangements. In two weeks of meetings in Asmara and Addis Ababa, Lake, along with Ouyahia, tried to negotiate amendments to the OAU peace plan. In Asmara, they failed to get Eritrea to accept Ethiopian demands that peace talks be contingent on an Eritrean withdrawal from all the occupied territories. Though Eritrea reiterated its acceptance of the OAU peace plan, it rejected any amendments to the technical arrangements.[32]

Meeting the mediators in Addis Ababa, the Ethiopian government requested three amendments to the technical arrangements. First, specific identification of all the areas occupied, by either side, and from which with-drawal should be made. Second, though the technical arrangements spoke of a UN peacekeeping force, the Ethiopians insisted on a much smaller OAU observer mission, arguing that bringing in the United Nations would change the "ownership" of the peace process. Third, Ethiopia demanded that there should be no restrictions on the composition of the civilian administration that would take over from areas vacated by the withdrawing Eritrean forces; in addition, armed militias should be allowed to patrol these areas. These amendments, Ethiopia contended, would allow a virtual return to the status quo that existed prior to May 1998.[33]

Despite the failure of the Lake-Ouyahia mission, the mediators invited the foreign ministers from the two countries for proximity talks in Algiers at the end of March 2000 to fine-tune the technical arrangements and speed up the implementation of the OAU Framework Agreement. After various postponements, the talks began on April 27, 2000, chaired by Ouyahia and attended by Assistant Secretary Rice and, representing the EU, Italy's deputy secretary of state for foreign affairs Maurizio Mellani. But after six days of negotiations, the proximity talks broke down against the backdrop of mutual recriminations. Ethiopian foreign minister Seyoum Mesfin blamed Eritrean representatives for refusing to discuss any substance of the agenda set by the OAU; instead "they wanted Ethiopia first and foremost as precon-dition to sign a ceasefire and framework agreement and modalities."[34]

In early May 2000, the UN Security Council made a last-ditch effort to avert the looming signs of war. The seven-member UN delegation, led by U.S. ambassador Richard Holbrooke, urged both sides "to refrain from resorting to force and further hostilities and to commit immediately, seriously, and without precondition to negotiations." Expressing "in the strongest possible terms the council's support for the OAU peace process," Holbrooke's mission tried to commit both sides to the deal "immediately, seriously, and without preconditions." In two days of back-and-forth talks between Addis Ababa and Asmara, Holbrooke warned Ethiopia and Eritrea that they could face sanctions if either side were to resume hostilities. Unable to persuade the two leaders from the brink of war, the Holbrooke mission gave up on its mediation efforts.[35]

Two days after the collapse of the Holbrooke mission, a ferocious war exploded along the contested border. Prime Minister Zenawi set the tone for the impending conflict: "We shall negotiate while we fight and we shall fight while we negotiate." In a coordinated series of assaults, Ethiopian forces launched what the defense minister billed as a blitzkrieg, starting on the Mereb-Setit western front, followed by Zalambessa on the central front line, and eventually in Bure on the eastern front. In the first four days of war, Ethiopian troops, backed by helicopter gunships and fighter jets, penetrated Eritrean lines, destroying eight divisions of the Eritrean army and cutting main supply lines for the remaining Eritrean troops on the western front. By the end of May 2000, Ethiopian forces had put fourteen of Eritrea's twenty-four divisions out of action, and the remaining ten divisions had suffered heavy losses. In addition, the United Nations estimated that about 750,000 Eritreans fled their homes and farms during the Ethiopian advance, some 60,000 of whom poured across the border into Sudan. On June 2, 2000, Meles announced that the military offensive had achieved its objectives of forcing Eritrea's withdrawal from all pockets of disputed border territory since May 1998 and virtually broken the Eritrean army.[36]

As the mediators scurried back to Algiers for proximity talks in late May 2000, Ethiopia had gained the upper hand on the ground and could use its military advantage to wring additional concessions from the negotiations. In marathon meetings in Algiers, Ouyahia, Lake, and Serri presented "a consolidated and revised" peace proposal to the parties, but they had to negotiate more with the Ethiopians than with the Eritreans. In translating its battlefield victories into diplomatic gains, Ethiopia insisted on continuing to hold on to strategic areas inside Eritrea until international troops were ready to occupy those areas, quibbled over the size of the buffer zone between the rival armies, and demanded international guarantees that Eritrea would not attack again. With Eritrea's bargaining position undermined by the string of battlefield losses, the mediators' compromise cease-fire agreement was more favorable to Ethiopia. Even after Eritrean acceptance of the cease-fire proposal in mid-June 2001, Ethiopian forces bombed a military airstrip on the outskirts of Asmara and sent thousands of reinforcements to the front line to help consolidate the military gains.[37]

The Algiers Peace Accord reaffirmed the parties' acceptance of the OAU Framework Agreement and the modalities for its implementation, and committed them to a fifteen-point cessation of hostilities agreement. Under the cease-fire provisions, the parties agreed to withdraw to positions held before hostilities began in May 1998 and allowed the deployment of a UN force in a fifteen-mile Temporary Security Zone (TSZ) until international arbitrators demarcated the 600-mile border. The TSZ, wide enough to prevent the two sides from shelling each other, would lie inside Eritrean territory. Two weeks after the deployment of the UN peacekeeping mission, Ethiopia was requested to submit redeployment plans for its troops from positions taken after February 6, 1999, that were not under Ethiopian administration before May 6, 1998. After the deployment of UN peacekeepers, Eritrean civilian administration, including police and local militia, would be allowed to function in the TSZ to prepare for the return of the population. The agreement stipulated that the interim deployment of forces would not prejudice the final status of the contested areas, which would be determined at the end of the delimitation and demarcation of the border and, if need be, through an appropriate mechanism of arbitration. The presence of Ethiopian troops in the disputed areas gave Addis Ababa a psychological advantage as the implementation mediation process began. In a major concession to Eritrea, the mediators allowed the implementation to be led by a UN force operating under the auspices of the OAU rather than an exclusively OAU process as Ethiopia had demanded. The OAU and the United Nations committed themselves to guarantee the agreement until the determination of the common border on the basis of colonial treaties and applicable international law. The agreement also empowered the international community to take "appropriate measures" under Chapter VII of the UN Charter in case either side failed to comply with the redeployment plan.[38]

The Algiers Peace Accord was an important first step toward the search for a comprehensive resolution of the conflict, entailing the demarcation of the borders, the resettlement of displaced civilians, and the rehabilitation of both countries. The mediators, particularly Lake and Ouyahia, remained engaged in efforts to find durable peace. In November 2000, with the cease-fire holding, the United Nations dispatched 4,200 UN peacekeepers in the TSZ. In December 2000, after talks in Algiers, Ethiopia and Eritrea signed a new agreement establishing three key bodies: an independent body appointed by the OAU secretary-general to investigate the incidents of May 6, 1998, and any other incident prior to that date that contributed to the war; a neutral Boundary Commission composed of five members with a mandate to delimit and demarcate the border; and a neutral Claims Commission to address the negative socio-economic impact of the crisis on the civilian population, including the impact on those persons who were deported. In April 2002, the Boundary Commission announced its findings that granted most of the disputed territory to Ethiopia, but Badme—to Ethiopia's consternation—went to Eritrea.[39]

CONCLUSIONS AND LESSONS

The entry of mediators in African conflicts is often conceptualized as a neat division of labor whereby structural factors impel disputants to invite meaningful third parties to help in conflict management. This characterization belies the competitive nature of invitation that makes entry a messy and unwieldy process. Internal conflicts exacerbate the problems of entry by increasing the stakes and multiplying the invited parties. Moreover, where there are multiple parties waiting for invitation, there is often a wide gulf between invitation and acceptance that compounds the entry of mediators. The notion of entry as a problem of creating order captures the puzzle of reconciling competitive mediation bids that accrue from invitation with credible mechanisms that combine the parties' acceptance and the mediator's leverage. Interstate conflicts, such as the Ethiopia-Eritrea border war, confront some of these problems, but the problems are less insurmountable where there are a limited number of disputants and where there are strong institutions to confer or deny entry.

1. As a first lesson, order in entry of mediators can be established from the outset by the presence of strong allies of both parties, in this case the United States and Rwanda. Their intervention created a negotiating framework that partially insulated the mediation from competitive interests and marginalized less weighty mediators. Although regional mediators converged around the conflict in the face of the United States–Rwanda intervention, they were not able to dissuade the parties from the parameters of the United States–Rwanda formula that became the benchmark for subsequent agreements.

2. The other significant element of the United States–Rwanda intervention was that once a working formula for a settlement was established, the mediation passed on to the OAU without marking a sharp discontinuity. Once the OAU adopted the initiative, it could draw from its experience of ad hoc mediation committees as a means of owning the conflict.

3. Institutional ownership legitimizes entry, helping to exclude alternative mediators but also expanding the terms of the agreement. The OAU's fact-finding mission that culminated in the Ouagadougou summit gave wider legitimacy to the framework that both parties could not wiggle out of.

In addition, the collective weight furnished by the agreement precluded potential entrants or at least limited their room for maneuver. Even when Eritrea, derisive of the OAU, moved decisively to the Arab world for economic and political support, its allies such as Libya and COMESSA could operate only within the strictures of the OAU framework. An equally significant phase in the role of mediators was the exhaustion of the committee model that the OAU had relied upon since its inception and, in this case, throughout the initial phases of the mediation. Both the heads of state and the interministerial committees were found wanting after the conclusion of the Ouagadougou summit. Although they had succeeded in making the mediation a collective African process, these institutions could not manage the vagaries of shuttle diplomacy that subsequent negotiations entailed. The room was thus open for a more flexible mediation framework within the OAU secretariat that eventually gave way to the OAU's special envoy.

The transition to the OAU special envoy occurred in the context of an uneasy stalemate in the war and intense negotiations not about the basic terms of the agreement, but about clarity and details. With competitive mediators finally marginalized from the conflict, the United States and the European Union could re-enter the mediation to complement the OAU efforts. The OAU's ownership in its exclusionary dimension paved the way for this re-entry; Africans needed to get their act together and establish credible mediation mechanisms before external actors could step in to help. Ownership claims are often exaggerated, but they cannot be underestimated in the context of competitive mediation bids, for ownership confers commitment and promises rewards and sticks.

4. Ownership is a selective mechanism, notably when the institutions for mediation are clearly delineated. Before Libya emerged as the pretentious African hegemon, dictating the rules and foisting claims, the OAU mediation environment was more certain, with key actors tasked with conflict resolution under the umbrella of the summit of heads of state. The Ethiopia-Eritrea conflict threatened this clarity, but it was not entirely obliterated when the OAU Secretariat and the Algerians reasserted their mediation roles. Algeria's mediation was critical because it brought an even-handed regional actor who could be authoritative without being partial, with a solid anchor in the OAU structures without the Libyan political baggage. At the same time, it pre-empted the escalation of the African-Arab dimension of the conflict that had been simmering, with the Ethiopian

accusation that Eritreans were courting Arab countries, once again excluding outside interference.

5. The U.S. re-entry though Special Envoy Lake departed from the initial intervention in several respects. Lake could use his status as former U.S. national security adviser to build on discreet American power in an exercise that required extreme caution and a low profile. He could operate unobtrusively, employing the instruments of suasion and coercion to push the parties to an agreement. Assistant Secretary Rice, on the other hand, in her high-profile diplomacy, had overexposed herself to the parties, perhaps in the quest of a quick agreement to rescue wayward friends. Furthermore, unlike Rice, Lake operated within larger multilateral structures of the United Nations, the European Union, and the parties' prior signatures to the OAU framework.

6. The mediation partnership of the United States, the European Union, and the United Nations marked a momentous phase in the conflict, lending collective leverage to an OAU process that needed more muscle. This partnership was facilitated by the settlement of prior conflicts over mediation ownership, allowing international actors to operate in an environment of relative stability and order. The Lake-Ouyahia-Serri partnership evidenced the coalescence of international and regional action that built on previous agreements, while seeking to overcome the flaws of these agreements. This partnership established a mediation balance that was acceptable to both sides. In addition, the multilateral nature of the mediation dispelled the accusation from both parties that the United States was favoring the other side. When pressure for UN sanctions gathered momentum toward the end of the conflict, the partnership shielded the mediators from accusations of partiality.

The outcome of the Ethiopia-Eritrea conflict partly demonstrates the triumph of stronger parties despite the good intentions of third parties. At critical phases of the negotiations, Eritrea, the weaker party, made most of the concessions. Ethiopia's determination to undo the invasion led to the escalation of the war in February 1999, July 1999, and May 2000, forcing Eritrea to sue for peace and, in the end, accept the terms of an asymmetrical agreement. Yet the successful entry of mediators ultimately helped limit the worst consequences of the conflagration.

8

CONCLUSIONS

The objective of this study has been to investigate the conditions for a successful entry into the mediation of internal conflicts. Confined exclusively to the entry phase of the mediation process, the investigation has been conducted on three theoretical premises. First, an understanding of gaining access to internal conflicts contributes to a better understanding of the mediation process. Second, an investigation on entry facilitates examination of the mediation process from the perspectives of both the intermediaries and the parties. And third, an objective comprehension of entry requires not only an understanding of the motives for such an initiative but also an identification of its underlying problems.

Guided by the aspects of the motives and the underlying problems of entry initiatives, the study focused on responding to the following important questions: Why is mediation entry considered? Why do prospective mediators propose themselves? How do parties choose a particular mediator? When is entry attempted? And finally, How is entry initiated?

Successful entry has been defined as a process through which a prospective mediator gains access to a conflict. Gaining access is dependent on consent or acceptability, involving the self-interests of the parties as well as those of the prospective mediators. Prospective mediators are motivated by their own self-interests in either initiating entry or accepting an invitation to mediate and parties to a conflict are equally motivated by self-interests in accepting mediation and entry of a particular mediator.

WHY MEDIATION IS CONSIDERED

Parties to any conflict are generally confronted with two policy options: dialogue and violence. Which policy a party pursues at a given time depends mainly on how it perceives the conflict's final outcome. It has been pointed out in chapter 1 that when a party perceives a conflict in a relative-gains mindset, its logical policy preference will be a military one. This is a competitive and zero-sum approach that aims at a unilateral solution. On the other hand, when a party perceives a conflict in an absolute-gains mindset, its logical and favorable policy preference will be dialogue. This is a cooperative and joint approach that aims at solutions that admit gains for the other side as well and thus ensures a greater likelihood of durability for the outcome.

The case studies have clearly demonstrated that when conflicts are perceived in competitive terms, the order of policy preference is clear: the military track is preferred over mediated negotiation. In all the case studies the governments perceived the conflicts in a zero-sum context. In Rwanda, for example, the government was resisting two major forces that had an objective of replacing it. On one side, the Tutsi-dominated RPF was challenging the Hutu-dominated power hegemony. On the other hand, the northern Hutu-dominated government was threatened by other Hutu from the southern and the central regions of the country that constituted the internal political opposition. Given that the two forces had an objective of replacing the regime in power, dialogue could not have been the government's preferred policy option. The government's initial preference of the military track was also a natural response to the RPF's military invasion.

The RPF's initial preference of the military track was dictated by the Rwandese political realities. On the one hand, the Hutu-dominated government's policy of excluding the Tutsi from participating in the country's political affairs could obviously not be changed by negotiations. On the other hand, the government's policy of denying hundreds of thousands of Rwandan refugees their right to return to their country could not be reversed by negotiation. The only viable policy to address the exclusionist and the refugee policies was therefore the military option.

In Burundi the Tutsi-dominated government's policy of excluding the majority Hutu has persistently been based on the Tutsi myths of their ethnic superiority and the notion of being threatened by the Hutu numerical strength. Set in zero-sum terms, the government's perceived solution to the conflict has been a total Tutsi dominance in all spheres of the country's public life. The government's policy preference in response to any challenge to the Tutsi political dominance has constantly been violence. The Hutus' violent anti-Tutsi reaction to this oppression has always been the logical response to the Tutsi-dominated government's violent offensive.

In Congo-Brazzaville, a living case of the security dilemma began from the moment that a multiparty system was introduced. Ethnic groups were no longer able to find security within the single-party bargaining and were thrown into open competition with each other, a situation reaffirmed by the spoils system firing and hiring after the first election. Thereafter neighborhoods began to look warily at former neighbors of different ethnic identity, starting a spiral of hostility that ended in brutal savagery. Political colleagues of the groups' political leaders felt immediately that they needed mediation to break the relative-gains unilateralist perceptions that animated the conflict.

In Liberia, Samuel Doe's growing paranoia after the 1985 elections, proven by the Quiwonkpa coup attempt and the signs of general restiveness following the ensuing ethnic repression to be well founded, was not open to any sense of shared or absolute gains. Doe was out to destroy his opponents and they were thus trained that it was necessary to destroy him. Thus suspicion not only called for mediation but also brought all its efforts to naught, as each side demanded the defeat of the other before any negotiations could take place. In addition to all the other lessons it illustrates, the Liberian situation shows clearly that a willingness to negotiate must precede effective mediation or else its absence will destroy the mediation attempts.

In Africa's Horn, the growing feeling that "it's us or them" rose after Eritrean independence to destroy the "friendly divorce" spirit that reigned in the early 1990s. Each step in the widening separation between the brother republics both derived from and contributed to mutual relative-gains attitudes. Relations ratcheted away from brotherly harmony into zero-sum perception and competitive effort to impose unilateral solutions. The uncertain boundary provided the occasion for explosion and the need for mediation.

In the Sudan, the government's perception of the country's national identity as characteristically Arab and Muslim has set the conflict on a confrontational and competitive course whereby the initial preference of violence for both parties became inevitable. From the government's point of view this meant that if the non-Arabs and non-Muslims could not be convinced to share the government's perception peacefully they had to be forced militarily to accept it.

At the same time, the case studies reveal that a party's policy preference is not exclusively a function of its own perception but also that of its opponent.

The insurgencies in Rwanda, Burundi, Sudan, and Liberia were actually forced by the governments to adopt the military track after the doors of political settlement were completely closed. It has been proposed in chapter 2 that the RPF's objective in the Rwandan conflict was a compromise political settlement in spite of the fact that it was the one that had initiated the military confrontation. This was in line with the movement's political objectives spelled out in its eight-point program. But a political settlement was initially impossible given the government's belligerent position. The RPF's initial military approach was thus dictated by the government's behavior. It was intended to serve a short-term objective: to force the government to the negotiating table.

In Burundi, the Hutu-dominated groups would have preferred a political settlement that had a genuine commitment of opening up the doors of all the national institutions that could guarantee the participation of all the Burundians irrespective of their ethnic, regional, religious, or gender differences. This desire was demonstrated by their participation in the political reforms that culminated in the June 1993 elections that brought, for the first time in the country's tumultuous history, a democratically elected and the first Hutu president to power. The sad events of October 21, 1993, forced the Hutu-dominated groups to adopt the military approach, not as the most preferred policy option but as the only viable policy option they had.

In Liberia, Doe's methods of winning election showed the opposition that peaceful power sharing and transitions to democracy were a sham. Interestingly, the shift from cooperative attempts to military attempts also involved a shift in opposition elites, from opposition party politicians to disgruntled associates of Doe from the military (Quiwonkpa) and the administration (Taylor), who had been trained in Doe's own military methods of taking and exercising power. This shift in elites, too, made mediation more difficult.

The abrogation of the 1972 Addis Ababa Agreement was responsible for the resumption of the civil war in the Sudan. After the abrogation, the southern Sudanese were left with no other alternative but to resort to violence. The subsequent Arabization and Islamization of the state reinforced the insurgency's preference for the military approach. As in the Rwandan and in the Burundian cases, the choice of the military track by the SPLM/SPLA in the Sudan was also dictated by the government's bellicose stance.

The other two cases were different, although without shaking the general proposition. In Congo, the security dilemma hit all parties, although the new democratically elected government did follow parliamentary rules when it called new elections after being put in the minority and then tried to lead a democratic electoral campaign. In the Horn, the conflict was an interstate war consummating a national liberation struggle for independence, and it is hard to say who began it, who was government, and who was opposition. In both cases, the spiral of relative-gains thinking caught up both sides in its whirlwind.

It was proposed in chapter 1 that in an already violent conflict, mediation is considered as a policy option specifically when the military track is too costly to pursue. Mediation then becomes a policy choice of last resort. It has been noted that from the parties' self-interests and cost-benefit considerations, mediation is considered as a policy option in one of two ways. The first is when a party abandons the zero-sum perception of the conflict's final outcome. This change of perception draws the party into a search for a joint and compromise solution. Hence, mediation becomes the most preferred policy option.

In Rwanda, although the government had responded positively to the regional intervention, only in 1992 was it seriously committed to the consideration of mediated negotiations with the RPF. The government took this decision when it was absolutely clear that, on the one hand, it could not succeed in defeating the RPF militarily, and on the other, it was too costly to continue to pursue the military track. This action supports the study's first hypothesis that when the costs of pursuing the objectives of the issues in the conflict increase, then mediation is likely to be accepted. In Burundi, the initiators of the October 21, 1993 coup succumbed to mediation when they were faced with a real danger of regional and international isolation. The Mahdi government in the Sudan accepted the 1987–1988 Obasanjo-Deng mediation initiative because it was seriously hurting at the battlefield. This was actually the only mediation initiative that had received perceptual acceptability from the government. That is, it was considered as a serious policy alternative to the military track.

In Liberia, the relations between war costs and peace gains were a bit more complicated. The government—either Doe or Sawyer of the IGNU—was basically uninterested in negotiation or mediation and was soon sidelined; once this happened, the real mediation took place among the various rebel factions. In no case was mediation the actually preferred policy, any more than it was for either combatant in the Horn. In Congo-Brazzaville, mediation became the preferred policy of the government when the rebellion began to bite, but then the government looked about for a preferred mediator. Between one that treated all parties as equal and sought to set up an outcome of reconciliation capped by a free and fair electoral decision and one that arranged a compensation rebel surrender, the government chose the latter, even though it could not produce the compensation in the end.

At another level, mediation is considered not as an alternative but as a complement to the military track. In this situation mediation becomes a short-term measure, particularly when the military track seems to be in trouble. This means that a party that embraces this expedient acceptability of mediation operates in a dual policy approach within an unchanged competitive mindset. This explains the Rwandan government's ready acceptance of the regional intervention. The acceptance had nothing to do with a real commitment to a compromise solution. It was intended to attract sympathy and external assistance. Buyoya's expedient acceptance of the regional mediation in mid-1998 was a typical example of the application of the dual-policy approach. It took two years of regional pressure, including a sanctions regime, to move Buyoya to accept the regional initiative. Even after accepting the regional mediation he continued the military track and his own internal political settlement program. Arusha then became a platform for public relations, endorsement of the Internal Partnership program, and lifting of the sanctions.

In the Sudan the acceptance of the 1989 Carter initiative, the 1990 Cohen initiative, the 1991/1993 Abuja initiative, and the 1993 IGAD initiative by the government were all expedient. Francis Deng captures the mood in which these initiatives had been accepted:

> A recurring pattern has been for the country's contending factions to approach mediated talks more as a public relations exercise than a genuine attempt to reach a settlement. None of the elements involved wants to be perceived as a warmonger not interested in peace. So, whenever a third party suggests mediation, the initial response is nearly always positive. But when the talks start, it soon becomes obvious that the positions of the parties are far apart and they have no intention of compromising.[1]

The Carter mediation was initiated immediately following the June 30, 1989, coup that brought al-Bashir's regime to power. The coup took place on the eve of abrogating the Islamic shari'a laws by the Mahdi government and at a time when a direct internal political settlement seemed imminent. The coup was engineered as a way to thwart these positive developments. It did not make sense for a government that had undermined such policies to immediately adopt a compromise stance itself. Its acceptance of the Carter mediation was therefore expedient because it was intended to demonstrate that the new regime was committed to a compromise settlement. It was within the same spirit that the Cohen mediation was accepted.

The government's invitation of the Abuja initiative also served a public relations function. The Abuja talks took place at a time when Africa and its continental organization (the Organization of African Unity) were placing internal conflicts at the center of their urgent priorities specifically because of the conflicts' impact on regional peace and security. Being the oldest conflict in the continent, the Sudanese government was aware that if it did not display peace overtures it would have been considered a pariah state. The government's uncompromising stance throughout the Abuja Process attests to this. The Sudanese government also invited the IGAD's mediation out of expediency. This decision was dictated by the difficulties associated with the sustenance of the military track and serious internal opposition to the regime, as well as regional and international isolation.

As suggested above, in Liberia, the rebel parties proceeded on both tracks until one gradually became less promising and more costly, making the other—the mediation—look more attractive. Although it is still not clear what tipped the balance at Abuja in August 1996 and 1997, the lesser parties were worn out and the undisclosed deal that Abacha offered Taylor looked better than continuing to fight. (Taylor was, of course, right in his calculation: he won the subsequent elections by threatening to return to war if he did not.)

In Congo, fighting became costly and unproductive for the rebels and Sassou offered them a life of peace and plenty in the army; he never abandoned his military option but he brought the rebel troops away from theirs. (When the plenty did not materialize, they became restive again, but it was too late: They had already handed in their arms.)

Finally, in the Horn, the parties were still not reconciled two years after the mediated agreement; they were constrained from renewing the military option only by exhaustion and by the international community—notably the UN Mission in Eritrea and Ethiopia—but they remained on a war footing. Under intense international pressure and heavy internal pressure from the cost of the repeated rounds of war, Ethiopia and Eritrea chose peace, but every step in that choice was fought diplomatically as it had been fought militarily, with an unchanged competitive mindset. One clear pattern emerging from these case studies is that the insurgency's perception of the nature of the conflict, and its choice of policy option, are conditioned by the state's internal behavior. It is the government's policies toward some sections of the society that lead to an emergence of an insurgency; it is also the government's policies that determine an insurgency's policy choice toward a conflict. While an insurgency's initial policy priority would be dialogue, this would work only when the government's policies create an appropriate environment for dialogue to take place.[2] It is usually because of the lack of a conducive environment for dialogue that violent internal conflicts emerge.

While it is the insurgency that generally resorts to violence first, this policy option is dictated by the government's behavior. For the insurgency, violence becomes not a preferred policy option but the only option. Even when the insurgency perceives a conflict in a win-win mindset it cannot get a compromise outcome without the cooperation of the government. As the adage goes, it takes two to tango. Without this cooperation, the insurgency's resort to violence becomes a short-term approach whose major objective is to win the government's cooperation. As in a competitive mindset where mediation becomes not an alternative but a complement to the military track, violence also becomes a complement to dialogue in a cooperative mindset.[3] Hence, the phenomenon of a dual policy approach applies to both the competitive and cooperative perceptions.

An important aspect of accepting mediation that was addressed in chapter 1 is that of asymmetry. The study has challenged the assumption that mediation is likely to be accepted by the weaker party rather than the stronger one on the basis of absolute, rather than relative, cost-benefit considerations. It has been argued that acceptance of mediation is a question of the parties' individual interests more than just a matter of power relationship. This means that irrespective of the parties' power balance in a conflict they will accept entry of mediators as long as the entry serves their particular interests concerned in their own cost-benefit terms. The acceptance of the early regional mediation by the government in Rwanda and the Abuja initiative by the Sudanese government confirms this proposition. These mediation initiatives were accepted regardless of the governments' relative military strength during those particular moments. This observation also confirms the idea of the mutually hurting stalemate as a component of ripeness for mediation entry—not as a perception of symmetry or asymmetry but as an internal calculation of costly impasse on either—and hence both—sides.

WHY MEDIATORS PROPOSE THEMSELVES

It was suggested in chapter 1 that mediators are motivated by self-interests. This is true whether mediators propose themselves or are proposed by others—third parties or parties to the conflict. This is also true whether the mediator is a state (of whatever size and strength), an intergovernmental organization, an NGO, or an individual person.

States are motivated by the conflicts' impact on their national interests defined in cost-benefit terms in relation to their objectives and to their self-preservation as entities. The degree of a conflict's impact on a state's national interest is a function of the state's moral principles, its physical proximity to the conflict, and its close bilateral relations, all elements in a state's interests as objectives. Intergovernmental organizations are motivated by their institutional objectives. Political and security organizations are driven by their peace and security objectives while regional integrative groups are motivated by their socio-economic objectives. This is equally true with NGOs and individual persons. But interests also—and most basically—refer to the essential element for any organizational entity, their self-preservation, system maintenance, and self-defense. Not only are states'—that is, governments'—considerations of self-preservation and vital interests involved but also regional organizations' concerns for their own existence and functioning and NGOs' attention to their own viability.

The Rwandan case provides an interesting and clear example of the association between self-interests and a motivation to intervene in an internal conflict. The strong historical ties and bilateral relations between France, Belgium, Zaire, and the Habyarimana regime explain the three countries' early response to the conflict. The countries' motivation was so strong that their initial response was to intervene militarily rather than to mediate. When the initial anxiety following the RPF's unexpected invasion subsided, the three countries were actively involved in a diplomatic offensive to encourage the regional leaders to intervene. Zaire's subsequent mediating role not only was motivated by Mobutu's close relationship with

Habyarimana but was also intended to revive Mobutu's declining personal status in the region.

The early concern and the active involvement of the three countries provides clear support for the study's hypothesis number three that a third party is likely to try to intervene or accept an invitation to mediate when the conflict threatens its interests. The early response of the three countries, which were closely related to Rwanda, could be contrasted with the conspicuous delay of the other major powers to get involved in the Rwandan conflict. Apart from other factors, the issue of how close in terms of national interest the other major powers were to Rwanda was a major factor in explaining their lack of urgency regarding getting involved in the conflict.

Self-interest accounted for the early regional response in Rwanda. Security interests motivated the region. Habyarimana's perception of the conflict as an interstate conflict raised the possibility of an interstate war between Rwanda and Uganda. The regional early response had an objective of preventing the internationalization of the conflict as it was already demonstrated by the French and Belgian response. The OAU's active involvement in Rwanda was motivated by the objective of reasserting its responsibility of attending to the continent's political problems. This was in line with the organization's redefinition of its vision and mission particularly in dealing with the destructive African conflicts.

The UN Security Council response to the Rwandan conflict was lukewarm. This was surprising for an international organization responsible for world peace and security not to have responded directly and immediately to such a dangerous crisis. Two major factors contributed to the unenthusiastic response. One, the Security Council members seemed to have been satisfied with the regional and the OAU early response. Instead of being involved actively and directly, the organization hid behind the regional and the OAU efforts. And two, together with some of the Security Council members who are really the UN decision makers, the United Nations' hands were, at that particular time, tied up in other hot spots. These included the Gulf, Yugoslavia, Angola, and Somalia. The UN Security Council's tepid handling of the Rwanda conflict put the organization and its key members at odds with the RPF government for the next decade.

The direct association between self-interest and the mediators' motivation to intervene has also been amply demonstrated by the Burundi case. As in Rwanda, the regional and the OAU response to the Burundi conflict was immediate and firmer. The prompt regional intervention was motivated by the three most important issues of African current political agenda: regional security, discouraging the continued role of the military in African politics, and encouraging democratic rule in Africa.

The UN's active involvement in Burundi could as well be explained by the organization's peace and security objectives. For the United Nations, Burundi was an opportune moment for damage control. The swift response was motivated by the organization's unsatisfactory handling of the Rwandan and the Somali conflicts. The Carter Center's involvement in Burundi was motivated by President Carter's moral values. Perceiving the Burundi conflict in a regional context, the center was more concerned with the conflict's humanitarian impact on the Great Lakes Region.

As in the Rwandan and the Burundi conflicts the OAU's involvement in the Sudanese conflict was motivated by the organization's peace and security objectives. Being the regional organization responsible for dealing with the continent's political problems, the Sudanese membership to the organization provided the legitimacy for the OAU's involvement. Humanitarian concerns and personal prestige were instrumental in motivating the involvement of Obasanjo, Deng, and Carter. The U.S. strategic interests in the Horn of Africa and beyond accounted for Cohen's initiative.

Nigeria's involvement in the Sudanese conflict was prestigious to the nation as an African major power and to Babangida's leadership. The IGAD's involvement in the Sudan resembles that of the Great Lakes Region's involvement in Rwanda and Burundi. It has been motivated by regional security concerns and the conflict's spillover effects on the members' individual political stability.

In Liberia, the IFMC and the Carter Center applied for the job of mediator in consonance with their interests defined as purpose. The IFMC kept coming back after being rebuffed for lack of capacity. Interestingly, the Carter Center reduced its activities after IGNU's and ECOWAS's disapproval of Carter's frank assessment and the subsequent ransacking of his center's regional headquarters; self-preservation of the mission meant operating thereafter at a more discreet level. The United States withdrew its mediation efforts after political authorities in Washington decided that post–Cold War Liberia no longer held any interest for the United States and the United States has no past or present responsibility for conditions in the country, a rather remarkable judgment but one clearly rooted in a (mis)perception of interest. ECOWAS offered and then imposed its services, deciding that conditions in Liberia were in its interest, but then tempered its mediation to keep harmony in the ECOWAS family, at the cost of some effectiveness.

In the Horn of Africa, the United States jumped in early, perceiving relations between two countries close to the Middle East to be very much in its interest. The OAU jumped in too, hoping for a positive mediation experience to buttress its claims of usefulness and thereby strengthen an organization that badly needed some accomplishments to show for its existence. Rwanda, as the OAU president at the time, made a useful contribution in helping to establish the formula for a settlement if there ever was to be one, and Algeria's President Bouteflika took on the task of completing the agreement as a personal assignment and part of his legitimization as a world leader. Mediation served the interests of the various candidates by reinforcing their images and promoting their purposes.

The same characteristics were present in Congo. Some early mediators—Senegalese and Central African leaders and the Francophonie—gently withdrew from mediation: the conflict put too much strain on their friendships and taxed their capabilities too much to be in their interest to pursue. Two potential mediators remained, one motivated and one reluctant. The Carter Center was interested in involvement to test its International Negotiation Network and strengthen its reputation consistent with its purposes. Ultimately, it lacked the capacity and had to cede its place to Gabonese President Bongo, Sassou's son-in-law, whose entry served mainly family interests.

None of this indicates which interests will be predominant and which will support mediation versus abstention. As in many social actions, a post hoc understanding of motivations is easier to produce than a prediction before the fact. Yet many of the mediations were understandable and even predictable when approached from the mediators' interests as a starting point. Given the various players' purposes and organizational concerns as various corporate entities, their attempt to enter into mediation could have been expected. Thereafter, there were a few surprises, of course, since human agencies still have the possibility of interpreting their own interests. The United States' withdrawal from mediation in Liberia is one surprise, as testified to by the debate within the administration. The Carter Center's involvement in a French-speaking country with no past experience with the former president is another (Burundi was approached through English-speaking Africa), until the center's interest in responding to a call addressed to it rather than to the president is noted.

How Parties Choose a Particular Mediator

It was proposed in chapter 1 that parties are motivated by self-interest in choosing a particular mediator. Concomitant with the cost-benefit calculations, a party chooses or accepts a particular mediator according to the role it expects the mediator to play in line with the party's interests. A state may be preferred if the party's objective of accepting mediation is to get a compromise solution. This preference is due to the resources a state commands and its ability to guarantee the compromise agreement. If the mediator were expected to play an empowering, legitimizing, or internationalizing role, an international organization would be the appropriate choice. If the objective of accepting mediation is just to buy time with no intentions of a compromise solution, then an individual person or an NGO would be an appropriate choice because they are generally not restricted by the deadlines that constrain states or international organizations.

However, determining a mediator is not always a matter of free choice for the parties to the conflict. Two terms used in describing this situation are "unavoidable mediator" and "patrons-preferred mediator."

An unavoidable mediator is one whose mediation initiative is difficult for the parties to reject. This could be a friendly country, or an organization where the parties are a member, or a regional and international body that has a pre-authorized agreement for such an intervention. Another example of an unavoidable mediator is one whose intervention is made on the pretext of humanitarian concerns. A patrons-preferred mediator is the one whose mediating role satisfies the interests not only of the parties but also of their patrons.

In Rwanda, the initial entry of the region and Mobutu as mediators was an example of the unavoidable mediation. The parties had no choice; they were presented with a fait accompli. The region was determined to intervene with or without the parties' consent. Regional entry was not resisted, however, because it served the parties' self-interests as well. This assessment supports the study's hypothesis number five that the more the parties believe that a potential mediator will help them attain their objectives, the more are the chances that his entry initiative will be accepted. The government wanted to use the regional intervention as a vehicle through which it could demonstrate that the conflict was between Rwanda and Uganda. If the region bought into this perception, the government hoped that Uganda would be forced to stop its support to the RPF. This would isolate the RPF from its logistical lifeline.

Mobutu's mediating role was not resisted by the government because of the close relationship between Mobutu and Habyarimana and by the RPF because it wanted to go along with the region's choice. The government believed that Mobutu's mediation would work in its favor. For the RPF the regional intervention provided international recognition and legitimization. It was also intended to provide world sympathy and support. It was as well a tactical move to prevent Mobutu's destructive potential regarding the regional peace efforts if he was not accepted as mediator.

At the later stage of the conflict, when the government failed to convince the region that the conflict was between Rwanda and Uganda, it started to withdraw its cooperation with the regional initiative and started searching for other alternatives. This led to the expansion of the regional initiative's support system from the regional to the international level. The expansion involved the active involvement of the United States and France and culminated in the Paris meetings that decided on the continuation of the regional mediation under Tanzania's facilitation.

The decision was a compromise on the parties' disagreement on the mediator and the venue. The government had wanted the negotiations to be held in Paris under the French mediation. The RPF had insisted on holding the negotiations in Africa under African mediation. The government's preference for the French mediation was based on the fact that the close bilateral relations between the two countries would have served its interests better than would the regional mediation. On its part, the RPF believed that its interests would be served better through the regional rather than the French mediation.

As in Rwanda, the regional and the OAU's involvement in Burundi was also unavoidable entry. However, unlike in Rwanda, the regional mediation did not serve the interests of both parties. The mediation was favorable to the Hutu groups because it guaranteed that they shared power with the Tutsi. It was, however, not favorable to the Tutsi groups because it undermined their monopoly of power. It was therefore supported by the Hutu groups and was vehemently resisted by the Tutsi groups.

Unlike the regional/OAU initiative, the UN mediation was favorable to and supported by both parties although it was also unavoidable. Whereas the Tutsi groups wanted to use the UN intervention to reverse the results of the June 1993 elections, the Hutu groups hoped to use the UN intervention to reaffirm the election results. Whereas the Hutu groups had hoped that the UN intervention would lead to the restoration of the toppled democratically elected government, the Tutsi groups had hoped that the UN mediation would derail the Hutu political victory and shift the power balance in its favor. The Tutsi groups seemed to have read the situation correctly because the latter is exactly what finally happened. Unlike the regional/OAU initial objective, which was to restore the democratically elected government to power, the United Nation's objective was to engage all the parties in order to get a compromise settlement. The unavoidable regional intervention in Rwanda and Burundi is a validation of the study's hypothesis number four that the more determined a third party is to intervene, the most likely that it will gain access.

Unlike Rwanda and Burundi, Sudan demonstrated a relative freedom of choice of mediators. In Sudan, only the OAU initiatives (minus the Abuja initiative) could be said to have been unavoidable. Although imposed, they nonetheless served the interests of both parties. Rather than considering them as an infringement to its sovereignty, the government perceived the OAU's interventions as acts that would have worked in its favor, that is, reaffirming its sovereignty. The SPLM/SPLA hoped that the OAU intervention would have provided recognition and legitimation.

The Obasanjo-Deng and the Carter initiatives were readily accepted by the parties when the mediators presented themselves. The Obasanjo-Deng initiative was accepted because both parties were really committed to negotiating a compromise solution. For the government this decision was mainly based on its unfavorable military position at that time. For the SPLM/SPLA, regardless of its relatively military strength then, negotiated settlement was still its preferred policy option. On the other hand, while the SPLM/SPLA accepted the Carter initiative with a real commitment to negotiate in good faith, the government accepted it for public relations purposes. This was equally true with the Cohen, Abuja, and IGAD initiatives, regardless of the fact that they were all the outcome of the government's own invitation.

In Liberia, all the mediators were to some degree "unavoidable," and the parties tried both to refuse and to make the most of the situation. The United States was the (reluctant) patron; neither Doe nor Taylor were much interested in mediation at all, in the beginning, but Doe grew to like the idea if it would save his job or his skin and Taylor accepted it only to the extent that it would lead to the removal of Doe at lesser cost. Each side greeted U.S. mediation in terms of its interest. When the United States withdrew, ECOWAS came in and its mediation, backed by ECOMOG, was unavoidable. With the murder of Doe, the mediation turned to the rebel parties, who accepted it only halfheartedly and with fingers crossed behind their backs, ready to bolt from any agreement at the first opportunity, as their interests dictated. Taylor finally accepted the definitive mediation of Abacha when, in some yet undisclosed way, his interests were served by the agreement and he felt he could win by elections more cheaply and legitimately than by violence.

In the Horn of Africa, unavoidable mediation was produced by the regional organization, the OAU, and by the patron, the United States. Others also appeared, notably Gaddafi, but they were accepted only by the side whose interests they favored. The forces responsible for acceptance were international pressure and exhaustion, forces that shaped the interest of the parties rather than shaping the mediation to fit a fixed sense of interest. In Congo-Brazzaville, Sassou actually invited a number of mediators, the invitation more than the mediation serving his interests by showing his reasonableness and desire for peace. He then accepted the mediation that served his interests by promising a one-sided solution, and the rebels accepted, against the wishes of their leaders, choosing their own very basic interests over politics.

The governments' resistance to the entry of the regional initiative in Burundi and the Horn support the proposition that strong-willed intervenors cannot be prevented from forcing their way into a conflict if they are determined to do so.[4] But both also demonstrated that an unavoidable mediator can be resisted for quite a long time. It took two years and a sanctions regime for the Burundi, Ethiopian, and Eritrean governments to finally accept the regional mediation. These delays demonstrate the validity of the study's hypothesis number one, that the higher the stakes a party attaches to the issues in conflict, the more likely that mediation will be rejected. In a violent conflict such as these, many precious lives were lost within such a long period of resisting mediation. Although the consideration of the mediation phase is beyond the scope of this study, it can safely be anticipated that a serious result of such a forced entry to mediation would be a lack of cooperation from the party that has been resisting the entry of the mediator.

Another aspect related to the choice of a particular mediator raised in chapter 1 is that of partiality. On the basis of cost-benefit calculations, it has been argued that impartiality is not a necessary condition for choosing or accepting a particular mediator. As long as the choice and acceptance of a mediator are related to a mediator's ability to deliver the expected outcome, even a biased mediator could be accepted. This proposition has been evident in all the case studies. Mobutu's mediation in Rwanda had been accepted by the RPF in spite of his closeness to the Habyarimana's regime. In Burundi, despite Buyoya's complaints that Nyerere was a biased mediator, he accepted Nyerere's mediation regardless of the initial resistance. In the eyes of the SPLM/SPLA, Nigeria had all the trappings of favoring the Sudanese government. Still, it did not resist the Abuja initiative.

All the cases show that conflicting parties accept mediation in terms of their interests, reckoned in cost-benefit terms, and often very neatly calculated. However, this conclusion is clearer on how the decision to accept is made than on what that decision will be. It shows that interests are quite malleable, often more malleable than the terms of the mediation, and if mediation is not deemed to be in the parties' interests now, the cost-benefit calculations behind those interests can be altered by such threats, warnings, promises, and predictions—the exercise of power[5]—such as sanctions, pressures, exhaustion, alternative outcomes, and so on. Thus potential mediators, especially unavoidable ones, work first on the parties' sense of interest, if necessary, to have their offers accepted, before they turn to working on the parties to have the substance of the mediation agreed to. The incapacity to wield such exercises of power is what limits the effectiveness of NGO mediators such as the Carter Center and the IFMC. By the same token, the parties can raise their resistance to such exercises of power by stubbornness, inability to "hear" and "feel" pressures, or definition of their interests.

WHEN ENTRY IS ATTEMPTED

A theoretical question related to timing that was posed in chapter 1 was whether timing matters when it comes to initiating entry. At issue is the level of conflict escalation at which entry should be attempted. The cases have demonstrated that the timing of the entry phase depends on the objective of entry, and more specifically on the objective of a compromise settlement versus objectives. In chapter 1, the timing of entry for compromise settlement was discussed under the concepts of *hurting stalemate* and *ripeness.* Entry is a function of ripeness, although the cases show various degrees of hurting for one or both parties. Entry can be attempted at any time, but in the absence of ripeness, the mediation must work to sharpen the parties' perceptions of stalemate before it can achieve acceptance for effective mediation. Otherwise, the intervention serves other purposes. The early regional response to the conflict in Rwanda, for example, served the parties' immediate objectives of attracting sympathy and external assistance for the government and recognition and legitimation of the RPF. The absence of a perception of stalemate by the parties let them use the early mediation for their own ends in the conflict. Fighting and negotiation continued simultaneously until March 1991 when the first cease-fire (the N'sele cease-fire) was agreed upon. "Unripe" entry was also practiced in Burundi with Buyoya's expedient acceptance of the regional mediation in April 1998 for reasons other than a compromise solution. Hence, the entry did not stop him from continuing with the military track and his internal political program.

In Sudan, the Carter mediation was accepted by the government not for a compromise settlement, as it was initiated just a few months following al-Bashir's coup and the beginning of the Islamic radicalization of the state. Though the timing of the initiative was not appropriate for a compromise solution, it helped to portray the new regime as a peace-loving administration. The Abuja initiative was launched when the government was doing fine at both the military and the diplomatic fronts—indeed a bad timing for a compromise settlement. Still, its entry was perfect for the government to display peace overtures when the continent was expressing serious concern about ongoing regional conflicts.

In Congo, Bongo's 1997 mediation was not aimed at compromise: it was aimed to produce leveraged surrender, exchanged for jobs in the army and amnesty for the troops, leaving their leaders out in the cold (and eventually under capital sentence). Yet timing mattered: the tide had begun to turn toward the end of 1999, away from the stalemate of mid-year, and Sassou used Bongo to take advantage of it. In Liberia, although the various diplomatic initiatives were focused on producing compromises of some sort, the ECOMOG military intervention was designed to save a member-state government and so responded to the military crisis, not to any stalemate.

Entry initiatives that had an objective of a compromise settlement were the July 1992 Arusha Peace Process for Rwanda; the January/September 1994 UN mediation in Burundi under Ould-Abdallah; the Carter Center and Francophonie demarches in Congo; repeated U.S., Libyan, and OAU efforts in the Horn; the IFMC, U.S., and various ECOWAS demarches in Liberia; and the 1988–1989 Obasanjo-Deng initiative in Sudan. All these initiatives could be explained by the concepts of hurting stalemate and ripeness for resolution. The timing for all the initiatives was crucial. The Arusha Peace Process for Rwanda began after the parties were seriously committed to a compromise settlement following a two-year period of fierce fighting. The commitment to negotiation came after each party realized that it was less costly to end the conflict through negotiation than continuing with the military track. Their genuine commitment to dialogue enabled them to stop fighting and sign a cease-fire agreement. To a large extent, the cease-fire was respected and held throughout the negotiation until a peace agreement was signed in August 1993.

The UN mediation under Ould-Abdallah in Burundi was initiated at a time when there was not exactly a power vacuum but an environment in which power did not entirely lie in the hands of one ethnic group. Whereas the military was still dominated by the Tutsi groups, political power was supposed to be in the hands of the Hutu groups following their overwhelming victory in the June 1993 elections. This was so, despite the president's assassination during the October 21 coup. The UN mediation was initiated when the army had disowned the October 21 coup. The only way out of this political confusion was through a negotiated settlement. This explains the success of Ould-Abdallah's mediation, the final outcome of which was the power-sharing arrangements of the Convention of Government.

In Congo-Brazzaville, the early demarches, including the Carter Center, the Francophonie, the Central African Republic's Patasse, and Senegal's Niasse, all responded to a mutually hurting stalemate between government and rebels in mid-1999. In the Horn, the various attempts, but most notably the persistent OAU and U.S. efforts to make mediation succeed, responded to fleeting moments of stalemate that the two sides had a hard time acknowledging at the same time. The mediators were looking for and trying to generate ripeness, rather than responding to a clear perception of it. Similarly, in Liberia, the various efforts to enter into mediation tried to seize on the objective evidence of a hurting stalemate to engage the parties and encourage the subjective perception of ripeness. The signs were present that the war was costly and unwinnable for any of the parties, but the recognition of a stalemate only egged the parties into further efforts to break out of it, thereby only producing more evidence of how costly and unwinnable it was.

The Obasanjo-Deng mediation in Sudan was initiated at the peak of the SPLM/SPLA's military successes. This was the only time that the Sudanese government had indicated some serious commitment to a negotiated settlement. The government was pushed to this position following a series of humiliating defeats at the battlefield. The government troops were unable to stop the SPLM/SPLA's advances, and its efforts to solicit enough external logistical support for the war were not paying off. This opportune moment for striking a negotiated deal was hijacked by al-Bashir's coup of June 30, 1989.

These attempts at entry underscore the sometimes short duration of ripeness, for even when perceived the moment often disappeared as the military balance shifted or the parties tried to break the stalemate. Timing is everything, but potential mediators often have to cultivate each party's perception of a ripe moment in order for them to have one to seize. Sometimes it even takes mediation as manipulation for the would-be mediators to actually contribute to the objective evidence of the stalemate so that the parties can become subjectively aware of it.[6] The sanctions against both states in the Horn and Buyoya in Burundi are perhaps too rare examples of mediators' concrete efforts to encourage that perception. Again, the inability of NGOs to do so, as in Congo and Liberia, left their attempts to gain entry completely at the mercy of the parties' own perceptions of how much they were stalemated and how much it hurt. States and movements, like people, can develop pretty obdurate defenses against feeling pain.

How the Entry Process Begins

Entry has been defined as a process between the time mediation is considered and when it is formally endorsed by all the parties and a specific mediator is agreed upon. Against the general assumption that entry is always initiated by mediators and not by the parties to an internal conflict, this study has shown that entry can be initiated by both the mediators and the parties. On the basis of cost-benefit considerations it has been argued that a party's self-interests can be a driving force for it also to take the initiative of considering mediation and inviting a mediator. This position has been supported by the Sudanese's government's invitations of the Cohen, Abuja, and IGAD initiatives and the Congolese government's multiple invitations.

The study has addressed two important challenges relating to the parties' initiation of entry. One is to overcome the perception of weakness arising from taking the initiative to invite for mediation. And the other is to convince the other party and the prospective mediator to accept the invitation. The fundamental question here is why the inviting party would think that the other party and the mediator would accept its invitation. There is no way that the inviting party could be in a position to know beforehand with certainty how the other party will react to its invitation.

However, as far as the reaction of the invited mediator is concerned, the hope of its acceptance is based on the perception that the invitation will be accepted because it is usually not expected. When it is extended it raises a strong temptation for its acceptance. Apart from serving the mediator's own personal interests, the invitation would be considered as an honor and a noble challenge worth taking. Hence, the inviting party would rely more on the mediator to convince the other party to accept mediation and the proposed mediator. The inviting party also banks its hopes on the mediator to overcome the problem of the perception of weakness. The mediator here is expected to play a double role. On one hand he is supposed to convey the invitation for negotiation, and on the other he is required to make it appear that he is the source of the initiative.

In the situation when prospective intermediaries take the initiative, they either propose themselves directly or are proposed by other third parties. The challenge here is to convince the parties to accept the intermediaries and accept mediation. The mediator's hope of being accepted is based first on the perception that parties are rational enough to make a cost-benefit judgment between continuing with the military track and pursuing a compromise solution. And second, the mediator hopes that his initiative will be accepted because it saves the parties from taking such an initiative themselves and suffering the humiliation of being perceived as weak.

One of the means for prospective mediators to ascertain the possibility of being accepted to play the mediating role is consultation. The consultation could be through a direct contact with the parties or through another third party, or could take the form of a problem-solving event. The Woodrow Wilson Center workshop on Sudan, for example, served a consultative problem-solving function that finally opened up the door for a series of mediation attempts.

LESSONS

The study has been an attempt to focus on entry, an important area of the mediation process that has so far not received considerable descriptive and analytical attention. Its major objective was to investigate and explain the environment through which a prospective mediator initiates a mediation process in an internal conflict. The use of more than one case study was intended to facilitate comparison. The case studies varied not only in the nature of the conflicts but also in their respective intermediaries. The characteristic of being internal, largely centralist conflicts was their common denominator, and even the one interstate conflict was the prolongation of an internal—but regionalist—conflict. The comparison has also been within a single case study and across case studies given that more than one actor tried to intervene in each case.

The following are the major and specific findings and conclusions of the study. It may be objected that these conclusions apply only, at best, to entry into mediation in Africa, since that is where the cases came from. However, there appears to be nothing in the foregoing that is specifically African or that can be explained only in African terms. As is often the case (but not always recognized), Africa offers lessons that are of use in understanding the rest of the world. Yet these findings and conclusions must be treated as tentative. Although some of them have received adequate descriptive and analytical attention elsewhere, they still require further theoretical and empirical investigation.

1. Entry is a process of creating order—in the conflict and its definition, in the parties' relations, and in the achievement of an outcome.

2. In initiating entry, both mediators and parties are motivated by self-interests. This is true in the processes of considering mediation, volunteering to mediate, choosing of mediators, and timing of entry.

3. Entry can be initiated by either the prospective mediators or the parties themselves.

4. Mediators with strong interests in particular conflicts will persist in their intervention attempts.

5. Acceptance of mediation is a question of the parties' individual interests more than a matter of power relationship. Regardless of a conflict's structure, parties can accept entry of a mediator provided it helps them attain particular interests. In other words, acceptance of mediation by a party is not always a function of weakness. A party can accept mediation from a point of strength and can reject mediation from a point of weakness.

6. Interests, particularly parties' interests in accepting mediation, are malleable and can be enlarged by pressure, threats, and promises.

7. Impartiality is not a necessary condition for choosing or accepting a specific mediator. As long as the choice and acceptance of a mediator are based on a mediator's ability to help the parties attain their expected outcomes; a biased mediator could also be acceptable.

8. The definition of the nature of the conflict is crucial to entry and mediation. Among the competing definitions held by parties and their allies, the choice of a definition that best corresponds to the changing reality will enable a prospective mediator to use its entry effectively.

9. To achieve entry and mediate compromise, mediators must penetrate—but not necessarily change—the zero-sum, relative gains, and security dilemma mentality of the parties. Though it would provide more stable agreements if change and reconciliation were to occur, third parties can also enter mediation that perceives outcomes satisfying each party's interests rather than joint gains.

10. Invitations for mediation from parties do not necessarily mean that they aim at compromise settlements.

11. Entry timing depends on the objective of the mediation. A mediation that aims at a compromise settlement requires entry timing that corresponds

with the conflict's ripeness for resolution. A mediation that has objectives other than a compromise settlement does not require ripeness.

12. When a conflict is not ripe but mediators' interests indicate an interest in entry, would-be mediators must make real efforts to ripen the conflict by inducing the parties to perceive the hurting stalemate in which they find themselves and the possibility of a way out. Ripening can involve efforts to cultivate both the subjective and the objective components of stalemate.

13. Subsidiarity is a strong but not absolute principle. Most entry in internal conflicts has been from the individual neighborhoods.

14. To achieve entry and begin effective mediation, a party must achieve control of the process, either coordinating or marginalizing competitors. Uncoordinated multiple mediation leads to outbidding and undermines conflict management. Thus entry is an exclusionary as well as an interventionist process.

15. There has been a pronounced dominance of Track One entry. Those who have attempted entry have generally been either states or regional organizations, those who have achieved entry have all been officials, and those who have succeeded in their mediation have all been state actors.

16. Regardless of the form the entry took (states or organizations) the dominant preference has been a collective approach.

NOTES

1. The Problem

1. Janice Gross Stein, ed., *Getting to the Table: The Process of International Prenegotiation* (Baltimore: Johns Hopkins University Press, 1989); I. William Zartman and Maureen Berman, *The Practical Negotiator* (New Haven, Conn.: Yale University Press, 1982).

2. Saadia Touval, "Gaining Entry to Mediation in Communal Strife," and C. R. Mitchell, "External Peacemaking Initiatives and Intranational Conflict," in *The Internationalization of Communal Strife,* ed. Manus I. Midlarsky (New York: Routledge, 1992); C. R. Mitchell, "The Motives for Mediation," and John B. Stephens, "Acceptance of Mediation Initiatives: A Preliminary Framework," in *New Approaches to International Mediation,* ed. C. R. Mitchell and K. Webb (New York: Greenwood Press, 1988); Thomas Princen, *Intermediaries in International Conflict* (Princeton, N.J.: Princeton University Press, 1992); and Stein, ed., *Getting to the Table.*

3. Oran Young, *The Intermediaries* (Princeton, N.J.: Princeton University Press, 1967); Saadia Touval and I. William Zartman, eds., *International Mediation in Theory and Practice* (Boulder, Colo.: Westview, 1985); Jeffrey Z. Rubin, ed., *Dynamics of Third-Party Mediation: Kissinger in the Middle East* (New York: Praeger, 1981); Louis Kriesberg and Stuart J. Thorson, eds., *Timing the De-Escalation of International Conflicts* (New York: Syracuse University Press, 1991); and Jacob Bercovitch, ed., *Resolving International Conflicts: The Theory and Practice of Mediation* (Boulder, Colo.: Lynne Rienner, 1996).

4. Stephens, "Acceptance of Mediation Initiatives," 52.

5. Ronald Fisher, "Prenegotiation Problem-Solving Discussions: Enhancing the Potential for Successful Negotiation," in Stein, ed., *Getting to the Table,* 206.

6. The one element of entry that has been much discussed is that of "ripeness." See I. William Zartman, *Ripe for Resolution: Conflict and Intervention in Africa* (New York: Oxford University Press, 1989); Touval and Zartman, eds., *International Mediation*; Kriesberg and Thorson, eds., *Timing the De-Escalation of International*

Conflicts; Mitchell and Webb, eds., *New Approaches.* Some work has been done on prenegotiation but does not deal directly with the problem or mediation entry; see Stein, ed., *Getting to the Table.*

7. The only exception is Touval, who has specifically dealt with the entry phase in the mediation of both interstate and internal conflicts; see Touval, "Gaining Entry." See also Mitchell, "External Peacemaking Initiatives"; Princen, *Intermediaries in International Conflict;* and Stephens, "Acceptance of Mediation Initiatives."

8. Harold Saunders, "We Need A Larger Theory of Negotiation: The Importance of Prenegotiation Phases," *Negotiation Journal* 1 (July 1985): 250.

9. Stephen John Stedman, "Negotiation and Mediation in Internal Conflict," in *The International Dimensions of Internal Conflicts,* ed. Michael Brown (Cambridge, Mass.: MIT Press, 1996), 363.

10. Stein, ed., *Getting to the Table,* 266.

11. I. William Zartman, "Prenegotiation: Phases and Functions," in Stein, ed., *Getting to the Table,* 6.

12. Stephen John Stedman, "Conflict and Conciliation in Sub-Sahara Africa," in *The International Dimensions of Internal Conflicts,* ed. Michael Brown (Cambridge, Mass.: MIT Press, 1996).

13. Zartman, *Ripe for Resolution;* Francis Deng et al., *Sovereignty as Responsibility* (Washington, D.C.: Brookings Institution Press, 1996).

14. Stephen John Stedman, "Conflict and Conflict Resolution in Africa: A Conceptual Framework," in *Conflict Resolution in Africa,* ed. Francis M. Deng and I. William Zartman (Washington, D.C.: Brookings Institution Press, 1991), 367–399.

15. I. William Zartman, ed., *Elusive Peace: Negotiating an End to Civil Wars* (Washington, D.C.: Brookings Institution Press, 1995); Mitchell, "External Peacemaking," 274.

16. Anthony D. Smith, *National Identity* (London: Penguin, 1991), 5.

17. Ibid.

18. Ann Mosely Lesch, *The Sudan—Contested National Identities* (Bloomington: Indiana University Press, 1998), 5–6; I. William Zartman, "Putting Humpty-Dumpty Together Again," in *The International Spread of Ethnic Conflict,* ed. David A. Lake and Donald Rothchild (Princeton, N.J.: Princeton University Press, 1998). See also the discussion of the "centralist" and "pluralist" models in Rasma Karklins, *Ethnopolitics and Transition to Democracy: The Collapse of the USSR and Latvia* (Washington, D.C.: Woodrow Wilson Center Press, 1994).

19. Lesch, *The Sudan,* 7.

20. Rubin, ed., *Dynamics of Third-Party Mediation,* 5.

21. Zartman, "Prenegotiation," 4.

22. Touval, "Gaining Entry"; I. William Zartman and Sadia Touval, "Mediation: The Role of Third-Party Diplomacy and Informal Peacemaking," in *Resolving Third World Conflict: Challenges for a New Era,* ed. Sheryl J. Brown and Kimber M. Schraub (Washington, D.C.: United States Institute of Peace Press, 1992). On the absence of legal sanctions in accepting mediation, see Stephens, "Acceptance of Mediation Initiatives," 52.

23. Mitchell, "External Peacemaking," 274; Stedman, "Negotiation and Mediation."

24. Ibid.

25. Zartman and Touval, "Mediation: The Role of Third-Party Diplomacy," 239; Touval, "Gaining Entry," 59; and Mitchell, "External Peacemaking," 276.

26. Saadia Touval, *Mediation in the Yugoslav Wars: The Critical Years, 1990–1995* (New York: Palgrave, 2002), 11.

27. Louis Kriesberg, "Varieties of Mediating Activities and Mediators in International Relations," in Bercovitch, ed., *Resolving International Conflicts,* 222.

28. See the report of the Thirteenth Meeting of the International Watch on Zaire, Washington, D.C., May 2, 1997.

29. Oliver Richmond, "Devious Objectives and the Disputants' View of International Mediation: A Theoretical Framework," *Journal of Peace Research* 35, no. 6 (1998): 717.

30. Kriesberg, "Varieties of Mediating Activities," 223.

31. Jacob Bercovitch and Allison Houston, "The Study of International Mediation: Theoretical Issues and Empirical Evidence," in Bercovitch, ed. *Resolving International Conflicts,* 23; F. Edmead, *Analysis and Prediction in International Mediation* (New York: UNITAR, 1971).

32. Bercovitch and Houston, "The Study of International Mediation," 23. See also Zartman and Touval, "Mediation: The Role of Third-Party Diplomacy," 250–51.

33. Stephens, "Acceptance of Mediation Initiatives," 56.

34. Touval, "Gaining Entry," 260.

35. Louis Kriesberg, *Social Conflicts* (Englewood Cliffs, N.J.: Prentice-Hall, 1982).

36. Kjell Skjelsbaek and Gunnar Fermann, "The UN Secretary-General and the Mediation of Internal Disputes," in Bercovitch, ed., *Resolving International Conflicts,* 76.

37. Bercovitch and Houston, "International Mediation," 11–32.

38. Zartman and Touval, "Mediation: Third-Party Diplomacy," 242.

39. Keith Webb, "Morality of Mediation," in *New Approaches to International Mediation,* ed. C. R. Mitchell and Keith Webb (Westport, Conn.: Greenwood Press, 1988), 16.

40. Mitchell, "Motives for Mediation," 29.

41. Peter Carnevale and Sharon Arad, "Bias and Impartiality in International Mediation," in Bercovitch, ed., *Resolving International Conflicts,* 39–53.

42. Mitchell, "Motives for Mediation," 46.

43. Ibid., 47.

44. Touval, "Gaining Entry," 255; Zartman and Touval, "Mediation: Third-Party Diplomacy," 243; Stephens, "Acceptance of Mediation Initiatives," 52–73; Princen, *Intermediaries.*

45. Stephens, "Acceptance of Mediation Initiatives," 52–73.

46. Ibid., 56.

47. Ibid.

48. Mitchell, "Motives for Mediation," 29–30.

49. Princen, *Intermediaries,* 16.

50. Mitchell, "Motives for Mediation," 37; Zartman and Touval, "Mediation: Third-Party Diplomacy," 244; Touval, "Gaining Entry," 261.

51. Mitchell, "Motives for Mediation," 34.

52. Touval, "Gaining Entry," 263.

53. I. William Zartman, "Internationalization of Communal Strife: Temptations and Opportunities of Triangulation," in Midlarsky, ed., *The Internationalization of Communal Strife,* 27.

54. Webb, "Morality of Mediation," 16–17.

55. Zartman, "Communal Strife," 27.

56. Ibid.

57. Mitchell, "Motives for Mediation," 40; Zartman and Touval, "Mediation: Third-Party Diplomacy," 244; Touval, "Gaining Entry," 257.

58. Mitchell, "Motives for Mediation," 42.

59. Ibid., 43.

60. I. William Zartman, "Inter-African Negotiations and State Renewal," in *Africa in World Politics,* ed. John Harbeson and Donald Rothchild (Boulder, Colo.: Westview, 2000), 243.

61. Mitchell, "Motives for Mediation," 31.

62. Touval, "Gaining Entry," 264.

63. On the former, see Hizkias Assefa, "World Council of Churches Mediation and the Sudan Civil War," in Mitchell and Webb, eds., *New Approaches,* 147–167. On the latter, see, Glynne Evans, *Responding to Crises in the African Great Lakes.* Adelphi Paper, no. 311 (New York: Oxford University Press, 1997), 39.

64. Assefa, "World Council," 160.

65. Ibid., 161.

66. Ibid.

67. Hendrik van der Merwe, "South African Initiatives: Contrasting Options in the Mediation Process," in Mitchell and Webb, eds., *New Approaches,* 183.

68. Touval, "Gaining Entry," 265; Marina Ottaway, "Ethiopia and Eritrea," in *Elusive Peace: Negotiating an End to Civil Wars,* ed. I. William Zartman (Washington, D.C.: Brookings Institution Press, 1995).

69. Loraleigh Keashly and Ronald J. Fisher, "A Contingency Perspective on Conflict Interventions: Theoretical and Practical Considerations," in Bercovitch, ed., *Resolving International Conflicts,* 235–58; Fisher, "Prenegotiation Problem-Solving Discussions," 206–238.

70. Fisher, "Prenegotiation Problem-Solving Discussions," 242.

71. Ibid., 210–11.

72. Vivienne Jabri, "The Western Contact Group as Intermediary in the Conflict over Namibia," in Mitchell and Webb, eds., *New Approaches,* 106.

73. Assefa, "World Council," 162.

74. Zartman, *Ripe for Resolution.*

75. Zartman, "Prenegotiation," 10.

76. Touval, "Gaining Entry," 258.

77. Richmond, "Devious Objectives," 707.

78. Sadia Touval, "Why the UN Fails," *Foreign Affairs,* October 1994, 50.

79. Kriesberg, *Social Conflicts,* 274–75.

80. Stephens, "Acceptance of Mediation," 58.

81. Ibid.

82. Touval, "Gaining Entry," 267.

83. Mitchell, "External Peacemaking," 272.

84. Karl W. Deutsch, "External Involvement in Internal War," in *Internal War: Problems and Approaches,* ed. Harry Eckstein (New York: Free Press, 1964), 100–110.

85. Mitchell, "External Peacemaking," 282.

86. Princen, *Intermediaries,* 63.

87. Ibid., 60.

88. Zartman and Touval, "Mediation: Third-Party Diplomacy," 248–49. See also Princen, *Intermediaries,* 61–62.

2. Rwanda, 1990–1992

1. For a detailed description of the origins of the conflict, see Alison Des Forges, *Leave None to Tell the Story: Genocide in Rwanda* (Washington, D.C.: Human Rights Watch, 1999); Gérard Prunier, *The Rwanda Crisis: History of Genocide, 1959–1994* (Kampala: Fountain Publishers, 1995); Catharine Newbury, "Background to Genocide in Rwanda," *Issue* 23, no. 2 (1995), 12–17; René Lemarchand, *Rwanda and Burundi* (New York: Preager, 1970) and idem., "Rwanda: The Rationality of Genocide," *Issue* 23, no. 2 (1995), 8–11; and Dixon Kamukama, *Rwanda Conflict: Its Roots and Regional Implications* (Kampala: Fountain Publishers, 1997).

2. Lemarchand, "The Rationality of Genocide," 9.

3. Kamukama, *Rwanda Conflict,* 42–43.

4. Des Forges, *Leave None to Tell the Story,* 47.

5. Ibid., 48; Prunier, *The Rwanda Crisis,* 74.

6. Prunier, *The Rwanda Crisis,* 91; Newbury, "Background to Genocide,"13.

7. Cyrus Reed, "Exile, Reform, and the Rise of the Rwanda Patriotic Front," *Journal of Modern African Studies* 34, no. 3 (1996): 487; Prunier, *The Rwanda Crisis,* 100.

8. For a detailed account of the launching of the war and its initial setbacks, see Prunier, *The Rwanda Crisis,* chapter 3.

9. Ibid., 96.

10. Reed, "Exile," 485.

11. Prunier, *The Rwanda Crisis,* 153.

12. Ibid., 152–53.

13. For an elaborate account of Uganda-RPF relations, see Prunier, *The Rwanda Crisis,* chapters 2 and 3; Kamukama, *Rwanda Conflict,* chapters 7 and 8; and Reed, "Exile."

14. Prunier, *The Rwanda Crisis,* 75.

15. Ibid.

16. Prunier, *The Rwanda Crisis,* 102–103; also Daniel Bourmaud, "France in Africa: African Politics and French Foreign Policy," *Issue* 23, no. 2 (1995).

17. Prunier, *The Rwanda Crisis,* 103–104.

18. Ibid., 122.

19. Christopher Clapham, "Rwanda: The Perils of Peacemaking," *Journal of Peace Research* 35, no. 2 (1998): 201.

20. Interview with Hutu political exiles, Dar-es-Salaam, August 1997, and Arusha, January 1998.

21. Saadia Touval and I. William Zartman, "International Mediation in the Post–Cold War Era," in *Turbulent Peace: The Challenges of Managing International Conflict*, ed. Chester A. Crocker, Fen Osler Hapson, and Pamela Aall, (Washington, D.C.: United States Institute of Peace Press, 2000).

22. Clapham, "Rwanda: The Perils of Peacemaking," 200.

23. This account and that which follows is based on interviews with officials of Tanzania's Ministry of Foreign Affairs, Dar-es-Salaam, August–September 1997, and with officials in the OAU Secretariat, Addis Ababa, August 1998.

24. "Declaration on Rwandese Refugees Problem," Dar-es-Salaam, February 19, 1991.

25. Confidential interview.

26. "Cease-Fire Agreement between the Government of the Republic of Rwanda and the Rwanda Patriotic Front," N'sele, Zaire, March 29, 1991.

27. Bruce D. Jones, *Peacemaking in Rwanda: The Dynamics of Failure* (Boulder, Colo.: Lynne Rienner, 2001); Clapham, "Rwanda: The Perils of Peacemaking," 201.

28. Prunier, *The Rwanda Crisis,* 149–150.

29. Jones, *Peacemaking in Rwanda.*

30. Herbert Weiss, "Zaire: Collapsed Society, Surviving State, Future Polity," in *Collapsed States: The Disintegration and Restoration of Legitimate Authority,* ed. I. William Zartman (Boulder, Colo.: Lynne Rienner, 1995).

31. Saadia Touval, "Gaining Entry to Mediation in Communal Strife," in *The Internationalization of Communal Strife,* ed. Manus I. Midlarsky (New York: Routledge, 1992), 270.

32. Prunier, *The Rwanda Crisis,* 159.

33. Ibid., 170–78.

34. I. William Zartman and Johanes Aurik, "Power Strategies in De-escalation," in *Timing the De-Escalation of International Conflicts,* ed. Louis Kriesberg and Stuart Thorson (Syracuse, N.Y.: Syracuse University Press, 1991).

3. Burundi, 1993–1998

1. For a detailed description and analysis of the origins of the conflict, see Lemarchand, *Rwanda and Burundi;* and idem., *Burundi: Ethnic Conflict and Genocide* (Washington, D.C.: Woodrow Wilson Center Press, 1996).

2. For detailed coverage of the events that led to the massacres, see Lemarchand, *Burundi,* 118–127.

3. Evans, *Responding to Crises,* 25. See also Stephen R. Weissman, *Preventing Genocide in Burundi: Lessons from International Diplomacy.* Peaceworks, no. 22 (Washington, D.C.: United States Institute of Peace, 1998), 6.

4. The commission was also mandated to investigate the 1988 Ntega-Marangara massacres.

5. Lemarchand, *Burundi,* 134.

6. René Lemarchand, "Political Instability in Africa: The Case of Rwanda and Burundi," *Civilisations* 16, no. 3 (1966): 4.

7. I. William Zartman, ed., *Governance as Conflict Management: Politics and Violence in West Africa* (Washington, D.C.: Brookings Institution Press, 1997), 2.

8. Lemarchand, *Burundi,* 178.

9. Leonce Ndikumana, "Institutional Failure and Ethnic Conflict in Burundi," *African Studies Review* 41, no. 1 (April 1998): 42.

10. Lemarchand, *Burundi,* 182.

11. Evans, *Responding to Crises,* 27; Ndikumana, "Institutional Failure," 30; Leonce Ndarubagiye, *Burundi: The Origins of the Hutu-Tutsi Conflict* (Nairobi: n.p., 1995).

12. "The Resolution of the Burundi Conflict: The Views of FRODEBU Party" (paper presented at the workshop on "The Experience of Individual and Institutional Mediators in African Conflicts," Arusha, Tanzania, January 21–23, 1998), 3. See also Ndarubagiye, *Burundi.*

13. René Lemarchand, "Genocide in the Great Lakes: Which Genocide? Whose Genocide?" *African Studies Review* 42, no. 1 (April 1998): 10.

14. Ahmedou Ould-Abdallah, *Burundi on the Brink, 1993–1995: A UN Special Envoy Reflects on Preventive Diplomacy* (Washington, D.C.: United States Institute of Peace Press, 2000), 84–89, 126–129.

15. Ibid.

16. "Cairo Declaration on the Great Lakes Region," November 29, 1995.

17. "Tunis Declaration on the Great Lakes Region," March 18, 1996.

18. Mohamed Sahnoun, *Somalia: The Missed Opportunities* (Washington, D.C.: United States Institute of Peace Press, 1994).

19. Ould-Abdallah felt that military intervention was inappropriate for Burundi's problems; see Ould-Abdallah, *Burundi on the Brink,* 99–100, 120–126.

20. Evans, *Responding to Crises,* 52.

21. United Nations, Report of the Secretary-General on the Situation in Burundi, UN Doc. S/1996/116 (February 15, 1996), 1.

22. Evans, *Responding to Crises,* 58.

23. Mohammed O. Maundi, "Regional Mechanisms for Conflict Resolution" (paper presented at the Eighth International Conference on Peace and Security in Southern Africa, Arusha, Tanzania, August 22–24, 1994), 12–14; Weissman, *Preventing Genocide in Burundi,* 11–12; Touval, "Why the UN Fails," 44–57.

24. Weissman, *Preventing Genocide in Burundi,* 12.

25. Ould-Abdallah, *Burundi on the Brink,* 71–84.

26. "Joint Communiqué of the Second Arusha Regional Summit on Burundi," Arusha, Tanzania, July 31, 1996.

27. Weissman, *Preventing Genocide in Burundi,* 25–26.

4. Congo-Brazzaville, 1993–1999

1. For general background on the Republic of the Congo, see René Gauze, *The Politics of Congo-Brazzaville,* trans. Richard Adloff and Virginia Thompson (Stanford, Calif.: Hoover Institution Press, 1973); Marcel Soret, *Histoire du Congo: Capitale Brazzaville* (Paris: Berger-Levrault, 1978); John F. Clark, "Congo: Transition and Struggle to Consolidate," in *Political Reform in Francophone Africa,* ed. John Clark and David Gardinier (Boulder, Colo.: Westview, 1997). For fuller details on the first two rounds of the conflict, see I. William Zartman and Katharina R. Vogeli, "Opportunities Seized, Opportunities Lost: Conflict, Coup, and Collapse in Congo-Brazzaville," in *Opportunities Missed, Opportunities Seized: Preventive Diplomacy in the Post–Cold War World,* ed. Bruce Jentleson (Lanham, Md.: Rowman & Littlefield, 1999).

2. Electoral figures are from Clark, "Congo: Transition and the Struggle to Consolidate."

3. Fuller details of the mediations are available in Zartman and Vogeli, "Opportunities Seized, Opportunities Lost."

4. Touval and Zartman, "International Mediation in the Post–Cold War Era."

5. For an evaluation of Bongo's and Sahnoun's roles, see Zartman and Vogeli, "Opportunities Seized, Opportunities Lost," 286–288.

6. Françoise Soudan, "Congo-Brazza: Les vraies questions," *Jeune Afrique,* no. 1915 (September 17, 1997), 13.

7. Sources for this round are the experience of the author in connection with the Carter Center mediation.

8. Françoise Soudan, "La paix des braves," *Jeune Afrique,* no. 2035 (January 11, 2000), 8–10.

9. Interviews with members of the Congolese delegation to the State Department, Washington, D.C., July 2000.

10. The purpose of the Congolese mission to Washington in the summer of 2000 was to plead for financial aid to pay off the surrendering militiamen, despite the major revenues Congo gains from its oil sales.

5. Liberia, 1989–1996

1. See, for example, Clement Adibe, "The Liberian Conflict and ECOWAS-UN Partnership," *Third World Quarterly* 18, no. 3 (1997): 417–488; Herbert Howe, "Lessons of Liberia: ECOMOG and Regional Peacekeeping," in *Nationalism and Ethnic Conflict,* ed. Michael E. Brown et al. (Cambridge, Mass.: MIT Press, 1997); Jeremy Levitt, "Pre-Intervention Trust-Building, African States, and Enforcing the Peace: The Case of ECOWAS in Liberia and Sierra Leone," *Liberian Studies Journal* 24, no. 1 (1999); Max Sesay "Civil War and Collective Intervention in Liberia," *Review of African Political Economy* 23, no. 67 (1996); Marc Weller, *Regional Peacekeeping and International Enforcement: The Liberian Crisis* (New York: Cambridge University Press, 1994); David Wippman, "Enforcing the Peace: ECOWAS and the Liberian Civil War," in *Enforcing Restraint: Collective Intervention in Internal Conflicts,* ed. Lori Fisler Damrosch (Washington, D.C.: Council on Foreign Relations Press, 1993).

2. The opposition parties proposed that Doe hand over power to a coalition government and organize new elections in exchange for a rebel cease-fire. Doe showed interest in the proposal, but Taylor rejected it on the basis that it technically left Doe in power.

3. For a detailed discussion of this theme, see the following: Comfort Ero, "ECOWAS and Subregional Peacekeeping in Liberia," *Journal of Humanitarian Assistance,* September 25, 1995, http://www.jha.ac/articles/a005.htm; Friends of Liberia, *Liberia: Opportunities and Obstacles for Peace.* A Report on the Abuja II Peace Process (Rosslyn, Va.: Friends of Liberia, December 1996); Amos Sawyer, *Dynamics of Conflict Management in Liberia* (Accra: The Institute of Economic Affairs, 1997); Reed Kramer, "Liberia: A Casualty of the Cold War's End," *Africa Notes,* July 1995.

4. Ero, "ECOWAS."

5. The United Nations established the United Nations Observer Mission in Liberia (UNOMIL) in September 1993 to help monitor the implementation of the Coutonou Agreement. By April 1995, UNOMIL comprised troops and observers from eleven states: Bangladesh, China, the Czech Republic, Egypt, Guinea-Bissau, India, Jordan, Kenya, Malaysia, Pakistan, and Uruguay.

6. We are grateful to the Carter Center for interviews and documentation on its role in Liberia.

7. *Africa News* (Washington, D.C.), July 19, 1994 and July 31, 1994.

8. Inter Press Service, "Liberia: Criticism over ECOWAS Co-Chairing Geneva Peace Talks," July 12, 1993.

9. *West Africa,* September 17–23, 1990, 2478.

10. Ibid., and *West Africa,* July 23–29, 1990, 2165.

11. R. Mortimer, "Senegal's Role in ECOMOG: The Francophone Dimension in the Liberian Crisis," *The Journal of Modern African Studies* 34, no. 2 (1996): 298.

12. Ibid.

13. Touval and Zartman, *International Mediation in Theory and Practice.*

14. Mortimer argues that the French objected to Senegalese involvement in Liberia because of that country's close ties with the United States, which Paris regards as an unofficial competitor in Africa. The French also interpreted Senegalese participation in the Gulf War as indicative of its gradual drift toward the United States and hence became defensive toward any further Senegalese-American interaction.

15. There were indications that the United States shared this view of the ECOWAS mission at least after the deployment of ECOMOG. Herman Cohen, for instance, made disparaging remarks about the mission that raised the neutrality question and strengthened Taylor's excuse for noncooperation with ECOWAS.

16. Mortimer, "Senegal's Role in ECOMOG," 298.

17. The United States had committed only $2.8 million to ECOMOG since the inception of the mediation. The $3.5 million aid announcement in September 1991 was therefore a clear sign of U.S. preparedness to support the Francophonie initiative in the mediation. Mortimer's account indicates, for instance, that the Ivory Coast and Senegal also got more of the new funds ($1 million each) compared with their anglophone counterparts (Ghana, Guinea, and Sierra Leone got $500,000, while Gambia received $250,000).

18. Kramer, "Liberia."

19. Ero, "ECOWAS."

20. *West Africa,* August 13–19, 1990, 2280.

21. For a discussion of the legality of the ECOWAS mission, see Levitt, "Pre-Intervention Trust-Building," and Sawyer, *Dynamics of Conflict Management in Liberia.* See also "The Duty to Interfere," *West Africa,* November 26–December 2, 1990.

22. *West Africa,* July 30–August 5, 1990, 2200.

23. *West Africa,* July 23–29, 1990, 2165.

24. I. William Zartman, *Cowardly Lions: Missed Opportunities to Prevent State Collapse and Deadly Conflict* (New York: Cambridge University Press, 2005).

6. Sudan, 1983–1993

1. For entry into the first civil war, see Hizkias Assefa, *Mediation of Civil Wars: Approaches and Strategies—The Sudan Conflict* (Boulder, Colo.: Westview, 1987).

2. A detailed background to the conflict is provided by Francis M. Deng, *War of Visions: Conflict of Identities in the Sudan* (Washington, D.C.: Brookings Institution Press, 1995); Lesch, *The Sudan;* Francis M. Deng and Prosser Gifford, eds., *The Search for Peace and Unity in the Sudan* (Washington, D.C.: Woodrow Wilson Center Press, 1987), 71–77.

3. Deng and Gifford, eds., *The Search for Peace;* Deng, *War of Visions;* Lesch, *The Sudan.*

4. Bona Malwal, "The Roots of the Current Contention," in Deng and Gifford, eds., *The Search for Peace,* 9–14.

5. Elias N. Wakoson, "The Dilemmas of the South-North Conflict," in Deng and Gifford, eds., *The Search for Peace,* 90–106.

6. Malwal, "The Roots of the Current Contention," 12–14.

7. Peter Nyaba, *The Politics of Liberation in South Sudan: An Insider's View* (Kampala: Fountain Publishers, 1997), 22; Lesch, *The Sudan,* 48.

8. Francis M. Deng, "Myth and Reality in Sudanese Identity," in Deng and Gifford, eds., *The Search for Peace,* 63.

9. Ibid.

10. I. William Zartman, *Governance as Conflict Management: Politics and Violence in West Africa* (Washington, D.C.: Brookings Institution Press, 1997), 1.

11. Nyaba, *The Politics of Liberation.*

12. Manifesto of the SPLM, July 31, 1983.

13. Nyaba, *The Politics of Liberation,* 22.

14. Lesch, *The Sudan,* 63; Lam Akol, "The Present War and Its Solution," in Deng and Gifford, eds., *The Search for Peace,* 21.

15. Akol, "The Present War," 23.

16. Ann Mosely Lesch, "Negotiations in Sudan," in *Making War and Waging Peace: Foreign Intervention in Africa,* ed. David Smock (Washington, D.C.: United States Institute of Peace Press, 1993), 125. On the "territorial model," see Smith, *National Identity.*

17. Deng, *War of Visions,* 506; Nyaba, *The Politics of Liberation.*

18. Nyaba's *The Politics of Liberation* provides a detailed background to the breakup. The splinter group then changed its name from SPLM/SPLA-United to the Southern Sudan Independence Movement, with the South Sudan Independence Army as its military wing.

19. Ibid.; Deng, *War of Visions,* 20.

20. Smith, *National Identity,* 6.

21. Lesch, *The Sudan,* 15.

22. Former minister of interior Ali Abdel Rahman, cited in Akol, "The Present War," 16.

23. Charter of the National Islamic Front, January 1987, reprinted in full in Deng and Gifford, eds., *The Search for Peace,* 78–89.

24. "The Government's Peace Program for Negotiations with the SPLM/SPLA," 5; see also Herman Cohen, *Intervening in Africa* (New York: St. Martin's, 2000), 68.

25. Mansour Khalid, "External Factors in the Sudanese Conflict," in Deng and Gifford, eds., *The Search for Peace,* 109–126.

26. Ann Mosely Lesch, "External Involvement in the Sudanese Civil War," in Smock, ed., *Making War and Waging Peace,* 85; I. William Zartman, "The Triangulation Problem," in Midlarsky, ed., *The Internationalization of Communal Strife.*

27. Lesch, "External Involvement," 85.

28. Mohammed Hassan, "Eritrean Independence and Democracy," in *Eritrea and Ethiopia: From Conflict to Cooperation,* ed. Amare Tekle (Lawrenceville, N.J.: The Red Sea Press, 1994), 110; Deng, *War of Visions,* 377.

29. Nyaba, *Politics of Liberation,* 152.

30. Christopher Mitchell, "The Process and Stages of Mediation: Two Sudanese Cases," in Smock, ed., *Making War and Waging Peace,* 152; Lesch, "External Involvement," 88.

31. Lesch, "External Involvement," 88.

32. Mitchell, "Stages of Mediation," 153.

33. Deng and Gifford, eds., *The Search for Peace;* Francis M. Deng, *Partners for Peace* (New York: African Leadership Forum, 1998).

34. Deng, *Partners for Peace,* xv.

35. "Kampala Document of a Proposed Conference on Security, Stability, Development, and Cooperation in Africa," Kampala, Uganda, May 23, 1991.

36. Deng and Gifford, eds., *The Search for Peace,* xvi–xvii.

37. Deng, *War of Visions,* 506–507.

38. *Africa Confidential* 29, no. 8 (April 15, 1988), 1; Lesch, "Negotiations in Sudan," 119.

39. Lesch, "Negotiations in Sudan," 114–117.

40. Mitchell, "Stages of Mediation," 115.

41. Lesch, "Negotiations in Sudan," 121.

42. Ibid.

43. Mitchell, "Stages of Mediation," 155.

44. Ibid.

45. Lesch, "Negotiations in Sudan," 126.

46. Ibid., 127–128; Cohen, *Intervening in Africa*, 72–75.

47. Cohen, *Intervening in Africa*, 79–80.

48. "OAU Declaration on the Political and Socio-Economic Situation in Africa," Addis Ababa, July 1990.

49. Interview with Father Carroll Houle of People for Peace, Nairobi, October 1997.

50. Ibid.

51. Ibid.

52. Nyaba, *The Politics of Liberation,* 69.

53. Lesch, *The Sudan,* 173.

54. Ibid.

55. "Museveni Opens Sudanese Peace Talks in Entebbe," *Foreign Broadcast Information Service,* FBIS-AFR-93-037 (February 22, 1993), 5; "Sudanese Minister Hails Moi's Role in Peace Process," *Foreign Broadcast Information Service,* FBIS-AFR-93-037 (February 26, 1993), 7.

56. "Sudan against Peace Talks Summit: Report," Agence France-Presse, May 14, 1993.

57. Lesch, *The Sudan,* 173–177.

58. Ibid., 155.

59. Ibid.

60. Ibid., 160.

61. "U.S. Review of Sudan Terrorist Link Gains Urgency," *Washington Post,* June 27, 1993.

62. "Sudan Criticizes IMF for Suspending Its Membership," Xinhua News Agency, August 10, 1993.

63. Inter-Africa Group, *IGAD Mediation of the Sudanese Conflict* (Addis Ababa: Inter-Africa Group, July 1994), 1.

64. Ibid., 11.

7. Ethiopia-Eritrea, 1998–2000

1. Christopher Mitchell, "External Peacemaking Initiatives and Intranational Conflict," in Midlarsky, ed., *The Internationalization of Communal Strife,* 284. For other summaries of this approach, see Mitchell, *The Structure of International Conflict* (New York: St. Martin's, 1981); J. H. Laue, *The Functions of the Intermediary in Third-Party Processes* (Fairfax, Va.: Center for Conflict Analysis and Resolution, 1990); James Wall, "Mediation: An Analysis, Review, and Proposed Research," *Journal of Conflict Resolution* 25, no. 1 (1981): 157–180; and Louis Kriesberg, "Coordinating Intermediary Peace Efforts," *Negotiation Journal* 12, no. 3 (October 1996): 341–352.

2. For some of the early and recent studies on borders in Africa, see Saadia Touval, *The Boundary Politics of Independent Africa* (Cambridge, Mass.: Harvard University Press, 1972); Ian Brownlie, *African Boundaries: A Legal and Diplomatic Encyclopedia* (Berkeley: University of California Press, 1979); Carl Widstrand, ed., *African Boundary Problems* (Uppsala: Scandinavian Institute of African Studies, 1969); A. I. Asiwaju, *Partitioned Africans: Ethnic Relations across Africa's International Boundaries, 1884–1984* (London: C. Hurst, 1984); Ravi L. Kapil, "On the Conflict Potential of Inherited Boundaries in Africa," *World Politics* 18, no. 3 (July 1966): 656–673; Crawford Young, "Self-Determination, Territorial Integrity, and the African State System," in *Conflict Resolution in Africa,* ed. Francis M. Deng and I. William Zartman (Washington, D.C.: Brookings Institution Press, 1991), 320–346; and Steven R. Ratner, "Drawing a Better Line: Uti Possidetis and the Borders of New States," *American Journal of International Law* 90, no. 4 (October 1996): 590–625. On the OAU, see I. William Zartman, "Africa as a Subordinate State System in International Relations," *International Organization* 21, no. 3 (1967): 545–564.

3. *Addis Tribune,* July 31, 1998.

4. Chris Landsberg, "Horn of Africa: A Blow to Africa's Renaissance," *Los Angeles Times,* July 12, 1998, 2.

5. The first quote is from Michela Wrong, "Eritrea Likely To Reject Border Peace Plan," *Financial Times* (London), June 5, 1998, 5. The quote from Assistant Secretary Rice is from Scott Stearns, "Ethiopia-Eritrea Stalemate," Voice of America, Correspondent Report, no. 2-233353 (June 12, 1998).

6. Laeke Demessie, "Ethiopia-Eritrea: Governments Blame Each Other for Border Clashes," Inter-Press Service, June 3, 1998; Karl Vick, "School Attack Shocks Ethiopians," *Washington Post,* June 6, 1998; "Ethiopia and Eritrea Continue Fighting," *New York Times,* June 6, 1998.

7. Sam Kiley, "Third Front Opens after Both Armies Step Up Hostilities in Race to Control Red Sea Port," *The Times* (London), June 12, 1998; "Eritrea Accuses Ethiopia of Attacking Zalambessa," PanAfrican News Agency, June 9, 1998; Ghion Hagos, "Eritrea, Ethiopia Troops Fighting in Assab Front," PanAfrican News Agency, June 11, 1998.

8. Ghion Hagos, "Ethiopia to Expel Undisclosed Number of Eritreans," PanAfrican News Agency, June 12, 1998; "Tense Stalemate in Border Conflict," *Addis Tribune,* June 19, 1998.

9. The White House, Office of the Press Secretary, "Ethiopia, Eritrea Agree To Halt Air Strikes," Washington, D.C., June 14, 1998.

10. Paul Ejime, "OAU Worries over Eritrea, Ethiopia Border Crisis," PanAfrican News Agency, June 4, 1998; Paul Ejime, "Summit: Ethiopia-Eritrea Conflict Tasks OAU," PanAfrican News Agency, June 6, 1998; Paul Ejime, "Ethiopian Minister Gives Conditions for Peace with Eritrea," PanAfrican News Agency, June 7, 1998.

11. Ethiopian Foreign Ministry, "Statement by the Minister of Foreign Affairs of the Federal Democratic Republic of Ethiopia on the Aggression Carried Out by the State of Eritrea on Ethiopia to the Sixty-Eighth Ordinary Session of the Council of Ministers of the Organization of African Unity, June 1998, Ouagadougou," Washington, D.C., Embassy of Ethiopia.

12. "Daily News Update," Eritrean News Agency, June 10, 1998.

13. "OAU Mission on Ethiopia-Eritrea Conflict Begins Work," PanAfrican News Agency, June 18, 1998; "Eritrea Accuses Ethiopia of Violating Moratorium," PanAfrican News Agency, June 19, 1998; Carol Pineau, "Eritrea—Air Strikes," Voice of America, Correspondent Report, no. 2-234205, June 19, 1998.

14. "Tense Stalemate in Border Conflict," PanAfrican News Agency, June 19, 1998.

15. Rosalind Russell, "OAU Says Ethiopia-Eritrea Mission Falters," Reuters, June 19, 1998.

16. Cited in ibid. See also Dianna Cahn, "OAU-Ethiopia-Eritrea," Voice of America, Correspondent Report, no. 2-234220, June 20, 1998.

17. Cited in Carol Pineau, "Eritrea/UN Reaction," Voice of America, Correspondent Report, no. 2-234690, June 28, 1998.

18. Cited in Gitau Warigi, "No End In Sight to Border Conflict, As Kenya Steps In," *The East African* (Nairobi), July 20–27, 1998.

19. Raymond Bonner, "Cut Off by U.S., Ethiopia and Eritrea Easily Buy Weapons," *New York Times,* July 23, 1998, 10; Rupert Cornwell, "Fears of New War in Horn of Africa," *The Independent* (London), July 25, 1998, 12; "United States to Suspend Sales of Weapons and War Material," PanAfrican News Agency, July 31, 1998.

20. Ghion Hagos, "Ethiopia Increases Defense Budget," PanAfrican News Agency, July 10, 1998.

21. "Ethiopia-Eritrea Border Talks End," PanAfrican News Agency, November 9, 1998; "No Breakthrough Yet at Eritrea-Ethiopia Talks," PanAfrican News Agency, November 8, 1998.

22. "UN Urges Eritrea, Ethiopia to Accept OAU," PanAfrican News Agency, January 30, 1999; "Bill Clinton Comments on Ethiopia-Eritrean Conflict," PanAfrican News Agency, January 22, 1999.

23. "Ethiopia Says Dispute with Eritrea Has Reached Critical Stage," PanAfrican News Agency, January 5, 1999.

24. "Tensions Rise In Ethiopia, Eritrea," Associated Press, November 21, 1998.

25. "U.S. Mediator in Eritrea-Ethiopia Conflict Arrives," PanAfrican News Agency, December 4, 1998; "U.S. Envoy Meets Meles over Border Conflict," PanAfrican News Agency, January 15, 1999. In March 1999, an Ethiopian official suggested that the capture of Badme had created an opportunity for outside mediators to move in with a new initiative, "perhaps even a joint initiative of the U.S., Italy, and Libya." The proposal was rejected by both the United States and the OAU.

26. Ghion Hagos, "Meles Reiterates His Stand for Ending Border Conflict," PanAfrican News Agency, April 28, 1999.

27. "Ethiopians Push into Eritrea," BBC News, May 15, 2000.

28. Ghion Hagos, "Rwanda, Uganda Launch New Mediation Effort," PanAfrican News Agency, May 11, 1999.

29. "Eritrea Will Work 'Indefatigably' for Peace, President Issayas Tells OAU," Eritrean News Agency, July 14, 1999; "Ethiopia Dismisses Eritrea's Acceptance of OAU Plan as 'Meaningless'," BBC News, July 17, 1999.

30. "OAU Delegation Visits Eritrea," Pan African News Agency, August 26, 1999.

31. "Ethiopia: OAU to Talk Over Ethiopia-Eritrean Conflict Settlement," Pan African News Agency, October 30, 1999.

32. Patrick Gilkes, "Interview with Eritrean Foreign Ministry Official," *BBC Focus on Africa,* March 9, 2000; "Ethiopia-Eritrea: Fighting Flares Up as Peace Envoys Visit," IRIN, February 25, 2000; Alex Last, "Envoys Mediate in Horn Dispute," BBC News, February 27, 2000.

33. Martin Plaut, "Horn Conflict: Devil in the Detail, More than 200,000 Troops Assemble on the Border," BBC News, March 13, 2000.

34. "Ethiopia-Eritrea Talks Collapse," BBC News, May 5, 2000; "Ethiopia Keeps All Options Over Border Conflict with Eritrea," PanAfrican News Agency, May 6, 2000; "Talks on Eritrea-Ethiopia Conflict in Algiers," PanAfrican News Agency, May 2, 2000.

35. "Holbrooke: Horn 'Close to War'," BBC News, May 10, 2000.

36. "Days After U.N. Talks, Ethiopia and Eritrea Resume Border War," Reuters, May 12, 2000; Patrick Gilkes, "Ethiopia's War Strategy," BBC News, May 19, 2000.

37. "Ethiopia Attacks as Eritrea Accepts Peace Plan," Reuters, June 10, 2000.

38. "Organization of African Unity Proposal for an Agreement on Cessation of Hostilities Between the Government of the Federal Democratic Republic of Ethiopia and the Government of the State of Eritrea," June 12, 2000, Addis Ababa; "Ethiopia and Eritrea to Sign Peace Deal," Reuters, June 15, 2000; Justin Pearce, "Analysis: What the Peace Deal Means: Ethiopians in Eritrea Are to be Replaced by Peacekeepers," BBC News, June 18, 2000.

39. "Agreement Between the Government of the Federal Democratic Republic of Ethiopia and the Government of the State of Eritrea," Algiers, December 12, 2000.

8. Conclusions

1. Francis Deng, "Mediating the Sudanese Conflict: A Challenge for the IGAD," *CSIS Africa Notes,* no. 169 (February 1995), 4–5.

2. Zartman, ed., *Elusive Peace.*

3. Zartman, *Ripe for Resolution,* chapter 6.

4. Touval, "Gaining Entry," 269.

5. I. William Zartman and Jeffrey Z. Rubin, eds., *Power and Negotiation* (Ann Arbor: University of Michigan Press, 2000).

6. Touval and Zartman, "International Mediation in the Post–Cold War Era."

INDEX

AACC. *See* All Africa Conference of Churches
Abuja Peace Accords, 105
Addis Ababa Agreement, 19, 28, 124, 178
African Leadership Forum, 138
Afwerki, Isaias 155–156, 159, 163. *See also* Ethiopia-Eritrea conflict; Sudan
Akol, Lam, 131
al-Bashir, Umar, 132, 139–141
al-Dhahab, Abd al-Rahman Suwar, 132
al-Mahdi, Sadiq, 132, 135, 138
All Africa Conference of Churches, 19, 104, 107, 111, 118–120
All-Liberian National Conferences, 104, 106
Angola, role in Congo-Brazzaville crisis, 92, 93
Annan, Kofi, 165. *See also* United Nations
Anyanya, 124, 126, 127
Arabism, 132
Arap Moi, Daniel, 136, 141
Arusha Peace Process, 27
Aubervillois, 87. *See also* Zulus

Babangida, Ibrahim, 46, 112, 144
Bagaza, Jean-Baptiste, 57, 80, 81
Belgium
   mediation in Rwandan conflict, 49
   role in Rwandan conflict, 41, 43, 54
Bizimungu, Pasteur, 36, 45
Boley, George, 111
Bongo, Omar, 89–90, 92, 94–99, 192–193
Boutros-Ghali, Boutros, 66, 71, 73, 94–95, 98. *See also* United Nations
Bowen, Hezekiah, 111
Brazzaville. *See* Congo-Brazzaville crisis
Burundi
   causes of crisis, 27, 57–58, 59
   Charter of National Unity, 60
   Coalition of Opposition Political Parties, 74

Mohammed O. Maundi is with the Tanzanian Mission to the United Nations in New York.

I. William Zartman is director of the Conflict Management Program and former director of the African Studies Program at Johns Hopkins University's Nitze School of Advanced International Studies in Washington, D.C.

Gilbert M. Khadiagala is acting director of the African Studies Program at Johns Hopkins University's Nitze School of Advanced International Studies in Washington, D.C.

Kwaku Nuamah is the project coordinator for the Council on Foreign Relations' G8-Africa Project in Washington, D.C.

GETTING IN: MEDIATORS' ENTRY INTO THE SETTLEMENT OF AFRICAN CONFLICTS

This book was set in the typeface American Garamond; the display type is American Garamond Bold. Cover design by Hasten Design Studio, Washington, D.C. Page makeup, copyediting, and proofreading by EEI Communications, Inc., Alexandria, Va. Production supervised by Marie Marr Jackson. Peter Pavilionis was the book's editor.